Reminiscences

of

Rear Admiral Elliott B. Strauss

U.S. Navy (Retired)

Copyright © 1989
U.S. Naval Institute
Annapolis, Maryland

Preface

Each generation of naval officers considers that it served at just the right time, and that seems to be particularly demonstrated in the oral history of Rear Admiral Strauss. At the conclusion of this memoir, he looks back and considers all the changes that have been made in the Navy since his retirement. In most cases, he does not view them as changes for the better, because he recalls a time when things were done smartly, when naval officers were accomplished sailormen, and when the attainment of a particular rank denoted a high level of experience.

In his case, pride in the Navy and professional accomplishment were legitimately inherited, for his father, Joseph Strauss, was a four-star admiral, quite a rarity in the years before World War II. The memoir describes the son's growth as a battleship-cruiser-destroyer officer in the years leading up to World War II--on the shakedown cruise of the light cruiser Concord, in the gunnery department of the battleship Arkansas, in various four-stack destroyers, and as navigator of the new light cruiser Nashville. Ashore he served at the Naval Torpedo Station and Naval Training Station at Newport, and he had a fascinating tour as assistant naval attaché in Great Britain in the mid-1930s. He also acquired a taste of staff duty while serving as flag lieutenant for Commander Atlantic Squadron, Rear Admiral Alfred Johnson.

He returned to London in 1941 to be a naval observer, but the attack on Pearl Harbor intervened and he was assigned to Commander U.S. Naval Forces, Europe, who, at the request of Admiral Lord Louis Mountbatten for a U.S. naval officer on his staff, assigned Strauss to that duty. He served there during the early war period, but on the departure of Mountbatten, was transferred in 1943 to the planning staff of COSSAC. Strauss provides an insider's view of the great wartime British leader, as well as recollections of the Dieppe raid, the landings in North Africa, and the plans for the cross-channel invasion of Normandy in 1944. When Admiral Sir Bertram Ramsay was made Allied Commander in Chief, Commander Strauss became a member of Ramsay's small U.S. naval planning staff and remained there until August 1944.

By now promoted to captain, Strauss commanded the attack transport Charles Carroll as the Pacific war was moving toward victory, worked with the irascible Admiral Kelly Turner at the founding of the United Nations, and served as first commanding officer of the light cruiser Fresno. He again had a taste of British duty with a tour as a student in the Imperial Defence College.

In the early 1950s he served on the OpNav staff, commanded a Destroyer Flotilla, and then was involved as a U.S. representative in Europe during the establishment of the NATO military command. Following retirement he was a dean at Bucknell University and later served overseas with the Agency for International Development.

Undoubtedly because of his several tours in Britain, Admiral Strauss is an unabashed Anglophile. He is a great admirer of the late Lord Mountbatten, one of the few Americans designated by Mountbatten to be an official representative at his funeral. Admiral Strauss is a thoroughgoing gentleman, cosmopolitan in outlook; his manners and even speech patterns reflect the gentility for which the British have long been noted.

Martha Reamy did the original transcribing of the taped interviews. Admiral Strauss and I have both contributed to the editing in the interests of improving the smoothness, clarity, and accuracy of the final version. The admiral has been quite cooperative in checking details in connection with the annotating footnotes. Joanne Patmore of the oral history staff produced the final smooth version of the transcript; Susan Sweeney of the oral history staff did the detailed indexing of the volume.

Paul Stillwell
Director of Oral History
U.S. Naval Institute
December 1989

REAR ADMIRAL ELLIOTT B. STRAUSS
UNITED STATES NAVY (RETIRED)

Elliott Bowman Strauss was born in Washington, D.C., on 15 March 1903, son of the late Admiral Joseph Strauss, USN, and Mrs. (Mary Sweitzer) Strauss, and grandson of the late Brigadier General N. B. Sweitzer, USA. He attended Hotchkiss School in Lakeville, Connecticut, and entered the U.S. Naval Academy, Annapolis, Maryland, on appointment at large in June 1919. He was graduated and commissioned ensign on 7 June 1923, and subsequently progressed in rank to that of captain, to date from 1 May 1943. On 1 July 1953, he was transferred to the retired list of the U.S. Navy and advanced to the rank of rear admiral on the basis of citation for actual combat.

After graduation from the Naval Academy in June 1923, he had four months' duty in the Bureau of Ordnance, Navy Department, Washington, D.C., then reported to the plant of William Cramp and Sons, Philadelphia, to assist in fitting out the USS Concord (CL-10). He served on board that light cruiser from her commissioning, 3 November 1923, until September 1925, during her shakedown cruise to South Africa. He next served in the USS Hannibal (AG-1), assigned to survey duty on the southern coast of Cuba, and from November 1926 until November 1927, served in the USS Arkansas, flagship of Battleship Division Two, Scouting Fleet.

He remained at sea for two years, serving successively in the destroyers Toucey (DD-282) and Blakeley (DD-150), then had a tour of shore duty at the Naval Torpedo Station, Newport, Rhode Island. In June 1932, he joined the USS Manley (DD-74), operating in the Atlantic, and later in the Pacific, and from May until September 1934 served as her executive officer. He returned to Newport, for a tour of duty at the Naval Training Station, after which from November 1935 until September 1937, he was Assistant U.S. Naval Attaché at the American Embassy, London, England. While there, he was a delegate to the Third Assembly, International Union of Geodesy and Geophysics, at Edinburgh, in 1936, and on 12 May 1937, was awarded the British Coronation Medal, at the coronation of King George VI of England.

Upon his return to the United States in the fall of 1937, he was designated aide and flag lieutenant on the staff of Rear Admiral Alfred W. Johnson, USN, Commander Training Detachment, U.S. Fleet, and was attached to the flagship, USS New York (BB-34). He later served in the same capacity when Admiral Johnson was made Commander

Atlantic Squadron, U.S. Fleet. During the period October 1939 until December 1940, Lieutenant Commander Strauss commanded a destroyer, the USS Brooks (DD-232), after which he served as navigator of the USS Nashville (CL-43), light cruiser, until 29 October 1941, participating in the expedition which took the first Marines to Iceland in July 1941.

He returned to London, England, as a U.S. naval observer just prior to the outbreak of World War II in December 1941, and served on the staff of Admiral Lord Louis Mountbatten, Chief of Combined Operations, during the early war period, taking part in the Allied raid on Dieppe, 19 August 1942. In November 1943 he reported to Commander U.S. Naval Forces, Europe, and was assigned duty with Task Force 122, later serving on the staff of the Allied Naval Commander in Chief, Admiral Sir Bertram Ramsay until August 1944.

He was awarded the Bronze Star Medal, with Combat "V", and the following citation:
"For meritorious achievement as the United States Naval Representative on the Staff of the Chief of Combined Operations in the Dieppe Raid, and while serving on the Staff of the Allied Naval Commander in Chief during the Invasion of Normandy. Embarked as an observer in a British destroyer which rendered close fire support during the Allied raid on Dieppe on August 19, 1942, Captain (then Commander) Strauss obtained information of great value to the United States and Great Britain in the planning and execution of subsequent operations. Ordered to the Normandy beaches on D plus 2-Day, he applied his comprehensive knowledge of the build-up procedure in solving far-shore shipping problems which threatened to delay the operation. Serving with distinction, skill and courage despite enemy air and ground attack throughout these missions to halt German aggression, Captain Strauss upheld the highest traditions of the United States Naval Service."

On 12 October 1944, Captain Strauss assumed command of the USS Charles Carroll (APA-28), an attack transport, which finished her share of the follow-up operations in connection with the Southern France campaign and sailed on 25 October for Norfolk, Virginia. Assigned to Transport Division 52 Pacific Fleet, she left on 4 January 1945 for the South Pacific carrying supplies and personnel to Guadalcanal, Manus, and Bougainville. In February, with Transport Squadron 18, she became a part of Amphibious Group Four, Task Force 51, in preparation for a major operation, and on 1 April 1945, successfully landed her assault troops and their equipment on the designated beaches at Okinawa Jima. She had aboard the late Ernie Pyle, beloved newspaperman who covered her assault operations in his articles shortly before his death. The <u>Charles Carroll</u> served as flagship of Commander Transport Division 63 from May until July 1945.

Detached from that command on 6 August 1945, Captain Strauss returned to the United States for duty in the Office of the Chief of Naval Operations, Navy Department, Washington, D.C. From July until September 1946, he was attached to the Military Staff Committee of the Security Council of the United Nations in New York, serving as a naval adviser to the first General Assembly of that body in January 1946, then reported to the Federal Shipbuilding and Drydock Company, Kearny, New Jersey. There he had charge of fitting out the USS <u>Fresno</u> (CL-121), and from her commissioning on 27 November 1946, until December 1947, commanded that light cruiser.

He returned to London, England, and from 6 January to 10 December 1948, was a student at the Imperial Defence College. In February 1949, he reported to the Navy Department to serve as head of the Strategic Applications and Policy Branch of the Strategic Plans Division, under the Deputy Chief of Naval Operations (Operations). Two years later he was detached for sea duty organizing and in command of Destroyer Flotilla Six, and in March 1952 was again ordered to the Office of the Chief of Naval Operations where he was head of the Long Range Plans Branch.

On 11 August 1952, he was ordered to the Office of the Deputy for Defense Affairs, Office of Special Representative in Europe for Mutual Security Administration, Paris, France. On 28 September 1953, after his retirement in July of that year, he was ordered detached from that assignment, but to continue duty in Paris as Staff Assistant Secretary of Defense for International Security Affairs (Office of Foreign Economic Defense Affairs), with his duty station in the U.S. Mission to NATO and European Regional Organization, Paris.

From August 1956 until March 1957 Rear Admiral Strauss was Director of Engineering at Bucknell University, Lewisburg, Pennsylvania.

On 6 April 1957, Rear Admiral Strauss was named Chief of the new American Foreign Aid Mission to Tunisia. There he directed a $5.5 million program providing commodities and technical assistance for the rest of the fiscal year ending 30 June, a program which in 1958 had risen to more than $20 million, and by the time of his detachment in August 1960, had put more than $100 million into the

Tunisian economy. In 1960 he served as personal representative of the Secretary of State as a member of a three-man team to evaluate the effectiveness of the mutual aid program to Pakistan, this assignment extended from September 1960 to January 1961. In January 1961 Rear Admiral Strauss initiated, as Director, the Agency for International Development (AID) mission to the Malagasy Republic and served there until February 1963. He retired from AID in May 1963. In July 1965, Rear Admiral Strauss became a public member of the Foreign Service Inspection Corps. He was a member of the team inspecting Embassy, Tel Aviv, and Consulate General Jerusalem, July to September 1965.

In addition to the Bronze Star Medal with Combat "V," Rear Admiral Strauss has the American Defense Service Medal; European-African-Middle Eastern Campaign Medal; Asiatic-Pacific Campaign Medal; World War II Victory Medal; Navy Occupation Service Medal, Europe Clasp; and National Defense Service Medal. He was made an honorary Commander of the Order of the British Empire and has the Croix de Guerre of France, with palm.

Rear Admiral Strauss was married in 1951 to Miss Beatrice Schermerhorn Phillips, daughter of former Ambassador and Mrs. William Philipps of Beverly, Massachusetts. He has three children by a former marriage: Elliott MacGregor Strauss, Armar Archbold Strauss, and Lydia Saunderson Strauss Delaunay. His usual residence is 2945 Garfield Terrace, Washington, D.C. 20008.

Authorization

The U.S. Naval Institute is hereby authorized to make available to individuals, libraries, and other repositories of its choosing the transcripts of four oral history interviews concerning the life and career of the undersigned. The interviews were recorded on 27 October 1986, 30 October 1986, 10 November 1986, and 17 November 1986 in collaboration with Paul Stillwell for the U.S. Naval Institute.

The undersigned does hereby release and assign to the U.S. Naval Institute all right, title, restrictions, and interest in the interviews. The copyright in both the oral and transcribed versions shall be the sole property of the U.S. Naval Institute. The tape recordings of the interviews are and will remain the property of the U.S. Naval Institute.

Signed and sealed this _25th_ day of _November_ 1989.

Elliott B. Strauss
Rear Admiral Elliott B. Strauss, USN (Ret.)

Strauss #1 - 1

Interview Number 1 with Rear Admiral Elliott B. Strauss,
U. S. Navy (Retired)

Place: Admiral Strauss's home in Washington, D.C.

Date: Monday, 27 October 1986

Interviewer: Paul Stillwell

Q: Admiral, to begin at the beginning, or even before that perhaps, I know you have a distinguished family background in the military service. Perhaps you could describe that.

Admiral Strauss: My father was in the class of 1885 at the Naval Academy.* I used to say he was in the class of '85, but I can no longer do that because there's a new '85 along. I had a grandfather in the Army, Brigadier General Nelson B. Sweitzer, and I jokingly say we don't speak of him, but he was in the class of 1853 at West Point.** In the Civil War he served a great deal of time on McClellan's staff.*** It may be of interest that his first commission,

---
*Joseph Strauss (1861-1948) reached the rank of four-star admiral during the course of his active service. For a brief biography, see <u>Dictionary of American Naval Fighting Ships</u>, Volume III (Washington, D.C.: U.S. Government Printing Office, 1968), page 565.
**Nelson Bowman Sweitzer stood 24th in the class of 1853; one of his classmates was Philip H. Sheridan, later a general, who stood 34th. Sweitzer retired in 1888 as a colonel, having achieved the temporary rank of brevet brigadier general in 1865.
***Major General George B. McClellan, USA, commanded the Division of the Potomac in the early part of the Civil War. Not particularly successful, he was relieved and ran against Abraham Lincoln for the presidency in 1864. Sweitzer was his aide de camp from 1861 to 1863.

Strauss #1 - 2

as a second lieutenant of dragoons, was signed by the later President of the Confederacy--then the Secretary of War--Jefferson Davis.*

I had a great-uncle, Charles McGregor, who was in the class of '64 at the Naval Academy. I have one of his academic reports, with "Annapolis" scratched out and "Newport, Rhode Island," written in, because the Naval Academy was switched up to Newport when they thought there was a possibility of Annapolis being overrun by the Confederacy. I think that's probably a rundown on my background.

Q: Could you sketch the highlights of your father's career, please.

Admiral Strauss: My father had quite an unusually distinguished career. He was still an ensign at the age of 35, but in those days an ensign, I think, roughly corresponded--in prestige and the jobs he got--to a commander today. He specialized in ordnance and at one time was the Chief of the Bureau of Ordnance. His first command was the Montgomery, which was a gunboat. I might say that when I was born he was in the monitor Arkansas, and my mother received a telegram, appointing me as a

―――――――――
*Jefferson Davis (1808-1889) was U. S. Secretary of War, 1853-57, and President of the Confederate States of America, 1861-65.

member of the Arkansas's mess when I was three days old.

Among other assignments, my father was the second captain of the newly commissioned Nevada. Captain Sims was his predecessor and put the ship in commission.* My father was taken out of the Nevada and appointed a temporary rear admiral and was sent to Europe to lay the North Sea mine barrage, 56,000 mines, which were laid between the Orkneys and the coast of Norway. I can almost say that this was the main U. S. naval operation of World War I, that and the Sixth Battle Squadron.** As you know, World War I wasn't a U.S. naval war, but I think that these two things mark it. He was made by the British an honorary Commander of the Order of St. Michael and St. George.

Later on, he went back and swept up the mines. That took something over a year. From there he came back to the General Board and then was made Commander in Chief of the Asiatic Fleet.*** In those days, the highest rank on the active list was rear admiral. You were made a vice admiral or an admiral for a particular appointment, and when you

---

*Captain William S. Sims, USN, became prospective commanding officer of the Nevada (BB-36) in November 1915 and put her in commission the following March. He subsequently became a four-star admiral and served as Commander U. S. Naval Forces Operating in European Waters during World War I.
**The five ships comprising Battleship Division Nine--USS Delaware (BB-28), USS Florida (BB-30), USS New York (BB-34), USS Texas (BB-35), and USS Wyoming (BB-32)--arrived at Scapa Flow in the Orkneys on 7 December 1917 to reinforce the British Grand Fleet as the Sixth Battle Squadron.
***Admiral Strauss served as Commander in Chief Asiatic Fleet from 4 February 1921 to 28 August 1922.

came back you cut off your stripes and reverted to your regular rank, which he did. He finished his career on the General Board.* He was also the first budget officer of the Navy, a job he did not want, but acceded to Secretary Denby's wish.**

Q: It was quite an honor for your father to have been a four-star admiral as commander in chief.

Admiral Strauss: Yes.

Q: And his memory has been honored with the naming of a destroyer after him.

Admiral Strauss: That's right, the DDG-16 was named after him.***

Q: What are your earliest memories of your father and of your own home life?

Admiral Strauss: I think the earliest I remember of him is

---
*The General Board consisted of a group of senior flag officers who provided direction to the Secretary of the Navy during the first half of the 20th century on such subjects as naval strategy and ship characteristics.
**Edwin Denby was Secretary of the Navy from 1921 to 1924.
***The USS Joseph Strauss (DDG-16), a 4,500-ton guided missile destroyer of the Charles F. Adams (DDG-2) class, was built by the New York Shipbuilding Corporation and commissioned on 20 April 1963.

when he was inspector of ordnance in charge of the Naval Proving Ground at Indian Head. Then Indian Head was both the smokeless powder factory and the proving ground for all the Navy guns. Of course, this latter had to be stopped when the range of guns was such that it endangered ships in the Chesapeake. Then the proving ground went to Dahlgren.

From there he went to sea, and I remember going from place to place, sort of following him until he came back to Washington for duty. I was at the Naval Academy when he was CinC of the Asiatic Fleet and my mother and sister went out to the Far East with him. And I missed this, because at that time the duty in the Asiatic station was very interesting indeed. And the CinC was allowed a naval yacht called the General Alava. His family could travel in her, which my mother and sister did. I think if that went on today, Jack Anderson would find it of great interest and would write articles about it.*

Q: Was there any predominant homestead that the family returned to several times?

Admiral Strauss: My family had a house in Washington for over 50 years at 2208 Massachusetts Avenue--from 1911 until

---

*Jack Anderson is a muckraking syndicated newspaper columnist who takes great delight in exposing things that government officials often would prefer not to become public knowledge.

my mother died some time in the Seventies. It's now the Embassy of Togo, so I don't know what strange rites go on in the living room.

Q: With your father off on sea duty, did your mother have the principal role in rearing the family?

Admiral Strauss: Yes. During the time that he was in Scotland for the war, she was in complete charge for a total of three years.

Q: What influence on your own life would you attribute to your parents?

Admiral Strauss: Well, understandably, I admire my father greatly, both as a naval officer and as a human being. And I was very lucky in my choice of mothers, because my mother educated me until I entered the third grade in school.

Q: Was she a teacher by training?

Admiral Strauss: No, it was just that she thought I ought to learn something. She was quite right, and she proceeded to deal with it.

Q: Did you have any siblings?

Admiral Strauss: I have one sister.

Q: How close were you during the growing-up years?

Admiral Strauss: Well, we were brought up together until I went away to school. She's one of my very few relatives and a very close relative, and I see a lot of her. She lives here in Washington.

Q: What are your early memories of school after you began? Did you go to a public school?

Admiral Strauss: I went to a Friends school here very briefly, and then went into Washington public schools and stayed there from the third grade up until the first year at Western High School. I left then and went to Hotchkiss School in Lakeville, Connecticut, and stayed there two years--the same two years. That is, I did the first year twice because I lost two out of three falls with Latin. And I would have stayed except I left to cram for the Naval Academy at Shadman's School in Washington, which took very mediocre material and seemed to prepare it to pass the examinations for West Point and the Naval Academy.

Q: Contrary to Latin, were there any subjects you were

Strauss #1 - 8

particularly strong in?

Admiral Strauss: English. I did reasonably well in English, both at Hotchkiss and afterwards at the Naval Academy.

Q: Do you recall the hoopla and so forth involved when your father took over the Nevada?* That must have been a proud moment for the family.

Admiral Strauss: I don't remember very much about it. We'd just entered the war, and the ship's movements and so forth were supposed to be a secret. Of course, we knew where he was, but there wasn't much talk or much demonstration about it. It was a red-letter day for me, the few times I was allowed to visit the ship.

Q: How much contact did you have with him while he was over in Europe during the war?

Admiral Strauss: Really none. He came back for very short periods--as I remember, once or twice--and that's the only contact that we had with him. He wrote very often. I would say certainly once a week or more.

Q: As is the case with many Navy families, your mother

_____
*Captain Strauss commanded the ship from 30 December 1916 to 14 February 1918.

must have been an efficient manager to keep the household running in his absence.

Admiral Strauss: Yes. We rented 2208 Massachusetts Avenue and moved to the Dresden, an apartment house in Washington. And one of the things I remember was that Mrs. MacArthur, whose son was a brigadier general in France at the time, lived just opposite us. When my father was made a KCMG, Knight Commander of St. Michael and St. George, General MacArthur had a similar decoration from the British.* And I remember my mother and Mrs. MacArthur congratulating each other on this.

Q: You probably took an avid interest in news from the war as well.

Admiral Strauss: Oh, yes, yes. Newsreels at that time were avidly watched, because they really gave us the best idea of what was going on in Europe.

Q: What are your recollections of the cram school?

Admiral Strauss: It was very rugged. There were no warm

---

*Brigadier General Douglas MacArthur, USA, served with the 42nd Division in France during World War I. MacArthur (1880-1964) eventually rose to the rank of General of the Army during World War II. Graduated from the U.S. Military Academy in 1903, his final tour of active duty was during the Korean War.

baths. You had to go to the YMCA to have a bath, but it was efficient. The man who ran it was called Mr. Shadman. He had one arm, and the story was that he'd lost the other one beating a boy to death who hadn't done his studies. I think that was perhaps apocryphal. Shadman's was a good cramming school and seemed to get a great many of its students into the service academies.

Q: What was the method that he used? Did he work from old Naval Academy entrance exams?

Admiral Strauss: A great deal, but subjects like geometry and geography, I think he taught pretty much from the bottom to try to get people started. For instance, I had had no geometry when I went there.

Q: What do you remember about the process of actually getting into the Academy?

Admiral Strauss: There were two examinations, a February examination and an April examination, and they were taken at a public school on 13th Street. And we were examined in arithmetic, algebra, geometry, English, geography, and American history. I think that was it. And you got in or not on those examinations. There was no looking at your

Strauss #1 - 11

SAT or anything like that.* And I had passed few examinations up to that time, so I was very gratified when I found out that I had passed. I worried about it a great deal from the time that I took them until the time that it was announced.

Q: Evidently, Mr. Shadman's course had paid off.

Admiral Strauss: It did. I don't think I would have got in unless I had had that experience. So I took the examinations in April and entered on the 12th of June of that year. And up until 1919, when my class entered, candidates could enter as midshipmen when they became 16. Some midshipmen entered in the September, just before the beginning of the academic year if they became 16 by that time. From my class, you had to be 16 by 1 April of the year you entered, and I was 16 on the 15th of March, so I had a 15-day leeway, which was very useful.

Q: You must have been the youngest in the class.

Admiral Strauss: Just by the accident of my birth I was, yes.

Q: What do you remember of the process of getting in--the

---
*SAT--Scholastic Aptitude Test, which is now used as one of the measuring devices for potential midshipmen.

plebe summer indoctrination and so forth?

Admiral Strauss: I think when one was dressed in a white working uniform with a stencil across your chest and a sailor's white hat with a blue band around it and a load of uniforms and equipment, you sometimes wondered whether you had done the right thing in entering. We had a lot of work in machine shops and that sort of thing and, of course, a great deal of drill during the plebe summer until the academic year started. We weren't allowed out of the Naval Academy grounds, but it was a busy life and, I think, reasonably happy.

Q: Why the work in machine shops?

Admiral Strauss: Just to teach you how you how to chip and file, and it acquaints you with this side of manual training.

Q: Had it been taken for granted during your growing-up years that you would go to the Naval Academy?

Admiral Strauss: I think fairly much. At one time I thought of being a chemist, but that didn't get very far. So I would say that up until the time I was 16 that I more or less planned to go there.

Q: Did your family background and experience give you an advantage over your classmates who were strictly civilians?

Admiral Strauss: Yes, I think so because of knowing a little bit of how the Navy worked and personalities in it, because, of course, it was a comparatively small organization at that time. The naval figures loomed up much more prominently, I think, than they do today. Yes, I would say it was of some advantage.

Q: Did you know some of your classmates previously as sons of naval officers?

Admiral Strauss: Yes, a few of them I did know as Navy juniors.

Q: How would you describe the atmosphere of life in Bancroft Hall?*

Admiral Strauss: It was austere. For instance, the wing that I was in had no running water. You had pitchers and wash basins. You, of course, made your own beds and took

---

*Since early in the century, Bancroft Hall has been the dormitory for Naval Academy midshipmen. It was named for George Bancroft, who was Secretary of the Navy when the Naval Academy was established in 1845.

care of the room, which was rigorously inspected. When you got to be a first classman, the corridor boys were allowed to make your beds, and you paid them a little bit. This wasn't a part of the regulation, but nobody seemed to bother about it, and it was always done.

Q: Who were the corridor boys? Were they Navy men?

Admiral Strauss: No, no. They were mostly colored civilians from Annapolis.

Q: What do your remember about the academic part of the Naval Academy?

Admiral Strauss: A great deal of it was, of course, professionally directed. I think the number of hours spent on engineering subjects, which included things like mechanical drawing, probably were greater than any other single subject. But the courses in English and history were very good. My impression about the Naval Academy is that the instructors for the most part were umpires between you and the books rather than professors in the normal sense of the word. There was an English professor, C. Alphonso Smith, who I think would have been distinguished in any academic organization. And there were others, but on the whole, as I say, they were referees between you and the blackboard.

Q: Could you give an example how this umpiring system worked?

Admiral Strauss: Well, you were given an assignment in some subject, say navigation, and there would be questions in it, and you responded to the questions. The professor had a little book, and he would make marks in it and that was it. If you asked a question or if you made a mistake, of course, they would correct it or give you some advice, and this varied from professor to professor. Some of them were much more forthcoming than others.

Q: I've gathered that there was more emphasis on rote memorization than analytical thinking.

Admiral Strauss: That isn't altogether fair, because your responses and your written examinations in a great many cases involved ratiocination. But what you say is true, that there was a great deal of rote learning.

Q: What do you remember about the duty officers and the disciplinary organization at Bancroft Hall?

Strauss #1 - 16

Admiral Strauss: I think that, on the whole, they did a very good job. They were, again, austere. They were there to enforce discipline, and they did it. And I don't mean to say that they were harsh, but it was done as officers to subordinates, really.

Q: Well, I think, too, it would depend on the personalities of the individuals. Some would be more harsh in their enforcement of the regulations than others.

Admiral Strauss: That's quite true, that there were some most helpful. For instance, we dedicated our Lucky Bag, the yearbook, to one of the duty officers, Commander Slayton, because we felt he was helpful and sympathetic.* And then there were others that behind their backs you characterized as quite otherwise.

Q: I've gathered that the Superintendent, Admiral Wilson, was very popular with the midshipmen.

Admiral Strauss: Admiral Wilson and Admiral Scales, they were both--Admiral Wilson had had a rather more distinguished career and looked the part of an admiral.**

---
*Commander Charles C. Slayton, USN.
**Rear Admiral Archibald H. Scales, USN, was Superintendent of the Naval Academy from February 1919 to July 1921; Rear Admiral Henry B. Wilson, USN, was Superintendent from July 1921 to February 1925.

Both of them were well liked, but probably Admiral Wilson was more a midshipman's idea of what a senior officer should look like, and perhaps act like.

Q: He wore his cap at sort of a jaunty angle.

Admiral Strauss: Yes. And he'd had quite a good war record. I think he was in command of convoys and so forth.

Q: You mentioned the cloistered life you lived initially. How did that gradually ease up as time went on at the Naval Academy?

Admiral Strauss: Well, each year there was a certain relaxation. A plebe had a pretty hard time between the work and the upper classmen.* The third class was a little bit better off and the second class even more so. Then the first class were treated in some ways as budding officers. They were allowed to go out the Naval Academy gate every afternoon and had considerably more freedom. Still, nobody could smoke except in the Smoke Hall, and that was a first class privilege, and midshipmen weren't allowed to ride in automobiles. I believe nowadays the first classmen can have automobiles. Once my father was

---
*A plebe is a midshipman in his first year at the Naval Academy; a third classman or youngster is in his second year; a second classman is in his third year; and a first classman is in his fourth year.

visiting Annapolis, and he was in a car with Admiral Wilson. The latter signaled me to get in. I reminded him that I wasn't allowed in automobiles, but he said he would remove the prohibition for the occasion.

Q: Prohibition of alcohol was the law of the land during your time at Annapolis, which probably made it even more a desirable thing to drink.

Admiral Strauss: Exactly. Yes, yes, I remember being a very freshly caught ensign and was out in Carvel Hall and then I sat at a nearby table to Lieutenant Fechteler, one of the Naval Academy duty officers.* He invited me over and gave me a drink. I realized then that I had really become an officer.

Q: How much of a social life did you have as a midshipman?

Admiral Strauss: Well, as a plebe, none. As a third classman you could invite girls down to dances, and most of us did that. I certainly did. And then occasionally, officers who'd had connections with your family would invite you to luncheon or dinner, and sometimes people in

---

*Lieutenant William F. Fechteler, USN, who eventually became a four-star admiral and served as Chief of Naval Operations from 16 August 1951 to 17 August 1953.

Annapolis would. But social life wasn't particularly brisk. The Naval Academy dances were well attended, and they were enjoyable. Then, athletic events, people came down for them.

Q: Did you take part in sports yourself?

Admiral Strauss: I'm afraid in a rather desultory manner. I was on the class swimming team, and I did some wrestling, but I was on the staff of the Log, which was a monthly publication. That was about it.

Q: Was that an outgrowth of your strength in English?

Admiral Strauss: I wrote for them a bit, but I drew pictures for them more than writing.

Q: The Log is now a midshipman humor magazine. Did it have that orientation then as well?

Admiral Strauss: Yes.

Q: This was probably a relief from the heavier material you had in your classes.

Admiral Strauss: It was, yes.

Strauss #1 - 20

Q: The Army-Navy football game, of course, was an annual event for the whole nation.

Admiral Strauss: That was a thing we sort of lived for, yes.

Q: What do you remember about the trips to the Polo Grounds in New York to see those?*

Admiral Strauss: Oh, the marches there and then afterwards you went to the theater. That was really almost the high point of the year. The year worked up to that sort of as a crescendo, and then after that the winter was a long, long anticlimax.

Q: Did the regiment of midshipmen go up together to New York on a train?

Admiral Strauss: Yes, that's right, and they went up on the train and then we marched to the Polo Grounds.

Q: Were the normal rules relaxed on the train so that you didn't have to observe the usual strict behavior?

---

*The Polo Grounds, at Eighth Avenue and 155th Stret, was the home park of baseball's New York Giants. It was also the site of the annual Army-Navy football game until the game was moved to Philadelphia.

Strauss #1 - 21

Admiral Strauss: Yes, and there was a custom that you always pulled the blinds of the car down going through Baltimore. I don't know what the origin of that was, but that was supposed to give the team good luck.

Q: Were midshipmen much sought after for dates in New York?

Admiral Strauss: I think a number of them made arrangements beforehand, yes, to meet girls and so forth.

Q: Were there any of the officers in the battalion or regimental organization that you particularly remember, especially those who later became famous?

Admiral Strauss: Well, Bill Fechteler, who afterwards became Chief of Naval Operations, I remember very well. Floyd Stewart Crosley, whose father was Admiral Crosley, was a duty officer.* He'd lost an eye in an engine room accident and was kept on the active list for a while with one eye because this was service incurred. I remember him.

Q: Are there any incidents you recall specifically about Fechteler? He certainly was a swashbuckling sort.

---
*Lieutenant (junior grade) Floyd S. Crosley, USN.

Admiral Strauss: No. We admired him. He was easy to get along with. He had a brother. His sister Amy married a classmate, Bob Hicks, and his brother, as I remember, who was also a naval officer, was killed in an airplane accident.*

Q: Do any of your fellow midshipmen especially stand out in your mind?

Admiral Strauss: Well, of course, Arleigh Burke became justly famous.** As a midshipman he wasn't well known at all.

Q: Did you know him during that time?

Admiral Strauss: I didn't, no. Buck Walsh, who was afterwards coach of the crew.*** Vin Conroy was a football hero and was much admired.**** Roland Smoot, from Utah, had

---
*Ensign Robert I. Hicks, USN; Lieutenant Frank C. Fechteler, USN, was graduated in the Naval Academy's class of 1918 and subsequently served as an aviator on board the aircraft carrier Langley (CV-1). He was killed in an airplane crash near Detroit on 18 September 1922.
**Midshipman Arleigh A. Burke, USN. In World War II Burke was Commander Destroyer Squadron 23 and chief of staff to Vice Admiral Marc Mitscher, Commander Task Force 58. Burke was Chief of Naval Operations from 1955 to 1961. His oral history is in the Naval Institute collection.
***Midshipman Charles S. Walsh, USN.
****Midshipman Vincent P. Conroy, USN.

a very fine war record.* I'd put him up just under Arleigh Burke. Mickey O'Regan was class president and went on to be a flag officer.** Some of the Marines I remember quite well. My roommate Dick Cutts went on to be a brigadier general.*** He was an expert shot. Lamson-Scribner became a major general in the Marines, and George Good became a lieutenant general in the Marines.**** Those are some that come to my mind.

Q: Did you have an aptitude for the mechanical and professional subjects?

Admiral Strauss: I did quite well in engineering subjects. As a matter of fact, I only ranked "one" in anything once, and that was mechanical drawing. In English I stood well up in the class. I had some difficulty with navigation, because it was a mathematical subject.

Q: How much emphasis was there in the coursework on leadership, or was that a sort of a by-product?

---

*Midshipman Roland N. Smoot, USN. Smoot, who commanded several destroyer squadrons in World War II, eventually became a vice admiral. His oral history is in the Naval Institute collection.
**Midshipman William V. O'Regan, USN. During World War II, as Commander Submarine Division 42, O'Regan commanded a wolf pack known as the "Mickey Finns."
***Midshipman Richard M. Cutts, Jr., USN.
****Midshipman Frank H. Lamson-Scribner, USN; Midshipman George F. Good, USN.

Strauss #1 - 24

Admiral Strauss: No, you were marked on military leadership, and there was a certain amount of lectures and talks about it. On the midshipmen's cruises that was emphasized.

Q: The class of '22 had that famous controversy over who would finish first in the class. Did you observe that with interest?

Admiral Strauss: Yes, I did. I did very much, because I knew Jerry Olmstead very well.* I saw him a great deal and I didn't run into Leonard Kaplan until years later, when I put the Fresno in commission in 1947 at the Federal Shipbuilding Company, Kearny, New Jersey.** He was the naval constructor superintendent of our commissioning, and I got to know him then and liked him very much. I thought he was a very conscientious and able officer and very easy to get along with.

Q: How had the popular sentiment been running back in '22? Was one the favorite over the other?

---

*Midshipman Jerauld L. Olmstead, USN, had the top standing at the graduation of the Naval Academy's class of 1922.
**Midshipman Leonard Kaplan, USN, finished second in the class of 1922 and was the victim of prejudice and mistreatment because he was Jewish. His entry in the 1922 yearbook was printed on a perforated page that could be removed from the book by those who so desired.

Strauss #1 - 25

Admiral Strauss: Oh, yes. I think that Jerry Olmstead was certainly more forthcoming and more likable, and then there was, of course, certain amount of prejudice against Kaplan.

Q: Olmstead unfortunately came to a sad end soon after that.*

Admiral Strauss: Yes, yes.

Q: Did you have any contact with Rickover at all?**

Admiral Strauss: I didn't hear his name until afterwards. I remember Olmstead had a roommate called Kenneth Baker who was a very attractive ne'er-do-well.*** And he would have bilged much sooner except that Jerry Olmstead kept an eye on him and helped him out. And when finally he was called upon to resign for not having passed his subjects, he wrote a resignation and he said that, "Owing to my extensive pool hall and other interests in the Middle West, I cannot continue as a midshipman and request that my resignation be

---
*Ensign Olmstead died at Brooklyn, New York, on 21 August 1923 as a result of poliomyelitis. For more on the Kaplan-Olmstead rivalry, see Norman Polmar and Thomas B. Allen, Rickover: Controversy and Genius: A Biography (New York: Simon and Schuster, 1982), pages 53-58.
**Midshipman Hyman G. Rickover, USN, who for many years ran the Navy's nuclear propulsion program and eventually became a four-star admiral.
***Midshipman Kenneth Baker, USN.

accepted." Well, they told him that this wasn't a suitable resignation and to rewrite it. So he wrote from Midshipman Kenneth Baker to the Superintendent, via the commandant, via the Third Battalion Officer, "I resign. K. Baker."

Another duty officer that I remember was J. J. Brown.* Lieutenant Commander J. J. Brown came into Baker's room one Sunday morning, and Baker had his feet up on the desk. Brown said, "Why aren't you at chapel, Mr. Baker?"

And Baker said, "I'm a Mohammedan, and I don't think that I should be required to attend Christian worship."

And Brown said, "Oh, yes, I agree." He said, "But you know Mohammedans are sun worshipers and they get up every morning at 5:30 and go on the roof of Bancroft Hall and worship the sun, and so you will have to do that." And that was the end of that conversation.

Q: Did Mr. Baker become a Christian again at that point?

Admiral Strauss: I can't remember.

Q: Did you have a leadership position within the regiment or your battalion or company?

Admiral Strauss: First classmen changed stripes every two

---
*Lieutenant Commander John J. Brown, USN.

months. Then the last three or four months you had your permanent stripes. I got to be a midshipman lieutenant with two stripes, but then permanently I was a midshipman ensign.

Q: What were the duties that went with being a midshipman lieutenant?

Admiral Strauss: It was mostly on the drill field that you counted as a company commander or a platoon commander. As far as the academic work, or work within the Academy, your midshipman rank had very, very little to do with it. For instance, the regimental commander took charge of the regiment and a battalion commander commanded each battalion, but that's about it.

Q: After four years you become a very accomplished driller at the Naval Academy.

Admiral Strauss: Yes, yes. One of the nice things about being a midshipman officer, you carry a sword instead of an eight-pound rifle.

Q: Did you take an interest in sailing?

Admiral Strauss: Only within the requirements of the curriculum.

Q: What do you recall of your summer cruises?

Admiral Strauss: They were made in coal-burning battleships, and for the youngster cruise we went through the Panama Canal and to Hawaii. And you spent half your time in the engineering and half the time on deck. And the watches in the firerooms were very strenuous indeed. I weighed about 115 pounds and handling the coal buckets--which were 70, 80 pounds--was, I remember, quite a job. We coaled ship quite frequently, and that was an all-hands job. You never really got the coal out of your system until you had a chance on September leave. I know that I had ring of coal dust around my eyes so I looked like Theda Bara for quite a long time after the cruise was over.[*] Unfortunately, my half in the fireroom was in going to Panama and going to the tropics. Then, when we got up in good weather, I was shifted back to the deck. The other half who had the good weather going down and then the shoveling coal in better weather were luckier.

Then second class cruise we made to Europe, and we went to Christiana just shortly before it was rechristened Oslo. And that was a very pleasant cruise. We went to

---
[*]Theda Bara was a movie star who wore heavy makeup in the era of silent films.

Lisbon also, so that was an outstanding cruise.

Q: You were probably in Norway pretty close to the midsummer's night celebration, when it's light almost the entire day long.

Admiral Strauss: Yes, the crew was reluctant to go to bed in daylight.

On first class cruise, we started out in the Connecticut, and she lost a propeller at the Kingston joint and tried to go ahead on one propeller. Then she lost that propeller and had to be towed. We were shifted over to the North Dakota for the rest of the cruise.

Q: The old Olympia went along on some of those cruises, I believe.

Admiral Strauss: She made my first class cruise.

Q: What ships were you in the first two years?

Admiral Strauss: I was in the New Hampshire, then the Kansas and then the Connecticut cum North Dakota.

Q: Those were mostly pre-dreadnought types.

Strauss #1 - 30

Admiral Strauss: Oh, yes. They were real old-timers.*

Q: What were the living conditions like on board?

Admiral Strauss: Well, of course, we slept in hammocks, and before you started the cruise, you rigged the hammock in your room and tried out on it. And the first few days you spent balancing and wondering whether you were going to fall out. After a while, you would see people in a hammock with one leg over one side and their head on the other, swinging back and forth without any trouble at all. The food was ample, but certainly no cordon bleu among the cooks.

Q: You have a real problem getting fresh food during a long voyage.

Admiral Strauss: Of course, also water was a problem. As I remember, we were allowed a gallon of fresh water a day, and that was to do everything--drinking and cleaning your teeth and so forth. You had to bathe in salt water, and you had to scrub your hammocks in salt water; to get them clean was really quite a job with a scrubber and salt water soap and salt water. If it rained hard, you were lucky, because then you could get a hammock really clean.

---

*The USS New Hampshire (BB-25) was commissioned in 1908, the Kansas (BB-21) in 1907, the Connecticut (BB-18) in 1906, and the North Dakota (BB-29) in 1910.

Q: And I believe the Naval Academy officials discouraged parents from providing too much spending money for overseas liberty, didn't they?

Admiral Strauss: Yes, they did. And I've forgotten what our allowance was. I'm not sure, but if you said $3.00 a month as a plebe and $10.00 as a first classman, it wouldn't surprise me. You also had money on the books from your pay. You couldn't draw this, and most people saved it up to buy their uniforms when they graduated, because that took quite a lot of money.

Q: What do you recall about the overseas liberty ports you went to?

Admiral Strauss: Well, we certainly enjoyed Christiania and Lisbon. In Christiania we were struck by the number of rowing boats with women at the oars and men sitting idly in the stem. There was a beach for women only, where they bathed nude. Bluejackets at the gun telescopic sights had a "third class liberty."

Panama was the first port we hit on youngster cruise after leaving the United States, and I remember that avocados were five cents apiece, and at the commissary down there you could get a marvelous meal for about 50 cents.

Everything seemed so very cheap. Then Hawaii was delightful. And the only two hotels on Waikiki beach were the Royal Hawaiian and the Moana. It was a very pleasant cruise. We came to Seattle coming back and that was nice. The people in Seattle turned out for the midshipmen. They gave them tickets to prize fights and took them into their homes. They were very hospitable.

Q: What sorts of things did you do ashore in Hawaii?

Admiral Strauss: Oh, swam, danced at the Moana Hotel.

Q: Was your ship able to go into Pearl Harbor itself? I know at one time there was a sandbar across that channel.

Admiral Strauss: As I remember, we anchored out.

Q: Was there tactical training as part of these cruises?

Admiral Strauss: Yes. The battleships tried to do maneuvers as a unit. Of course, you went through all the drills--fire drill, battle stations, and those. You spent a great deal of your time, besides shining brightwork and scrubbing the deck, in drills.

Q: It's really an ideal opportunity to apply the things

you've learned in class.

Admiral Strauss: Yes. And the fact that they start you out shoveling coal and scrubbing decks and shining brightwork, I think, is a good introduction, because you shouldn't have authority over men unless you know what they do and know how to do it as well as they do.

Q: How were you treated by the enlisted men in the crew?

Admiral Strauss: The relationship was rather a difficult one, because you weren't enlisted and you weren't an officer. I think that the book says that a midshipman is an officer in a qualified sense, but we got along very well. For instance, in the boiler room you'd be shoveling coal alongside a fireman second class, and you were boat's crews along with the bluejackets.

Q: Today, of course, it takes some really highly trained and very skilled professional enlisted men to run these complex ships. How skilled were they in that time? Were they a rather rough-hewn lot?

Admiral Strauss: They certainly, on the whole, were not educated people. The average bluejacket could read and write. Some of the petty officers, of course. such as the machinist's mates and signalmen and so forth were very well trained at their jobs, and there were certain ratings that were better educated than others. Radiomen, signalmen, yeomen, machinists, certainly. The second class seamen and the corresponding firemen weren't educated on the whole.

Q: Were there any aspects of the seagoing life that you found that you particularly enjoyed?

Admiral Strauss: I enjoyed standing watches, as a junior officer of the deck, for instance, where you had some control over things.

Q: There is, indeed, a satisfaction in giving an order and having this massive piece of steel follow your directions.

Admiral Strauss: Yes, yes, that's certainly true.

Q: Another big event of that era was the naval disarmament conference in Washington.* What was the reaction among the midshipmen to that?

Admiral Strauss: I don't think they knew it was going on.

---

*On 6 February 1922, the Washington Naval Treaty was completed at the conclusion of an international conference that began the previous year. The United States, Great Britain, Japan, France, and Italy agreed to a program of tonnage limitations for capital ships.

Strauss #1 - 35

That's sad to say, but, on the whole, it was just something that didn't impinge on them.

Q: There was a spin-off effect, though, in that there didn't seem to be as many opportunities coming up for naval officers.

Admiral Strauss: Well, that was true. The class of '22 for a while thought that a large proportion of the class wouldn't be commissioned. When they were finally able to commission them, a number who had made other plans didn't take advantage of that and stayed in civilian life.

Q: Did that have an effect on your class at all?

Admiral Strauss: No, I don't think that we thought it was going to hit us, and it didn't.

Q: How did you spend your September leaves?

Admiral Strauss: I spent them here in Washington with my family. I think all three September leaves.

Q: Did you have a choice on what your first duty would be following graduation?

Admiral Strauss: I applied to go to the West Virginia and got it. And then the West Virginia was not yet commissioned, and they kept on putting off her commission.* They sent those of us who were destined for her here to Washington, and we were at the optical school in the Navy yard for a while. And I heard the Concord, which was going to go in commission, was going around South Africa for her shakedown cruise. So I asked if I could be assigned to her, and I was. I was way the junior ensign in the Concord. I went to Philadelphia. She was commissioned in Cramp's Ship and Engine Building Company, which made beautiful ships. They made them so well that I think they went broke. But I put the Concord in commission.**

Q: Could you amplify on that statement? In what ways did you observe that she was particularly well built?

Admiral Strauss: I couldn't say that I saw that the Concord was well built, but all Cramp ships, like Bath ships, had a tradition.*** They didn't have many

---

*The USS West Virginia (BB-48), the last battleship allowed to be completed under the terms of the Washington Naval Treaty, was commissioned 1 December 1923.
**The light cruiser Concord (CL-10) was commissioned 3 November 1923. She was 555 feet, 6 inches long; 55 feet, 4 inches in the beam; and had a standard displacement of 7,050 tons. She was armed with 12 6-inch guns, four 3-inch guns, and ten 21-inch torpedo tubes.
***Bath Iron Works, in Bath, Maine, has for many years been considered one of the premier destroyer-building shipyards in the United States, particularly in the quality of the ships it delivers.

breakdowns, and when they went to sea they didn't have to come back to have their turbines realigned or anything like that. I, as an ensign, wasn't capable of saying that this particular ship was well built, but Cramp ships on the whole had a reputation for being well built.

Q: I take it, though, that she did perform well while you were on the cruise?

Admiral Strauss: Yes. When we went in commission, it was a fascinating cruise because we crossed the ocean. We spent some time, a few days, in Algiers, which was an experience. Mr. Bodley, the representative of Barclay's Bank of London, lived in an old mansion. He gave a ball for the officers and furnished the young ladies. The ballroom was lighted only by candles, a very romantic setting.

When we were getting under way to leave Algiers, a French tug was pushing us out, and that class of cruisers had propellers that stuck way out from the side of the ship like ears. The propeller cut the tug, and she sank right there in Algiers harbor. So that held us up. I remember the tug captain, with tears in his eyes, saying, "La remorquer est coutée." The propeller was slightly bent. We had to have a board of investigation. For a while we thought we might have to go into Bizerte in Tunisia, a country where afterwards I spent three and a half years, to have the propeller either replaced or mended.* Actually, they were able to hammer out the dents, and we went on and finished the cruise.

We went through the Red Sea, and we stopped at places that are household words now, but in those days most people had never heard of. We stopped at Djibouti and Berbera. We spent Christmas at Berbera in British Somaliland. We went to Zanzibar and Mombasa and Tamatave in Madagascar. Twenty-odd years later, when I went back, people would say, "Is this your first visit to Madagascar?"

I'd say, "Oh, no. I was here in 1923."

Then we went to Durban. We went to Lourenco Marques in Portuguese East Africa, then Durban, Port Elizabeth, Cape Town. And I always thought then if I were exiled from the United States that Cape Town was the place I'd go back to, because it was delightful from the standpoint of scenery, climate. The Earl of Athlone was the governor general, and I saw Captain Campbell, Royal Navy, who had two Victoria Crosses.** He was captain of the Q-boats in

───────────────
*Admiral Strauss worked in Tunisia in the late 1950s, following his retirement from the naval service, as an official of the Agency for International Development (AID). He discusses that experience in interview number four.
**As commanding officer of the Q-ship Farnborough, Commander Gordon Campbell, Royal Navy, sank the German U-83 67 miles west of Fastnet on 17 February 1917. On 8 August of the same year, he was skipper of the Q-ship Dunraven when she made a determined, barely unsuccessful attack on the U-61.

the World War. He organized the Q-boats. You know what the Q-boats were. They were disguised merchant ships that would drop their false sides and unmask their guns.

Q: It all sounds very exotic. Are there any special highlights from those ports that you remember?

Admiral Strauss: Well, I remember in Durban they had rickshaws, and the rickshaw men would have African headdresses with feathers and horns of animals. I had my first motorcycle ride, a wild one, from the Kilindini docks, where the ship was, into Mombasa.

Q: This was still very much the colonial era. Did you see the British and French influence where you went?

Admiral Strauss: Oh, yes. In Madagascar it was completely a French colony. Djibouti was also, and in Djibouti they had a French naval yacht called the <u>Diane</u>, which was kept there to chase Arab dhows crossing the Red Sea with slaves. The French officers had the life of Riley there; they'd either have their wives or their mistresses installed ashore. I asked one of them, "Have you really chased any?"

He said, "Oh, yes." He said, "Last month we stopped a dhow with African slaves going across." So it was a French colony, very French. Berbera, very British. We went to church in the Anglican church on Christmas Day, and the rector wore a pith helmet. In Zanzibar you could smell the cloves offshore before you got there. Then after Cape Town, we went to what had just ceased to be German Southwest Africa. We went to Walvis Bay, and at that time Walvis Bay was spelled "Walfish" or "Walvis." Its name had four or five different ways of spelling it, and we decided that "Walvis" was the best way and told this to the Hydrographic Office. And it has since been standardized as Walvis Bay, I think, from the representation of the Concord on that trip.

Then from Walvis Bay, we went to St. Helena. That was quite an experience, because the only vehicles were horse-drawn vehicles. There were no motorized vehicles. I remember going up to the governor's house in a carriage and seeing ladies in broad hats and gloves and the gentlemen without their waistcoats bowling on the lawn. It was a sort of 17th century scene revisited. The house was Longwood, where Napoleon lived.*

When we left, an American merchant seaman who had lived there for a long time asked if we could take him back to the United States under a law which allowed men-of-war to take on board distressed American seamen. A lot of

---

*Napoleon Bonaparte, the defeated French Emperor, lived in exile on the island of St. Helena from 1815 until his death in 1821.

distraught ladies came down to see this man off. We took him on board and assigned him to the third division, of which Lieutenant Couble was the division officer.* Couble said, "I don't want this man in my division. He's probably a bum. Why do you assign him to me?" So he told him to do some task, to clean up something.

The man came back in 20 minutes and said, "It's clean. What else do you want me to do?" He was probably the hardest working and most able seaman in the ship.

Q: Why were the ladies distraught?

Admiral Strauss: Well, I think he had a team of affectionate ladies, and he was leaving them, you see, and they were upset. I imagine he was quite a man with the ladies from what evidence we could see. Then we went to Recife, which was then called Pernambuco and were there for Mardi Gras, where everybody was sort of dancing in the streets and in parades. They had a custom. A lot of people would have glass tubes of perfume under pressure, and they would try to squirt you in the eye with this. If they did, it didn't do any permanent harm, but it stung quite a lot, I remember.

Q: How well were Americans received in these ports that

---
*Lieutenant (junior grade) Alexander J. Couble, USN.

you visited?

Admiral Strauss: We were the first American man-of-war to visit them, really, since the war. I would say we were received very hospitably indeed. As a matter of fact, when we first started, the officers rather vied to go to these parties we were invited to. Later on, they got sort of blasé, and the captain would say, "We have got to have four officers to such and such a dinner."*

"Oh, my heavens." And so we might have to draw straws to see who was assigned to go. No, I can't think of anyplace where we were not well received. We arrived in Zanzibar when the battle cruiser HMS Hood was also there. After our 7,500-ton ship, the forecastle of the Hood looked like the White House lawn. The English in Zanzibar, understandably, were more enthusiastic about the Royal Navy officers than the U.S. Navy ones.

The only time that I remember any inhospitable attitude was on a midshipman cruise. We went to St. Vincent, and I could see the people there didn't like the officers or the men and midshipmen wandering around and peering into things. We were interlopers there, but on this particular shakedown cruise I don't think we experienced that anyplace.

---

*The first commanding officer of the Concord (CL-10) was Captain Orin G. Murfin, USN.

Q: Of course, the British and French had been great allies during the war just past, and so that spirit probably lingered.

Admiral Strauss: I think it did.

Q: What sort of shakedown was there for both crew and ship during this voyage?

Admiral Strauss: Well, we did all the drills and tested all equipment, but it was a goodwill tour as much as anything. We looked for any bugs with the machinery or the guns or anything like that. And, as I remember, there wasn't anything that was particularly needed to be done.

Q: Well, that speaks well for the job that Cramp did.

Admiral Strauss: Yes.

Q: Who was your first skipper?

Admiral Strauss: Orin Gould Murfin, who was afterwards a Commander in Chief of the Asiatic Fleet.*

---

*As a four-star admiral, Murfin was Commander in Chief Asiatic Fleet from 4 October 1935 to 30 October 1936. Admiral Strauss's father had been in that same billet in 1921-22.

Q: What impressions, if any, do you remember of him?

Admiral Strauss: Well, since I was 20, he seemed to me an old man. He was 47.* He was very fair but not particularly bonhomous. He'd been with my father on his staff in the mine force in World War I, so may have been more forgiving of my many imperfections.

Q: Did that help you at all?

Admiral Strauss: It may have. I might have got worse reports if it hadn't been for him.

Q: What were your initial duties in the Concord?

Admiral Strauss: I was signal officer to start with and assistant navigator. The navigator was Lieutenant Commander William Stetson Hogg.** Then after a while, I was assigned to engineering and was an assistant engineer, and Lieutenant Commander Jake Reeves was the engineer officer.*** He was afterwards a vice admiral. He was the captain that took the carrier Wasp in to relieve Malta

---
*Murfin was born 13 April 1876 and was graduated in the Naval Academy class of 1897, which produced a number of famous admirals, including H.E. Yarnell, A.J. Hepburn, T.C. Hart, W.R. Sexton, and W.D. Leahy.
**Lieutenant Commander William S. Hogg, Jr., USN.
***Lieutenant Commander John W. Reeves, Jr., USN.

during World War II.*

Churchill, you know, sent them that signal when they made two trips in there: "Who says a wasp can't sting twice?"**

Q: Reeves has a reputation as a rather hard-boiled officer.

Admiral Strauss: Oh, he was, he was, yes. Black Jack Reeves.

Q: What do you remember?

Admiral Strauss: I remember that it was rather the custom to get dressed in civilian clothes and ask your head of department if you could go ashore.

Q: You sort of took it for granted?

Admiral Strauss: Yes. I came up one time in civilian

---

*Reeves was commanding officer of the USS Wasp (CV-7) when that carrier made trips into the Mediterranean in April and May 1942, ferrying British planes that were flown off to the island of Malta.
**On 11 May 1942, the Wasp received the following message from British Prime Minister Winston Churchill: "To the captain and company of the USS Wasp. Many thanks to you all for the timely help. Who said a wasp couldn't sting twice?"

clothes. He made me go back and get into uniform to ask him whether I could go ashore or not.

Q: He had quite an interest in damage control. Did you see that in the Concord?

Admiral Strauss: The first lieutenant was Sarge Henry.* Damage control in those days wasn't taken that seriously. You'd have drills and close all watertight doors and so forth, but the fine points of auxiliary lights and escape gear, we hadn't got around to that yet.

Q: What sorts of drills do you remember?

Admiral Strauss: Well, gunnery, signal, fire, abandon ship, fire and rescue, where you send help over to another ship.

Q: Were there any other U.S. ships along on this voyage?

Admiral Strauss: No, we were by ourselves. When we got back, we had a spell in the yard. We joined the fleet, and an admiral called George Washington Williams took us over.** I don't remember too much about that, but I know

---
*Lieutenant Walter O. Henry, USN.
**The Concord served as flagship for Rear Admiral George W. Williams, USN, Commander Destroyer Squadrons Scouting Fleet.

Strauss #1 - 47

that we did maneuver with the fleet for a while.

Q: That class had a reputation of being rollers. What do you remember of her in heavy weather?

Admiral Strauss: Well they were ten-beam boats, which are always tender.* But, I didn't remember them as particularly bad sea boats. I mean, having afterward spent so much time in the four-stack destroyers, anything bigger always seemed pretty comfortable in retrospect.

Q: What was the life like for a junior officer on board, the accommodations and the mess?

Admiral Strauss: There was no junior officers' mess. Officers were all together at four tables, ascending by rank. The stateroom was comfortable. I haven't any particular impressions of it. It was a good ship. It seemed to me the officers were rather harder on junior officers than I remember afterwards. You see, I was the only ensign from '23 on board for the shakedown cruise. After that, we got a classmate of mine, Jimmy Thach, who got to be a vice admiral, and M. M. DeWolf in '24.**

---
*The Concord's length was 555 feet and her beam 55 feet, giving her a 10:1 ratio.
**Ensign James H. Thach, Jr., USN; Ensign Maurice M. DeWolf, USN.

Several of the class of '24 came on board.

Q: What are your recollections of Thach?

Admiral Strauss: He was a very able, very pleasant, very agreeable officer. I was one number senior to him. He would have been senior to me if he hadn't got so many demerits. His demerit factor as a midshipman just was enough to pull him down that one number.

Q: How much of a difference does it make on board a ship that you're one number senior?

Admiral Strauss: None.

Q: He, of course, had a brother who was very famous as an aviator.*

Admiral Strauss: Yes, that's right.

Q: Was there a good deal of camaraderie in the wardroom?

Admiral Strauss: Yes. In that way it was very good.

---

*John S. Thach, the younger brother, was graduated from the Naval Academy in 1927 and became famous as the inventor of the Thach weave used by fighter pilots. John Thach's oral history is in the Naval Institute collection.

Q: Did you have any regrets that you'd gone to the Concord instead of the West Virginia?

Admiral Strauss: No. I felt very lucky. I think probably going to a ship that big would have been better discipline. A junior officer in a battleship really got knocked around. He was a boat officer most of the time. As divisional officers, we in the Concord had pretty much the same duties as they would.

Q: You probably got to spend more time on the bridge in the Concord than you would have.

Admiral Strauss: Well, I think so, yes. I stood top watches very soon, since the ship needed all the watch officers they could get, whereas in a battleship I'd have probably been a JO for a long time.*

Q: In appearance, that class looked like overgrown four-stack destroyers. How would you compare the handling of them?

Admiral Strauss: They weren't as easy to handle. I was afterwards navigator of the Nashville, and from my past

---
*JO--junior officer.

Strauss #1 - 50

experience with the Concord and with four-stack destroyers, when the captain of the Nashville was going to turn to make a pier, I said in my mind, "He'll never do it." And he just came around nicely. And I don't think the Concord could have done it, and I don't think I could have done it with a four-stack destroyer.

Q: Did they have enough power to respond well?

Admiral Strauss: Yes. Oh, yes.

Q: Are there any experiences that stand out in your mind from the period after you got back from the cruise and joined the fleet?

Admiral Strauss: No, I don't remember too well. I remember Admiral Williams made us mark a big 10, for cruiser number 10, on the bow in the way destroyers had their numbers painted then and which all ships have today.* Captain Murfin hated that big number. The minute Admiral Williams was detached, the captain had it painted out right away.

Q: That's interesting. I never recall having seen a

---
*The use of the large destroyer-type hull number on the bow probably resulted from the Concord's role as flagship of the Scouting Fleet's destroyer force.

picture of one of those cruisers with a big number like that.

Admiral Strauss: Well, of course, the cruisers had small numbers. The Fresno had a little number on the bow, but this was a great big thing, covered the whole bow.*

Q: Were your operations all in the Atlantic?

Admiral Strauss: With the Concord, yes.

Q: Did you take part in any fleet problems?

Admiral Strauss: I don't remember that we did.

Q: Where was the ship based?

Admiral Strauss: Its home port was Philadelphia.

Q: Any recollections of the yard there?

Admiral Strauss: Not at that time. Afterwards, though, I really put two ships in commission in Philadelphia. I remember the yard much better then. I don't connect it too well with the Concord.

---

*As a captain, Strauss commanded the cruiser Fresno (CL-121) in 1946-47.

Strauss #1 - 52

Q: I think it was known as League Island.

Admiral Strauss: Yes.

Q: And there were probably a good many destroyers in reserve at that time.

Admiral Strauss: It seems to me that this was before they started putting destroyers into reserve in large numbers. Later, I put the Brooks back in commission. She had been one of those in reserve, but I don't know for how long. She was just taken out of reserve as things were heating up in Europe.

Q: How long did that tour of duty last in the Concord?

Admiral Strauss: I went to her in the autumn of '23, and I think I left her early in '25.

Q: That was a good, solid beginning tour. Where did you go from there?

Admiral Strauss: I went to the Hannibal. The Hannibal was a survey ship. We had three ships surveying between the

Isle of Pines and Cuba, the Gulf of Batabanó. Two of them, the Nokomis and the Niagara, were yachts. One of them was Helen Gould's yacht, which had been given to the Navy and converted for surveying.* Whereas the Hannibal was a decked-over collier with a top speed of seven and half knots, Scotch boilers, one-screw reciprocating engines. The commanding officer was Commander Christopher Raymond Perry Rodgers, who was the last of the famous Rodgers family in the Navy. He was a marvelous man.

Q: What do you recall about him?

Admiral Strauss: It is a sort of a wrong, curious statement to say that he was an aristocrat. And he really was. I mean, he came from a very distinguished family on both sides. He wasn't a snob, but he didn't have much to do with the lower classes. He was a very able captain.

Q: How close a relationship did he have with you as a junior officer?

Admiral Strauss: Well, my relationship with him was quite close, because his uncle, W. L. Rodgers, and my father were friends, and his grandfather, Simon Cameron, and my

---

*The USS Niagara (SP-136) was a steam yacht built in 1898 and purchased by the Navy in August 1917 from Howard Gould of New York City.

grandfather were friends, so there was a relationship. He was always very good to me.

There was another officer on board, Fred Jackson, who, alas, fell off between the ship and the brow in Philadelphia and was drowned.* He was delightful. He was the sort of person Rodgers liked. The rest of the crew and the rest of the officers he was very pleasant with, but this was a friend, if you know the difference.

Q: What was it about Jackson that made him more of a friend than the others?

Admiral Strauss: Well, I think he was more Rodgers's sort. His father was quite a distinguished clergyman.

Q: How much of an interest and in touch was your father keeping? Did he advise you on things on your career?

Admiral Strauss: Well, when it came, he rather advised me to take the assignment to a survey ship. He said that it was the epitome of seamanship. He had spent almost two years after graduation from the Naval Academy surveying in Alaska. They lent officers to the Coast and Geodetic Survey, and he and some of his classmen were assigned there and spent almost two years in Alaska. He thought it was

---
*Lieutenant (junior grade) Frederick H. W. Jackson, USN, died 8 October 1925.

Strauss #1 - 55

very good training.

Q: Now you say that this is the epitome of seamanship. Is that because of the need for precise navigation?

Admiral Strauss: No, you are in small boats, and you have to tow signals from one place to another, and you have to rig up things ashore. There is very little sort of war professionalism; well, it's seagoing. Admiral Cameron Winslow was asked how he became so proficient a battleship handler.* He said, "From maneuvering small boats."

Q: Could you please describe the method that you used for conducting a survey? Did you have some rudimentary charts you were working from?

Admiral Strauss: The charts of that area were Spanish charts made, I guess, in the 16th, 17th century. And some of the islands that they showed would be as much as ten miles out of place. And so that was about all. Well, the Hannibal was a mother ship. She was painted white and spar color, you know, like the old battleships. Attached to her

---

*Admiral Cameron McRae Winslow, USN, commanded the U.S. Pacific Fleet in 1915-16. Before that, he was commanding officer of the battleship New Hampshire in 1908-09 and was cited for heroism in connection with the cutting of underwater cables off Cuba in the Spanish-American War. The destroyer Winslow (DD-359) was named in his honor.

were four old steam launches and a houseboat, which was a decked-over coal barge with two stories. The ground floor was the officers' living quarters and the mess room and above that, tented over, was where the bluejackets lived.

The houseboat was towed from area to area, and the steam launches were attached to the houseboat. The *Hannibal* ran survey lines deeper than ten fathoms with a depth finder. We would set up signals either afloat or on the shore and take position on them with a quintant, which covered a larger angle than a sextant, and held horizontally, gave you your three-point position on signals. And you would run ten-mile lines back and forth, sounding with the lead. And then there was a chart man who would record the soundings. This gave the rough material for the eventual charts. You had a coxswain, a boat officer, a fireman, and two leadsmen. The sounding boat would steam along a ten-mile line and then go perhaps 500 yards over and then come back along another ten-mile line. This was repeated.

One time one of the boats with Ensign Quinn was still on the sounding line, and Lieutenant (junior grade) Tom Ochiltree had finished his sounding.* As Ochiltree headed back to the houseboat, they crossed. Quinn, who was actually on a line, thought Ochiltree would keep clear.

---

*Ensign Bertrand D. Quinn, USN; Lieutenant (junior grade) Thomas H. Ochiltree, USN.

Ochiltree had the right of way according to the rules of the road. Well, they were both wrong, and they collided and one of the steamers sunk in about four or five fathoms. And this was telegraphed back to Rodgers in the Hannibal. He was pacing the quarterdeck as he read the telegram. He said, "These two young gentlemen have achieved the impossible. They have collided while running parallel lines."

Q: Then they had the business of charting the wreck, probably.

Admiral Strauss: Oh, they got it up. They got it up.

Q: How did the lead line compare with the depth finder in accuracy? Was it more precise?

Admiral Strauss: Oh, yes, if it was well cast. You see, you could only use it up to ten fathoms. Very hard to use it beyond that. It could be exact. A bad leadsman might leave slack in it or something like that, but a good leadsman could be completely accurate up to ten fathoms. The depth finder, in those days, I think was probably very good, but I just don't know how accurate.

We had a rather sad thing happen. The leadsmen used

to shift sides after an hour or so, and one of them said, "I can't swing the lead on the port side." He said, "My arm won't do it." I noticed that the sides of his face didn't seem completely equal, and I reported this to the doctor. And the doctor looked him over and immediately sent him to the hospital.

I said, "What's his trouble?"

He said, "He's got a brain tumor."

And I said, "Can they do anything about it?"

And he said, "No, I don't think so." I don't know what happened to him. The tumor had affected one side of his face and one of his arms.

We used to keep a spoon towing astern, and we would catch, I suppose, the proportion of five barracuda to perhaps one yellowtail or an edible fish. And if we got an edible fish, we put it on the coals of the furnace, the boiler, and had that for luncheon. One luxury we did have was Filipino messboys on the houseboat, and they would take off their clothes and put on a fireman's glove and dive down in the rocks and pull out langouste lobster, and we had all the langouste that we could eat. There were a lot of sharks around there, every kind of shark you can imagine--hammerhead sharks, tiger sharks--but they never bothered anyone. And when anybody would go swimming or the boys would go diving, we'd keep a man with a rifle there, but I never saw a shark bother anybody.

The only Cubans that we ever saw were sponge fishermen. There were a lot of them. They'd have these buckets with the glass bottoms, and you'd see them fishing. When we first got down there, Captain Rodgers wanted to call on the mayor of Batabanó, and he had assigned a classmate of mine named Wadbrook to be his sort of man Friday.* He sent word down that he was going ashore and told Wadbrook to get into a white uniform and come up on deck. Well, Wadbrook did. In the meantime, he had had his head shaved right down to the bone. Rodgers took one look at him and told him that, "I'm not going to use you." I think he took me ashore for this call on the mayor of Batabanó.

Q: Was Wadbrook deliberately trying to get out of it?

Admiral Strauss: No, a lot of people thought that having your head shaved was good for your hair. Quite a lot of bluejackets would have their heads shaved down in the tropics.

Q: In what way was that supposed to benefit your hair?

Admiral Strauss: The theory was that if you cut it off and

---

*Lieutenant (junior grade) William P. E. Wadbrook, USN.

it grew out anew, it would probably be stronger and thicker.

Q: Well, from your description it sounds like a very pleasant, fun-loving sort of life on that cruise.

Admiral Strauss: It was an interesting life. Of course, it was very tedious to live on the houseboat day in and day out. There was no recreation. Once during the survey season, we came up to Key West. The ship was semi-based on Key West. When we left Philadelphia, we stopped in Key West, and Key West at that period was absolutely wild. It was during Prohibition, and when the federal agents would come down there, the city police would tell all the bars and cafés to hide all their liquor. And it was like a wild West town really.

And we had quite an event there. Our navigator was named Smith.* He was a lieutenant (junior grade), and there was a place where we used to gather called the Duvall Club. It had a bar, and it had a gambling place, too. One evening I saw Smith in civilian clothes. I passed his room, and I said, "Going ashore, Smitty?" And he pulled the curtain in my face, which I thought was a little bit odd.

The next morning, the captain sent for us, and he had

___
*Lieutenant (junior grade) Harry T. Smith, USN.

a note and it said, "By the time you have read this, I will be off the dock and out with the tide. I cashed a bad check at the Duvall Club last night."

Well, immediately they went to search all the docks and the ships and the railway, and there was no sign of him. The captain was very upset about this. He said, "If Smith had said something to us, we could have made it good. A gambling debt is not cashable anyway." Nothing was heard of him until years later when he turned up again. In the meantime, he'd been dropped from the rolls of the Navy, and his father tried to make a law case out of the fact that since he was not borne on the Navy lists, he couldn't be a deserter. I don't know what eventually happened to him.*

The second navigator was named Pino, and after he left the ship he went down in the S-51.** So we had hard luck with navigators. The first navigator was the man Jackson, who I told you had fallen between the ship and the brow, so we had three navigators in a row who came to unfortunate ends.

Q: That was a rather star-crossed billet.

---

*The Naval Academy Alumni Association's Register of Alumni contains the following information concerning Harry Thurston Smith, class of 1922: resigned 4 October 1930 from the Navy as a lieutenant (junior grade), died 30 January 1973.
**Lieutenant (junior grade) Harlow M. Pino, USN, was lost 25 September 1925 when the submarine S-51 (SS-162) was rammed by the merchant steamer City of Rome and sank off Block Island, New York.

Admiral Strauss: Yes.

Q: Was it the feeling that Smith actually had killed himself, or that he just disappeared?

Admiral Strauss: We didn't know. We didn't know.

Q: Did you get into Cuba at all?

Admiral Strauss: Yes. We had liberty once or twice in Havana. I remember I was on shore patrol in Havana, but that's all.

Q: Prohibition wasn't enforced there, so that provided a means of relaxation.

Admiral Strauss: Prohibition wasn't in effect in Key West either.

Q: Except when the federal agents came.

Admiral Strauss: Yes.

Q: What was your specific role in connection with the surveying?

Admiral Strauss: I was one of the four boat officers. We had two civilian hydrographers attached to us, and they lived in the houseboat. They assigned the daily survey areas. The head of the houseboat was a mustang lieutenant. For bathing we had a sort of shower, a pierced bucket. But it was interesting. One of the things, most of the people turned black from the sun. I would keep peeling and never was able to get a tan.

Q: How much did you keep up professionally with the rest of the Navy? This almost sounds like detached duty.

Admiral Strauss: It was so detached duty that I'll tell you something that may be of interest. Rodgers was the second captain they sent after the great debacle of the Hannibal. The Hannibal reported directly to the hydrographer of the Navy and nobody else. His predecessor, had been Captain Conn, and before Conn was a man called Parker, a commander.* This thing was a pirate story, and I wrote it up for Shipmate.** The editor kept it for a long time, and then he sent it back to me because he thought it would do damage to the Navy to recount this

---

*Commander William T. Conn, Jr, USN, relieved Commander Edward C. S. Parker, USN, as commanding officer of the USS Hannibal (AG-1) in 1924.
**Shipmate is a magazine published by the Naval Academy Alumni Association.

story.

Parker was a terrific drunk, and he had some wild Indians among the officers and men. The doctor was an ally of his. And the executive officer was a lieutenant commander called S. L. H. Hazard.* And if Hazard had put the captain under arrest and reported it, I think that he would have been vindicated. Eventually, the captain was removed.

Some of the incidents recounted at the court of inquiry were startling. Boatswain Ullman, one of the very few of the crew who spanned both regimes, used to tell us some of these stories.** One time the court asked him if he could remember what took place on such and such a day. Ullman said, "Oh, yes, that was the day the captain tried to crucify the boatswain's mate." Apparently the captain had asked the boatswain's mate to have a drink with him.

The bluejacket said, "I don't think it right for me to drink with you on board." The captain then told the ship's carpenter to rig up a cross. Fortunately, he had more drink and forgot about it.

Some of the things that went on are unbelievable. One time, when the ship was in Key West, some of her officers had a row at a station dance about some woman. Her escort went to bed in his house on the station. The Hannibal officers went to his house, woke him up, and punched him.

---
*Lieutenant Commander Stanton L. H. Hazard, USN.
**Boatswain David L. Ullman, USN.

The captain, on learning of it, said, "We'd better get out of here," so he got the ship under way and stood out.

There was one occasion when some of the crew intended to attack Lieutenant Swanson, a mustang disciplinarian.* Ensign Walfrid Nyquist, in '21, stood with a pistol and told them to get back down the hatch.**

Parker was, of course, taken off the ship. He was eventually tried but was declared insane and ended up in St. Elizabeths. Parker's brother was a member of Congress and may well have exerted influence. How long he stayed in St. Elizabeths and what happened to him afterwards, I do not know. But that was the <u>Hannibal</u> at that time. The great lesson I tried to bring out in my article was the danger in not having a chain of command. Mind you, 99 commanding officers out of 100, or 999 out of 1,000, would not have behaved in this way. But you get a nut like that, and it shows what can happen.

Q: I'm sorry that <u>Shipmate</u> didn't publish it. If you still have a copy, we could append it to this account.

Admiral Strauss: I have a copy. I've thought of expurgating some of the names.

---

*Lieutenant Emil Swanson, USN.
**Ensign John Walfrid Nyquist, USN.

Q: I think the statute of limitations must surely have expired by now.

Admiral Strauss: No, the editor felt that to publish it in Shipmate would reflect badly on the Navy, you see, the fact that this had happened. But after all, it was 1922. That was a long time ago. These people, though, I'm sure none of them are still alive.

Q: Were the findings from the surveys compiled on board or just sent directly into the hydrographic office?

Admiral Strauss: The soundings were collected, and they were taken back to Philadelphia. The winter was spent in transferring these soundings, the data, to a chart. Of ten soundings, perhaps one of them would actually get onto the chart, sometimes more than that. But they were the whole basis of the final chart. We found that there was one boat that had recorded beautiful soundings, all of them right on the lines, where ours skipped. We found that those soundings weren't particularly reliable, that the chart man tried to make his sheet beautiful. We had to put all of the soundings together, to transfer them to a chart. We spent most of the winter in Philadelphia doing this.

Q: Was there any specific stimulus to this expedition--

that the fleet would be operating more in this area than it had been?

Admiral Strauss: It was part of an international effort which the French and the British did elsewhere in the Caribbean and in South America, all of which had been badly charted. It was a naval effort to make reasonable charts for that part of the world. The fact that the Navy might have to operate there was probably a consideration, but it was mainly for merchant shipping. The insurance rates for sugar carriers were very high at that time, and after we made the new charts, they went down.

Q: That's interesting. Well, if it hadn't been done in two or three centuries, I'd say it was certainly overdue.

Admiral Strauss: I'd say it was, yes.

Q: Let me raise the subject of the Naval Institute Proceedings. How was that regarded among the junior officers of the fleet in that time? Was it a useful professional magazine?

Admiral Strauss: Oh, I think so. I couldn't say how widely read, but among the serious officers that it was read with interest. I have a copy of an article my father

Strauss #1 - 68

wrote around 1900, on smokeless powder.* I've had two or three articles in the Proceedings.** I had one that I would like to have reprinted. It was called "Stars, Stripes and Gresham's Law," and it's about the ruination of the rank system in the services.

Q: When about was that published?

Admiral Strauss: March 1968.

Q: How long did this surveying tour last for you?

Admiral Strauss: It was a little more than a year. The next expedition went around November. I did not go on that. I was transferred to the Arkansas, which was just going back in commission after a refit. I first was assigned the secondary battery and then had turret three in the Arkansas. I was in her not a very long time. And then I had a ridiculous idea; I was thinking about leaving the Navy. I was going to get married, and my prospective wife's family wanted me to do other things. So I submitted my resignation, then went on leave and thought better of

---

*Lieutenant Joseph Strauss, USN, "Smokeless Powder, Proceedings, December 1901, pages 733-738. Commander Joseph Strauss, USN, "The Stability of Smokeless Powder," Proceedings, December 1910, pages 929-942.
**A listing of the younger Strauss's writings for the Proceedings is contained in an appendix at the back of this volume.

Strauss #1 - 69

it, I'm delighted to say, and withdrew it. I was over in North Africa when I withdrew it. I went to Rome and had the naval attaché there cancel it. So then I was ordered back to the destroyer Toucey.

Q: Maybe we could talk a little about the Arkansas from the time you were on board. You say she went back in commission. Was this modernization with the tripod masts and so forth?

Admiral Strauss: Yes. They took the cage masts off her. She had a catapult with a plane. The catapult was on my turret, and I had to be very careful, because if one didn't see that the boats and so forth were clear, you'd smash a boat up with the back end of the catapult. In addition, the captain's gig was right back there. All boats then were gasoline boats, and they had to be inspected every day to see that the bilges were clear of gasoline. The boat officer of the gig was Wiggles Weeden in the class of '24.* He was called up by the captain, who said, "Mr. Weeden, did you inspect the bilges of the gig this morning?"

And Weeden said, "Captain, I didn't, but I'm going to go down there right away."

He said, "Don't bother, Mr. Weeden. It's just burnt

_____
*Lieutenant (junior grade) William W. Weeden, Jr., USN.

up."

Q: What did you do as a turret officer? What do you recall of those duties?

Admiral Strauss: Oh, I was fascinated. I was started off as a 5-inch battery officer, and I didn't like that at all because there were too many guns. You had an awful hard time getting suitable crews who could man them. But the turret was a single unit, 12-inch/50-caliber, and that was a very fascinating job. I've always thought being a turret officer was one of the most professional jobs that there is.

Q: Why do you say that?

Admiral Strauss: Well, at that time the Navy existed to carry the turrets of the battleship. That was really their job.

Q: Everything else supported that.

Admiral Strauss: Yes. The screening and so forth was all done to protect these battleships and to get their turrets from one place to another to fight an engagement. So it was, I felt, the heart of the matter. They had constant drill. You know, getting the powder up and the shell and cutting down the time was a constant effort. We made a constant effort to try to cut a second off of here and a second off of there and at the same time make sure that the guns were properly boresighted. I remember the first short-range battle practice. We had a very fine officer, Cy Humphreys.* And he had one of the turrets. And in short-range battle practice, my turret got all 12 hits. But they weren't very fast. Cy Humphreys only got 11 hits, but he got an E out of it because the turret--bang, bang, bang--just that fast. I got credit for getting 12 hits; I don't think one other turret did.

Q: How fast would you say--maybe two or three rounds a minute per barrel?

Admiral Strauss: I would think a little faster than that-- perhaps 15 or 20 seconds between rounds.

Q: I've read that in that class of ship the guns were not in individual gun rooms--that really the turret officer could see the whole inside of the thing.

Admiral Strauss: That's right. From his booth he could see the whole gun chamber.

---
*Lieutenant (junior grade) Charles W. Humprheys, USN.

Strauss #1 - 72

Q: Didn't that present something of a safety hazard in that an explosion would really wipe out the whole turret?

Admiral Strauss: Yes, it did. You see, we wiped out a couple of turrets. In the <u>Mississippi</u>, I had a classmate who was killed in her turret explosion, Marcus Erwin.* And I had another one who got to safety down the shell hoist during a turret fire. He died just a little while ago--Levasseur.** He was a very little man, but he survived that explosion.

Q: He was in the <u>Mississippi</u> also?

Admiral Strauss: Yes. Then there was another officer, Henry Clay Drexler. He and his brother Louis Drexler both were in the Navy. Henry was killed in a turret explosion in a gun mount of a four-stack cruiser, the <u>Trenton</u>.*** So turret accidents weren't rare things in those days. Louis Drexler was killed in World War II.****

Q: Did you, as a result of these accidents, particularly

---
*Ensign Marcus Erwin, Jr., USN, was killed in a turret explosion on board the USS <u>Mississippi</u> (BB-41) while operating near San Pedro, California, 12 June 1924.
**Ensign Julian J. Levasseur, USN.
***Ensign Henry C. Drexler, USN, was killed on board the <u>Trenton</u> (CL-11) off Norfolk, Virginia, 20 October 1924.
****Commander Louis A. Drexler, Jr., USN, was killed 12 May 1945 while in command of a group of tank landing ships.

stress safety?

Admiral Strauss: Well, not so long before, I think when the ship was recommissioned, they put in sprinkler systems, which you could control right from the turret officer's booth.

Q: But you would still want to train your crew in making sure that the mushroom was well wiped off and that the gases were expelled.

Admiral Strauss: Oh, yes, yes.

Q: And what to do if a powder bag is broken and that sort of thing.

Admiral Strauss: Yes. There was a lot of drill to provide for that. I always remember that when you said, "Send up powder, send up powder," you might have a time getting the powder. But if you said, "Secure the turret," you could whisper and get it done.

Q: You mentioned it was hard getting the crews for the 5-inch guns. Why was that?

Admiral Strauss: Well, a gun captain had to be an organizer and a leader. You had to get people who could think quickly, do these jobs, and organize their gun crews, and there weren't all that many around.

I remember a couple of things that might be of some interest during that cruise. I was sent over to another battleship, the Wyoming, on an umpiring crew for target practice, and I took along with me a gunner's mate who was a superb man. He was a man I depended on a great deal. I told him to come in with a stopwatch to take the time of shots of a turret. And when I got in the turret, he wasn't there. The firing was ready to start and there wasn't anything I could do. Before the next turret firing, I said, "What happened to you?"

And he said, "Oh, I got lost."

And I said, "Well, you're going to stay right with me and we'll go in the next one together."

And when we got there he said, "Mr. Strauss, don't make me go in that turret."

And I said, "Why not?"

He said, "I just can't stand it." He said, "I would go to pieces." He had some sort of claustrophobia, you see.

And I said, "All right." And I didn't do anything about it because he was such a good man. That was his peculiarity, and I thought that the call on him to go into

Strauss #1 - 75

a turret needn't happen very often. He just had this quirk. I hadn't run into it before.

Q: Well, every one of us has a phobia of some sort.

Admiral Strauss: Oh, yes. I remember another time I went to practice. There was a very colorful man in the Navy-- his widow lives in Washington now--Hamilton Vose Bryan.* And he was a great sportsman. He got together a Navy polo team. And he was the wardroom treasurer of the Florida. I went over with the first lieutenant of our ship, Lieutenant Commander Bartlett.** And Bryan said, "Come and look at this, what I've done with the wardroom. See those curtains. I had those put in." And he said, "See that molding there. I had that done." And he said, "Look at those pictures. What do you think of it all?"

Bartlett said, "Well," he said, "I'll come in and I'll look around and I'll talk to the girls, but I certainly won't go upstairs."

Q: Sort of an un-nautical atmosphere.

Admiral Strauss: Well, Bartlett's remark killed Ham Bryan.

---
*Lieutenant Commander Hamilton V. Bryan, USN, was first lieutenant in the USS Florida (BB-30) in 1927.
**Lieutenant Commander Harold T. Bartlett, USN, was first lieutenant of the USS Arkansas (BB-33) in 1927.

Strauss #1 - 76

Q: Being compared to a house of prostitution.

Well, how did this assignment affect your status? Now you were getting a little more senior in the wardroom. Did you enjoy that?

Admiral Strauss: Yes. Because I had a turret, I was never in the junior officers' mess. The tables in the wardroom were divided up as senior first, second, third, and fourth wards. Fourth ward held the very junior people. I was in fourth ward.

Q: Did you stand deck watches in that ship?

Admiral Strauss: You bet. Oh, yes.

Q: What do you recall about those?

Admiral Strauss: Well, there were a lot of them, in port and at sea. We had four watch sections very often, which meant that you were on watch four hours and off 12. I have been one in three. I've never actually been watch and watch. The midwatch, midnight to 4:00 A.M., was the worst. I preferred the morning watch, 4:00 to 8:00 A.M. The sun rose, the ship woke up. I could send to the galley for a sandwich. The evening watch, 8:00 to 12:00 P.M., always seemed interminable.

Q: Who was your skipper?

Admiral Strauss: The skipper was Amon Bronson.* He was not a very able captain. I had the impression he was not enthusiastic about his job. He did what was required but appeared not to be professionally interested beyond that.

One of the officers on board was John Heffernan, who was afterwards Director of Naval History.** John was a lieutenant. John was the senior watch officer, and I was the junior, so I relieved John Heffernan. And I loved John and he was a great historian, but you'd say, "Are both anchors ready for letting go?"

"Well, yes, I'll see. Yes, I'm sure they are."

Q: Hesitating.

Admiral Strauss: Yes. And one time I remember, in maneuvering, Bronson had the conn and John Heffernan, a great historian, was the officer of the deck. And Heffernan would say, "At this time the houses of Aragon and Castile were at swords points. Aragon was winning."

And the captain interjected, "Right ten degrees rudder. Yes, Mr. Heffernan. Increase to 85 turns."

---
*Captain Amon Bronson, Jr., USN.
**Lieutenant John B. Heffernan, USN.

Strauss #1 - 78

Meanwhile, Heffernan would go right on, "Queen Catherine of Aragon . . ."

Q: His mind really was on other things besides the job at hand.

Admiral Strauss: Yes.

Q: That's got to be distracting to a conning officer.

Admiral Strauss: Yes. Bronson was long suffering. He didn't say, "Shut up."

Q: Was there a good deal of competition among the battleships?

Admiral Strauss: Yes. The executive officer of the <u>Florida</u> was Commander Mayo.* He once told his crew, "I want everything done bang-up, smartly." He said, "I want the ships around here to say, 'That was done right, that was done <u>Florida</u> fashion.'" So shortly after that, they were hoisting in a boat and one of the falls gave away, and the bow of the boat was hanging from the davit. So the word went around if you overturned a bucket of paint, for example, "Don't do that. That's <u>Florida</u> fashion."

---
*Commander Claude B. Mayo, USN.

Q: This is Ditty Box Mayo?

Admiral Strauss: Yes, that's right.

Q: Did you compete primarily in your own division?

Admiral Strauss: Yes.

Q: Probably with the Wyoming.

Admiral Strauss: There was the Florida, Utah, Wyoming, Arkansas.*

Q: Four ships.

Admiral Strauss: Yes.

Q: Did you have the flag on board at all?

Admiral Strauss: Yes, Commander Scouting Fleet was Vice Admiral A. H. Robertson.** From my very junior position, I had no contact with the admiral and remember nothing of

---
*These four ships comprised Battleship Division Two, the only battleship division in the Scouting Fleet in the Atlantic.
**Vice Admiral Ashley H. Robertson, USN.

him. I came to know the chief of staff, Captain R. Z. Johnston, very well, as afterwards we were in Newport at the same time.* Johnston had a Medal of Honor from the Veracruz operation. He was not selected for flag rank but years later received a promotion to rear admiral.

As for some of the other staff officers, Commander Draemel was also a friend.** I admired him greatly and predicted high rank for him. He became a rear admiral but for some reason stopped there. Commander Alan Kirk I probably knew as well as anyone in the Navy.*** His mother-in-law, wife of Captain Frederick Chapin, had introduced my mother and father to one another. I first met Alan when he was a lieutenant commander. We were together in London during World War II when he commanded the U.S. section of the naval expeditionary force for the invasion of Normandy.

Q: Did athletics play a part in the fleet then?

Admiral Strauss: Yes, they had boat races, and then they had pistol competition ashore, a number of things like that. They had baseball teams. And boxing, I remember

---

*Captain Rufus Z. Johnston, USN. In 1914, while serving as executive officer of the battleship New Hampshire, he was adjutant in the Second Seaman Regiment during its landing at Veracruz, Mexico.
**Commander Milo F. Draemel, USN.
***Commander Alan G. Kirk, USN. Kirk's oral history is in the Columbia University collection.

Strauss #1 - 81

they did for happy hour and so forth. I don't know if there was any inter-ship boxing.

Q: Then after that you went to the Toucey, you said.

Admiral Strauss: I went to the Toucey, and the captain was H. H. Frost, who was quite a man. He wrote On a Destroyer's Bridge, and he wrote We Build a Navy.* And actually he gave me a couple lines in the credits for each book that were very welcome.**

I don't know whether you know anything about Frost, but he was a lieutenant commander and he got promoted to commander in the ship. He went on the staff of Commander in Chief of the Pacific Fleet. He was a commander but was a tactician and strategian and had a great influence on the Navy. Nowadays you never think of a commander having much influence, but when Admiral Reeves took over the fleet, he said that the first thing he was going to do was to "de-Frost" the Navy.*** Frost got a mastoid infection and it went into his spine, and he died of spinal meningitis as a

---

*Commander Holloway H. Frost, USN, On a Destroyer's Bridge (Annapolis, U.S. Naval Institute, 1930). Lieutenant Commander Holloway H. Frost, USN, We Build a Navy (Annapolis: U.S. Naval Institute, 1929).
**In On a Destroyer's Bridge, Frost wrote the following: "Many of the methods of coöperation between the bridge and engineer department, which are so essential to the efficient operation of a destroyer, were worked out in conjunction with Lieutenant (J.G.) Elliott B. Strauss, engineer officer, U.S.S. Toucey."
***Admiral Joseph Mason Reeves, USN, was Commander in Chief U.S. Fleet, 1934-36.

commander, which was a great loss.* I always had a great admiration and respect for H. H. Frost.

Q: Why would Reeves make a comment like that?

Admiral Strauss: I don't know. He disagreed with a particular strategy, or whatever it was that Frost was advocating.

Q: That's a clever thing to say, in any event.

Admiral Strauss: Yes. If Frost had had another name, Reeves couldn't have said it. I didn't admire him particularly for it.

Q: How was Frost as a ship's captain?

Admiral Strauss: He was a fine captain. He wasn't a terribly clever ship handler. But I remember one time coming alongside the tender we caught one of the guys in a boat boom of the tender, and it pulled down a part of our topmast. Admiral Clark was Commander Destroyers Scouting Fleet, and he said, "If you get this fixed up with your ship's company, you won't hear anything more about it. But if you have to call on outside help, I'll have to have a

---
*Frost died 26 January 1935.

board of investigation."* So we got it fixed up. Well, that could have happened to anybody.

Frost was very loyal, up and down. It was the time when people were getting into trouble for bringing liquor on board ships. There were several incidents. And Frost got us all together, and he said, "I'm your friend." He said. "If you get into trouble, I'm here to get you out of it." But he said, "If any of you bring so much as an ounce of alcohol on board, I'll see myself that you get a general court-martial."

Q: Well, at least you knew where you stood.

Admiral Strauss: Yes. I thought he was a fine man and a dedicated officer.

Q: How would you assess him in terms of leadership?

Admiral Strauss: Well, he was not a swashbuckler. He wasn't a Bill Halsey type.** I think he was probably more a Spruance type.

---

*Rear Admiral Frank H. Clark, USN, embarked in the USS Concord (CL-10).
**Admiral William F. Halsey, Jr., USN, Commander Third Fleet during the latter part of World War II in the Pacific was aggressive and publicity-conscious; Admiral Raymond A. Spruance, USN, Commander Fifth Fleet, was methodical and quiet.

Strauss #1 - 84

Q: As one of his department heads in that ship, how close were you to him?

Admiral Strauss: I was his engineer. After he left the ship, he wrote to tell me I had passed my promotion exams before this was announced.

He used to say there were only two jobs in a ship--the captain and the engineer.

Q: Well, that's very flattering.

Admiral Strauss: Well, in a destroyer of those days it had some truth.

Q: What do you recall of the engineering plant?

Admiral Strauss: Well, of course, my last contact with any engineering was that type of plant. They had all reciprocating pumps, 150 pounds boiler pressure, and it was a job keeping these things going. The pumps would break down, or the condensers would salt up. You had to be working at them all the time. And eventually. after Frost left the ship, they put the Toucey out of commission along with a number of other ships.* It was claimed they had

---

*The USS Toucey (DD-282) was decommissioned 1 May 1930 at Philadelphia.

microscopic cracks in the boiler tubes, and we had to emery off several pipes and look at them with magnifying glasses. I could never see any cracks, but the division engineer came on board, and he took a look around and he said, "No, this ship's got to be decommissioned." So they decommissioned the Toucey and I don't know how many of the others.

Then we put the Blakeley into commission. The captain was a very nice man; he was W. G. B. Hatch, in '13.* One time, after working on a frustrating job on that plant, I snapped at him. Before I could apologize, he smoothed it over. From the Blakeley I went to shore duty in Newport, Rhode Island, in the Torpedo Station.

Q: Are there any operations that stand out from either of those destroyers? What sorts of duty did you have?

Admiral Strauss: We went to Guantánamo for the winter and would hold maneuvers down there: tactical exercises, simulated shore bombardment, that type of thing. And then the summer around Newport, based on Newport, doing pretty much the same operations.

Q: That's a pretty comfortable operating schedule.

---
*Lieutenant Commander William G. B. Hatch, USN, who had been commanding officer of the Toucey (DD-282) before she went out of commission.

Admiral Strauss: Yes.

Q: How well did your stomach adapt to the four-stack life? Did you have any problems with seasickness?

Admiral Strauss: Oh, I've been seasick from time to time. I was seasick in the Concord. Anybody who's been to sea a long time in any weather and says he hasn't been seasick, I don't believe him.

Q: Anything else about these ships that you want to put on the record?

Admiral Strauss: No. The discipline--even in those small ships under hard-lying conditions--I think was excellent. There was team spirit. I sort of have a feeling it was better than it is nowadays. Maybe the current times require a looser organization and a looser structure.

Q: Well, there's a good deal of togetherness between officers and men in such a small vessel, and literally you are all in the same boat. You share a good deal of the hardship.

Admiral Strauss: I remember that we were in a storm off of

Hatteras one time, and the Manley was really taking a good battering. And the chief machinist's mate said afterwards, "You know, when we go to sea, I always get seasick." He said, "I didn't get seasick that time. I was too scared."

Q: You mentioned the plans that your future wife's family had had for you. At what point in the sequence did you get married?

Admiral Strauss: After the Arkansas, I went to Washington very briefly for the communications school. Communications school really meant you did decoding and then took the messages to the different offices. One incident which I remember: I took a message to the Director of Naval Intelligence, where I was routinely to give it to the deputy director, Captain David Le Breton.* He had not come back from a late lunch. I tried to give the message to the director, Captain Alfred Johnson.** Johnson told me to keep the message and to wait for Captain Le Breton and to say, "Captain, I have been waiting for your return to give you this message.

It was between the communications school and Toucey that I got married.***

---
*Captain David M. Le Breton, USN, assistant director of naval intelligence.
**Captain Alfred W. Johnson, USN, director of naval intelligence.
***Strauss was married to Lydia Archbold on 14 February 1928.

Q: How had you met your future wife?

Admiral Strauss: I met her up in Bar Harbor when the Concord went there for Tennis Week. The British North Atlantic Squadron used to go to Bar Harbor for Tennis Week also.

Q: Was she from a Bar Harbor family?

Admiral Strauss: No, I guess you would say a New York family, but her mother had a house in Bar Harbor and a house in Washington.

Q: Where did she settle then when you went to sea?

Admiral Strauss: We built a house in Newport, and she stayed there.

Q: Was that why you landed in Newport for your first shore duty?

Admiral Strauss: Yes, it was. I was ordered there at that time, and I had the high-sounding title of explosives officer at the Torpedo Station. My division's main job was making primers for the Navy. It made primers for both fixed ammunition and for bag ammunition.

Q: So they did other things besides just torpedoes there, evidently.

Admiral Strauss: Well, our main relationship with torpedoes was we loaded the warheads. We made the detonators and we made the igniters for the torpedoes. And we made fuzes for medium-caliber guns. Actually, we made some for major caliber guns, 14-inch guns, too. But the bulk of the job was primers. We loaded tetryl, and the place where we loaded tetryl boosters was isolated because we were always afraid the tetryl would go up. Besides the explosive danger, it was very bad for people's kidneys, and we put them in rubber gloves and masks. And I used to try to go down once or twice a day to the tetryl plant, and I'd see the people putting on their masks, you know, as I approached.

Q: They didn't wear them most of the time.

Admiral Strauss: No, and I would say, "You damn fools. I don't care whether you get sick." I said, "You're not putting a mask on to please me; you're putting them on for yourself."

One of the jobs in primers is called bridging. You may know this; I'm sure you do. You put a piece of fine platinum wire, soldered on the two ends, into the primer. When you turn the electricity on, this heats up and ignites a wisp of gun cotton, and then that ignites the black powder. The platinum wire is about half as thick as a normal hair. It is quite a delicate job, soldering both ends. Well, it's called "bridging." The factory brought in, I think, about ten women to be bridgers, because they thought that with their small hands they'd do better than the men.

Well, actually, the best woman bridger was about equal to the lowest man bridger. If you ask me why, I don't know. So we took them off of bridging and put them on gauging, because all these parts had to be gauged--the maximum, the minimum, which they had to stay between. Then the men did all the bridging. And once a year we had to make fulminate of mercury to keep our hands in on its manufacture. We didn't allow women to do it because you couldn't blow up a woman, and nowadays they talk about having them in combat. Back then they weren't allowed to have anything to do with the explosives.

Q: Was that a real danger?

Admiral Strauss: Fulminate, yes; tetryl, no. I don't

think so. And TNT, no.* But one of the things that struck me there was everybody in the place knew to a couple of millimeters the tolerances on an igniter or the flask of a torpedo, but one had ever seen a warhead explode. There was only one person on the place, and he was a civilian ordnance engineer, who had ever seen a torpedo go up.

Well, I was in a very junior position, but I suggested that we ought to actually fire a torpedo against something that would really test it. Because the test they did, they'd hang the torpedo on two chains, pull back the torpedo, and let it hit a steel plate. If the ball left the exploder, well, that was considered a satisfactory test. As you know, in the war the performance of torpedoes was a fiasco.

After I left, I heard that they had got two destroyers that the Navy had handed to the Coast Guard, and the Navy Department said that these could be used as targets, provided they weren't destroyed beyond the position where they could be repaired. Well, what the hell? To my mind, that was a grave lapse, the fact that mechanically they knew everything about a torpedo as a boat, but as an explosive device they really didn't know anything. And we paid dearly for it.

Q: Ralph Christie was involved in the development of a

---
*TNT--trinitrotoluene, a potent explosive.

magnetic exploder.*

Admiral Strauss: He was the torpedo officer at the time I was attached to the Torpedo Station.

Q: What recollections do you have him?

Admiral Strauss: Well, he was very up and coming and very agreeable. He and his wife I liked very much. He was a very able officer, as he proved himself.

After I left there, as my next job I went as exec of the Manley, and the Manley was the ship attached to the Torpedo Station that took torpedoes out to test their running performance. But the explosive officer job was an interesting job.

Q: It sounds like essentially there was a factory there.

Admiral Strauss: Yes, there was. It was a torpedo factory. And the manufacturing officer, my boss, was Gordon Hutchins.**

Q: Were these civil service employees?

Admiral Strauss: Yes, yes. The head of the primer plant
_____
*Lieutenant Commander Ralph W. Christie, USN.
**Lieutenant Commander Gordon Hutchins, USN.

was an old-timer civilian. They wanted to get rid of him, but he had political clout, and he never did anything they could really fire him for. To the men it was a job. They were supporting their families. The women on the whole were doing it till they could get married; they were doing it to make a little extra money. And very often you'd come in, where they were working, and you'd see them sort of slapping one another. And they would go in the women's restroom and just stay in there and they'd make tea. Well, I finally got to put an external switch on the tea electric line, so that they couldn't make tea all day long. That practice wasted work time.

Q: Had you had an opportunity to go to postgraduate school when you came ashore?

Admiral Strauss: Well, the only school--I went to the Imperial Defence College, now called the Royal College of Defence Studies, but that was a good deal later.

Q: No, I'm wondering, though, if you had an option of going to PG school rather than the torpedo factory at that time.

Admiral Strauss: It was never suggested. I was ordered from sea to take the explosives officer job.

Q: It sounds like the sort of job that would usually be held by an ordnance PG. How did you get assigned to it without that background?

Admiral Strauss: I don't know. My predecessor, F. M. O'Leary, was not a PG.*

Q: Evidently that wasn't a prerequisite.

Admiral Strauss: No, it certainly wasn't. I certainly wasn't an ordnance PG. I can't remember who, if any, of the officers of the station were ordnance PG's.

Q: But you picked it up fairly quickly, I take it?

Admiral Strauss: Well, of course, at first you had to depend on the people who were engaged in the work. But I found that the difference was they knew the job lots better than I did, or people in my position did, but they wouldn't accept any responsibility. You know, they'd come around and say, "This is failing because of so and so. What should we do?"

"Well, let's increase the thickness then."

"Will you take responsibility?" And it very often was

_____
*Lieutenant Forrest M. O'Leary, USN.

that.

Q: So your job was not so much how it got done, but to make sure that it did get done.

Admiral Strauss: Yes, yes. And I remember one time they had an automatic machine for turning out the bodies of the primers, and the manufacturing officer got rid of it. And I said, "Gee, you only brought this thing in here a year ago and it cost so much."

And he said, "This new machine will make them that much faster and it will pay for itself." He was, of course, right.

Q: Did you get involved in the Newport social season?

Admiral Strauss: Oh, yes.

Q: It was quite a colony of naval officers up there at the War College.

Admiral Strauss: Yes, the War College and Training Station.

Q: Well, Admiral, I think that this probably would be a convenient place to break it off. Is there anything else you wanted to mention about that Newport tour?

Admiral Strauss: Some of the British North Atlantic Squadron visited there, and we had quite a "do" for them. I was assigned as liaison officer with the squadron commander, the British admiral, Sir Matthew Best.* The Training Station had a dance, which Admiral Best and a number of his officers attended. At the end of the dance, the band played the "Star-Spangled Banner." They had not been alerted to play "God Save the King." This was finally taken care of, but the pause was embarrassing.

Well, I could go on a long time about the Torpedo Station, but I think you're right. It probably is a good place.

---

*Rear Admiral Matthew Robert Best, Royal Navy, Commanding Second Cruiser Squadron.

Interview Number 2 with Rear Admiral Elliott B. Strauss,
U.S. Navy (Retired)

Place: Admiral Strauss's home in Washington, D.C.

Date: Thursday, 30 October 1986

Interviewer: Paul Stillwell

Admiral Strauss: The Manley had bow number 74. She was left over from World War I, and her stern had been blown off during World War I by explosion of depth charges on the fantail. The explosion killed the executive officer, Dickie Elliott, who was hit in the head by one of the compensating balls from the compass.*

The first captain when I was on board was Norman Gillette, who was a very fine officer, quiet, easy to get along with.** He was relieved by Lieutenant Commander Edwin Dowling Gibb. Gibb was quite a different type of officer. He was probably the best, albeit the most dangerous, shiphandler I've ever known. Just after he took over, we were assigned to go to New London to be present for the annual Yale-Harvard boat races. We had a berth alongside a long pier facing a brick building. We came down the pier at about five knots, and I thought we were going into the brick business. He ordered all engines full

---

*Lieutenant Commander Richard M. Elliott, Jr., USN, was killed on 19 March 1918. Thirty-three enlisted crew members were also killed by the explosion, which occurred while the ship was on convoy duty.
**Lieutenant Commander Norman C. Gillette, USN.

speed astern, started off the bridge and said, "Tie her up, Strauss." We stopped--well, you could have got no more than a calling card between the brick wall and the bow, and that was my introduction to Ted Gibb. We became very good friends and kept up over the years.

I went to the Manley on the West Coast. This was under Captain Gillette's command, and we came down the West Coast, through the canal, and back to Newport, where we were stationed to test torpedoes. Coming down the West Coast of the United States, I think just off lower California, I saw the greatest gathering of sea turtles that I'd ever imagined. They were like polka dots for as far as you can see. We made our way through them.

Later on, the Manley was assigned to be a guard for the President, who was cruising in the Nourmahal, Vincent Astor's yacht, on a fishing expedition.* This was on the East Coast. He caught a sea turtle and presented the ship with its flippers, which in a way I thought was an insult until I found that the flippers, perhaps, were the best part of the turtle for making soup.

Q: Was Roosevelt President by then?

Admiral Strauss: Roosevelt was President, yes. He was a
_____
*William Vincent Astor was a wealthy yachtsman and Naval Reserve officer. For more on Astor and the Nourmahal, see Jeffery M. Dorwart, Conflict of Duty (Annapolis: Naval Institute Press, 1983).

great friend of Vincent Astor. They went out quite a number of times together. The President's senior aide was in our ship. He was Wally Vernou, and with him were two of his junior aides.* One of them was Stuart Blue, who was afterwards sunk in the Juneau in the Pacific.** He had his 31st birthday in the Manley, and Froggy Pound said, "Here you are, Blue, 31 years of age and the only thing you've ever accomplished is the President calls you by your first name."***

Q: Did you have any impressions of Vernou? I've heard he was a very punctilious man and a good seaman.

Admiral Strauss: The only time I ever saw him at sea was on this occasion, and there wasn't much chance to evaluate him. He was certainly a pleasant and a very good shipmate for the short time he was on board. He had a complete absence of pomposity with his juniors.

Q: I would think that the President would want an engaging individual as his companion and aide.

---
*Captain Walter N. Vernou, USN, naval aide to the President.
**Lieutenant (junior grade) John Stuart Blue, USN, was commanding officer of the USS Sequoia (AG-25), the presidential yacht. He was a lieutenant commander when the cruiser Juneau (CL-52) was lost in November 1942. His 31st birthday was on 29 August 1933.
***Lieutenant (junior grade) Harold C. Pound, USN, who was assigned as an aide at the White House.

Admiral Strauss: I think almost always. Is it all right to digress a bit?

Q: Certainly.

Admiral Strauss: One of the other President's aides that I knew was afterwards Admiral Forde Todd. He told several stories about the President and serving in that capacity as aide to Wilson.* It was a custom in those days for the President to receive citizens on New Year's Day. At one time the citizens were lined up to go by the President, and then-Captain Todd said a very elderly man came up to the President and said, "Mr. President, I'm so glad to be here." He said, "I lined up at 6:00 o'clock this morning. And here I am, and all I can say, sir, is, goddamn you, sir, goddamn you--uh, uh! My! What have I said?"

Then the other thing that he noted was a congressman who was very much a man of the people. He came through the receiving line with his front and back collar studs showing, and the thing that struck Captain Todd was when he got to the front door, he put his collar on to leave the White House. He wanted to show that he was a man of the people, you see. He didn't "dress up" for these occasions.

---

*Captain Forde A. Todd, USN, was naval aide to President Woodrow Wilson in 1913-14.

Q: You, perhaps, knew Todd when he was a cruiser division commander and you were in the Nashville?*

Admiral Strauss: Yes, I did. I knew him personally quite well, because although he was a South Carolinian, he loved Philadelphia and had married a Philadelphia girl, a Miss Barnes. When I was in Philadelphia putting the Blakeley back in commission, I saw a great deal of them.

Q: Did the Manley suffer any aftereffects from the problem during World War I?

Admiral Strauss: No. The construction on the after part was different. The dogs were different, and the mountings of the ports were different, but no, there was no trouble otherwise.

Q: You worked up to be executive officer in the Manley, didn't you?

Admiral Strauss: Yes, you're right. Under Gillette I was engineer. Spike Kelty in '20 was the exec.** And when he left, I fleeted up to be exec.

---

*As a rear admiral in the late 1930s, Todd commanded Cruiser Division Eight.
**Lieutenant John N. Kelty, USN.

Strauss #2 - 102

Q: What recollections do you have of the engineering plant in one of those old four-stackers?

Admiral Strauss: They were difficult to keep up, but they were basic. There wasn't a great deal that could go wrong with them. There's nothing delicate; it's just that they wore out. The pumps and the bearings would go, or the condensers might develop a leak, something of that sort. Otherwise, they ran. Sometimes there was water in the fuel oil. This became quickly evident; the stacks gave white smoke, and the smell of white smoke is different. One could note this even if below deck. If the water was in enough quantity, it could extinguish a boiler fire.

Q: But pretty reliable generally?

Admiral Strauss: Yes.

Q: What do you remember about the enlisted men from that era?

Admiral Strauss: On the whole they were reliable. I don't think that many of them could deal with the sophisticated equipment of today, the radars and sonars and so forth. But for the job of that time, they did it, and I think that the executive ability of a great many of the petty officers was very high. There were a few that had got there sort of by _anno domini_. I remember that we needed a chief watertender, and I got one after considerable difficulty because it was a rating that was very much in short supply. And I found out that his last few years he'd been in charge of the laundry in a shore station and really had had no experience with boilers since he was a fireman. So he was rather difficult to use in that particular job.

Q: How formalized was the training and advancement program to make sure that men did get the proper experience?

Admiral Strauss: I think very little. There were schools--the baker school and the radioman school and so forth, but on the whole the people learned on the job.

Q: Mostly school of the ship.

Admiral Strauss: Yes, exactly.

Q: Did you have classes as such on board, or did people just learn through doing?

Admiral Strauss: Depending on the ship and depending on its duties, you had classes. For instance, you'd have classes for new seamen to prepare them for their exams for higher ratings and so forth. To show the level of education of some of these people, I remember that on an examination for seaman first class a question was, "What paints are put on a ship's bottom?" And the answers, of course, were anti-corrosive and anti-fouling. On one examination a man wrote, "Annie Carusi" and "Annie Fowler" for the answers to this question. And there were a number of similar ones, but on the whole I think we got there.

Q: As the executive you were the chief disciplinary officer. Do you remember any interesting cases in that regard?

Admiral Strauss: Of course, the greatest trouble was over leave and occasionally absent without leave. Of course, if someone was slightly over leave, there was always a very good excuse that the bus broke down, and a standard one was, "The clerk at the YMCA didn't call me." That got to be a joke. I'm afraid that most of them weren't at the YMCA, but that was the story.

Q: That's when they become very imaginative, giving you the excuses.

Admiral Strauss: I remember one commanding officer was

told that the man was returning on the Pennsylvania Railroad, and his train was late. The captain said, "I run the ship, not the Pennsylvania Railroad. Three days under confinement."

Q: Were punishments usually fairly strict?

Admiral Strauss: Yes. Deprivation of liberty was the easiest one, of course. For graver offenses you did put men in the brig. I think a captain was allowed to--five days was the limit, three days on bread and water. I'm not too sure of those figures, but they stick in my mind.

Q: What were the living conditions like on board for both officers and enlisted?

Admiral Strauss: At that time men were in bunks, usually. In some parts of the ship they were three deep. The officers all had single staterooms, but they were small. The captain's cabin was just forward of the engine room bulkhead, and his was the largest. There was only one shower for all the officers and one head for all the officers. So that from that standpoint it wasn't very luxurious.

Q: How was the food on board?

Admiral Strauss: That depended on the mess treasurer and the commanding officer and the quality of the mess attendants that you were given. At that time, Filipino mess attendants were phasing out. The custom was colored mess attendants, and that was a great change, because their nourishment came out of the pay of the mess. The Filipinos would usually have a little fish or a little chicken and rice, whereas when we got black mess attendants, most of them could eat a whole chicken at one sitting. So the bill went up accordingly.

Q: You mentioned your work at the Newport Torpedo Station. Could you elaborate on that? You had had some experience there, so you knew what they were about.

Admiral Strauss: The *Manley* did the test firing for the torpedoes as they were finished. During the latter part of our stay in the ship, they were using the photographic head, firing it under targets to see whether it worked. Well, of course, it worked as far as the mechanism was concerned, but as the war proved, the warheads failed miserably. The detonators failed miserably in practice.

One thing I remember, that during the time that Lieutenant Commander Gillette was the commanding officer he went skating with my then-mother-in-law, Rose Saunderson.

And they fell down, and he broke some ribs and was on the sick list for a while. So I became commanding officer, and the first time I ever handled a ship was during the time that Shorty Gillette was in sick bay. And I remember the first time that I took it from alongside the Torpedo Station, which was on Goat Island, and took it out. That was quite a day in my life.

Q: Were there a few butterflies in your stomach?

Admiral Strauss: Oh, yes. And the first day, if I do say so, I did the thing perfectly. Made a landing right alongside and threw the lines out and got tied up. But the second and the third time it was blowing hard, and when I came in, I got blown off and had to go around and make a landing a second time.

Q: But your confidence builds as you have more and more of those experiences.

Admiral Strauss: Yes.

Q: You mentioned this photographic head. Could you describe that in more detail please?

Admiral Strauss: I wasn't in on the actual workings of the

thing. We fired the torpedo, and those responsible from the Torpedo Station did all the evaluation. Sometimes a torpedo sank, and our job was to try and retrieve it. But the actual performance, we in the ship didn't know very much about.

Q: In what way was it photographic?

Admiral Strauss: As I understand it, it was the shadow of the hull as it went underneath that actuated it.

Q: I see. So that was to be the detonator mechanism.

Admiral Strauss: Yes. You see, the idea was that you could be a certain distance under a ship and blow up there, and it would be more effective than just slamming into the side.

Q: Which was the rationale behind magnetic exploders also.

Admiral Strauss: Yes.

Q: Were there any actual warhead shots during this time-- any explosive warheads?

Admiral Strauss: No. As I said before, that the only

person that had ever seen a warhead explode was the ordnance engineer who was attached to the Torpedo Station, and this event hadn't happened at the Torpedo Station. So even though they were completely familiar with all the workings of a torpedo, all of its dimensions, its difficulties and so forth, none of the people there had ever seen a warhead blow up.

Q: The end of Prohibition came while you were on board the <u>Manley</u>. People no longer had to be so covert about their drinking.

Admiral Strauss: No, but by that time there was very little, if any, in ships. I don't say there was none, but people had become so frightened at what could happen if they brought liquor on board that it had pretty well faded out. In some of the big ships, when they went into Guantánamo, they would smuggle cases of liquor on board. That did take place.

Q: How was the ship employed when she wasn't involved with these torpedo tests? Did you operate with the fleet at all?

Admiral Strauss: We did when the ship went to the West Coast. And during the time there, there was Prohibition, and the Navy--I started to say "as a whole," but that's an exaggeration. On Saturday many would go down to Agua Caliente, in Mexico, where there was plenty to drink. So that the Saturday exodus from San Diego, where we were based, to Tijuana was pretty widespread.

Q: What sorts of operations did you have with the fleet?

Admiral Strauss: We were plane guards for aircraft carriers. We did that a great deal. Then we would have tactical maneuvers. I can't remember that we had any gunnery practice out there. We had gunnery drills, but actual practice during the time we were there, I can't remember that we did.

Q: This would be principally the Lexington and Saratoga, I take it?

Admiral Strauss: Yes.

Q: Do you remember any interesting events from that plane guard duty?

Admiral Strauss: Well, I remember the first time that I saw a plane go over the bow and crash. We were sent over to see what we could do. We picked up a couple of signal flags and a little bit of debris, but that was about all. But they didn't stop the exercises; they went right ahead.

Q: Did the carrier keep you well informed on her intended maneuvers so you could keep up?

Admiral Strauss: No. On the whole, you were supposed to watch her and do what she did.

Q: I take it you still had enough speed from the engineering plant to be able to keep up with her.

Admiral Strauss: Yes, yes.

Q: That's where your "Annie Fowler" paint came in handy.

Admiral Strauss: Yes. We could make about 30 knots. During the year the ship had to make a full-speed run and had to make a smokeless run. That was part of the routine for the year.

Q: Did the skippers you had have a training program to bring you along so you would be eligible for command?

Admiral Strauss: I don't think that there was any organized program. We were supposed to learn on the job,

Strauss #2 - 112

and a good captain would give you advice. He'd give you a chance to handle the ship. Some captains might not be quite that forthcoming.

Q: And you'd learn a lot just by observation, of course.

Admiral Strauss: Yes. In a small ship like that, you have pretty much from time to time all the jobs in the ship. And everything is so close there that you get on to it.

Q: Was there a good deal of camaraderie between officers and crew because of that smallness and closeness?

Admiral Strauss: No. You knew them well and you knew each man really by name, and that was quite a thing. There was a certain informality about uniforms and things like that. There just had to be.

Q: But still a definite division between officers and enlisted.

Admiral Strauss: Yes, yes.

Q: Anything else on the Manley that occurs to you?

Admiral Strauss: We spent a winter in Boston, in the Navy

yard. And that was rather trying, because it was a very cold winter. We were tied up to a pier during all the cold weather, and we had very few officers. I think we were down to four officers at one time, so that the day's duty was pretty frequent. You didn't have much chance to get out of the ship. Ted Gibb, the captain, and I would go ashore in Boston, and there wasn't too much to do. During the better weather, the ship used to go back and forth through the Cape Cod Canal quite often. And that was all a very pleasant experience, except when it was foggy. When it was foggy, they'd make you lie off until it lifted. But I can't think of anything else particularly.

Q: The destroyer force still had the relatively recent memory of the destroyers that piled up at Point Arguello on the West Coast.* Were there precautionary measures taken to avoid that kind of thing subsequently?

Admiral Strauss: Not specifically. The account of the Honda disaster was widely promulgated. It was written up, and there was a Navy Department pamphlet giving most histories of groundings and collisions. Copies were distributed to all the ships, and I think most ships

---

*On 8 September 1923, seven destroyers ran aground on the rocky coast of California as the result of poor visibility and faulty navigation. For a detailed account see Charles A. Lockwood and Hans Christian Adamson, Tragedy at Honda (Philadelphia: Chilton Company, 1960).

studied that pretty well. But I don't think there were any specific instructions on the Honda disaster.

Q: Just the fact that people knew about it might make them a little more cautious.

Admiral Strauss: Oh, yes. Oh, yes.

Q: At that time, promotion for officers was certified by examinations. Do you recall studying for those?

Admiral Strauss: Oh, I do indeed. And I regret that they no longer pertain, because for several months before you took your exams, you spent a great deal of time studying up for them. Quite often somebody would say, "Let's go ashore," and you'd say, "No, I've got to work on my exams."

The exams for lieutenant (junior grade) and lieutenant and lieutenant commander took a lot of time. There were fewer exams for commander. And when I became a commander, it was during wartime and the exams stopped. So I never took any after that. But I can remember the ones I did take--for instance, the practical navigation and the theoretical navigation examinations. I had taken a correspondence course in international law, so I was forgiven the international law examination for lieutenant commander.

Q: From what you say, the exams served a useful purpose.

Admiral Strauss: Oh, they did. They familiarized you with the latest things, and they familiarized you with parts of the Navy that you perhaps hadn't experienced during your recent service. For instance, there were questions on aviation. If you'd been in a ship that had nothing to do with aviation, you had to learn something about aviation.

Q: Did you ever have any inclination or desire to go into either aviation or submarines?

Admiral Strauss: Yes. When I was a very young officer, I wanted to be an aviator, and I took the physical exam and they found that I had exophoria--that is, my eyes didn't line up quite right. It didn't interfere with vision, but they were afraid that if you got very tired, you might get double vision. I think today that that degree of exophoria nobody would have bothered about.

Q: The Navy could afford to be so selective because there were very few aviators.

Admiral Strauss: Yes.

Q: Well, from there you went back again to Newport to the Naval Training Station. What were your duties there?

Admiral Strauss: I was a training officer, a drill officer, and I had an additional job. I was in charge of the entire commissary setup. I was given that job because the previous holder of it had had some money difficulties and got into a good deal of trouble. I think he was court-martialed. So I was put in there to straighten the things out. And we had a gas station, a cafeteria, a shoe shop, a laundry. And, of course, to keep the accounts and to keep everybody happy was quite a job.

I learned certain things. When we set up the cafeteria, I was told by a food expert that the amount of coffee we would sell would depend on whether we had rich cream or not. And I had some trouble with the laundry because Mrs. Lieutenant A would want her socks starched, and Mrs. Lieutenant B would want them unstarched. I mean that isn't accurate, but it's the sort of thing that I was up against. But that was a lesson in itself.

I hadn't been there very long when one of my previous captains that I've referred to, Christopher Rodgers, came to see me. He said, "Someone down in the Bureau of Navigation asked whether you would like to be assistant naval attaché in Italy." And he, Captain Rodgers, replied, "Oh, he's just gone ashore there and it's his home port. I don't think he'd like it." *

And I said, "Please call them up and tell them that I would like it very much." But by that time, Savvy Forrestel had been nominated for the job.** So I said to Captain Rodgers, "Please tell your contact that if anything like this comes along, do please consider me."

Well, in a month or so they were setting up a junior assistant naval attaché in London and asked me whether I'd like that. I jumped at it.

Q: What stimulated your interest in going into that?

Admiral Strauss: Oh, to me it would be a fascinating job. I mean, rather than marching boots around a square it was the sort of thing that appealed to me.

Q: Is that what you were doing at Newport--dealing with the boot camp?

Admiral Strauss: Yes.

Q: Any specific memories about the training and

---

*Captain Christopher R. P. Rodgers, USN (Ret.), had previously been Strauss's skipper in the USS Hannibal in the 1920s. In the mid-1930s, he lived in Washington, D.C., and had a connection with the Office of Naval Intelligence, which supervised the attachés. The Bureau of Navigation controlled officer personnel assignments.
**Lieutenant Commander Emmet P. Forrestel, USN, who did indeed serve as assistant naval attaché in Rome.

administration of the recruits?

Admiral Strauss: It was, of course, an essential job to start them out. The first steps in their training change them from civilians to bluejackets, and they come in pretty woolly. And after two or three weeks you could see the change, that they became sailors.

Q: How large a number of people would be undergoing training during a given time, would you say?

Admiral Strauss: You know, I've forgotten now. I should remember. It was quite a while ago, and I've forgotten how many it was.

Q: Did you have a training vessel there?

Admiral Strauss: Boats, but that's all.

Q: What was in the curriculum?

Admiral Strauss: Well, there was quite a bit. You'd teach them about signal flags, light communication, something about guns, torpedoes. Then, of course, there was rifle practice. Besides their close-order drill, they'd practice on the range.

Q: But it's a pretty cut-and-dried thing. You don't have too much opportunity to innovate.

Admiral Strauss: Not really, no. It's a matter of teaching them discipline and morale and so forth.

Q: So that's why you found the attaché opportunity much more exciting?

Admiral Strauss: Well, I don't know. Maybe just because of how I'm made, it just appealed to me more.

Q: Why were you dealing with the commissary rather than a Supply Corps officer?

Admiral Strauss: Well you see, it was a line officer's job. It had been up to that time.

Q: Did you get into the Newport social swing while you were there?

Admiral Strauss: Yes, especially during August and the first part of September. That was the height of the season; there were more dances and so forth. They had dinner parties and dances, which were given by individuals then. I think there are still some, but all over that type of party is by subscription, usually for some particular charity nowadays. There are very few individually given dinners or dances anymore.

Q: There's more of a social consciousness now.

Admiral Strauss: Well, I think the main thing is that people have fewer servants. Servants are very expensive. And when you think that these people who serve at cocktail parties or dinners get $55.00 an hour--here and New York I think they get maybe $100--so if you get three people, that's $150, $165, you see.

Q: Makes for an expensive party.

Admiral Strauss: Yes, besides the liquor and the food and all the rest of it.

Q: How were naval officers perceived in society at large in that era? Were they given entrée to the best places?

Admiral Strauss: Certain of them certainly were. Others either didn't want to or didn't try. I think on the whole the Bellevue Avenue houses didn't care too much for the

Navy.* As a matter of fact, I heard one man, whom I never thought very much of, who said that if the Navy wasn't there, well, they'd have a chance for the summer colony to expand and so forth. The very rich people had the so-called villas, which were more or less palaces, up around there. I don't think the Navy loomed very large in their lives.

Q: How much association was there between the Naval Training Station and the Naval War College?

Admiral Strauss: A great deal. They were in one place, and the commandant of the Training Station was a colleague of the president of the War College. But, of course, the officers attending the War College wouldn't have too much chance to see the rank and file of the Training Station, although the officers would foregather at parties and so forth.

Q: Was there an opportunity for you to take advantage of the War College curriculum at all while you were there?

Admiral Strauss: No.

Q: Did you desire to attend the War College?
---
*Bellevue Avenue was the site of a number of beautiful mansions that housed the upper crust of Newport society.

Admiral Strauss: Not particularly. Curiously enough, the people in my class who did attend the junior War College on the whole never got very far. It seems to me that the ones chosen were those they didn't have a specific place for in other assignments.

Q: How was it perceived among naval officers as a whole during the mid-Thirties? Was it not seen as a desirable place to go?

Admiral Strauss: I think the senior War College, commanders and above, was, but the junior War College struck me--and I think it struck a number of others--as a parking place to put officers that they didn't quite know what to do with.

Q: How did you prepare yourself personally in the areas of strategy, tactics, and the other subjects taught at the War College?

Admiral Strauss: Well, on the job and reading, attending lectures when you could. That's about it. See, later on I went to the Imperial Defence College in London. The U.S. National War College was modeled on the Imperial Defence

College.

Q: It sounds like you had a very exciting opportunity there in London. Why don't you describe that, please.

Admiral Strauss: Well, that was really a very interesting tour. I got there, as I remember, in October of '35. In quick secession, I marched in the funeral of Admiral Beatty and in the funeral of Admiral Jellicoe.* Then in January of 1936 I marched in the funeral of King George V.** The whole diplomatic corps went into mourning for three months. The embassy had its stationery, as did all the other embassies, printed with a black border on it. And when I wrote the first letter to my family, they thought somebody in the family had died.

I might digress and say that life then was very formal compared to now. If anybody asked you to dinner at 8:00 or afterwards, you didn't ask what you wore. You wore a tailcoat and white tie, unless they said, "Don't bother to dress. Wear a dinner jacket," or something like that. The brigade of guards, if they went out in the evening with a

---

*Admiral of the Fleet David Beatty (1871-1936) commanded the British battle cruisers in the Battle of Jutland, 1916, and later served as First Sea Lord, 1919-27. Admiral of the Fleet John R. Jellicoe (1859-1935) commanded the Grand Fleet, 1914-16, and was later Chief of Naval Staff.

**George V (1865-1936) was King of Great Britain and Northern Ireland, and Emperor of India, 1910-36.

lady to the theater or dinner, had to be in a tailcoat and a white tie.

We made our official calls in a morning coat and top hat. You had three kinds of calling cards. The first class, you took yourself and left them with the person you were calling on. The second class, you went with the chauffeur, and the chauffeur handed the cards in. And the third class the stationer sent them to the people concerned. You were supposed to exchange calls with the whole diplomatic corps. And it's customary, if someone has a lot of honors after his name, you would put, "Admiral the Lord So-and-So, KBE, CB, etc." And for a really swell, you would have to put more than one "etc." And I remember I was thrilled to get a card once addressed to me, "Lieutenant Elliott Strauss, USN, etc." If anybody on earth didn't rate any "etceteras"--it was me. I still have that card someplace.

Q: Was there any substance to these calls, or were they merely getting-acquainted sessions?

Admiral Strauss: Well, your calls on the members of the Admiralty, the First Lord, First Sea Lord, and different sea lords and so forth, were really to meet them. And, of course, a great deal of the duties were seeing British naval officers and whenever you could, inspecting or visiting British naval facilities. But I remember the standard British Navy drink was pink gin. That's gin with this dash of Angostura bitters in it. And I remember lunching time after time and having a pink gin and then my host saying, "You can't fly on one wing, old boy," and having a second. Then in the afternoon I would be staring straight in front of me back in the office.

Q: How cordial was the spirit of cooperation between the two navies?

Admiral Strauss: Very good. I think we were looked on as a younger brother, but there was very little holding back in allowing us to see different facilities. One of the things that struck me is, I think, that the total number of people in the U.S. Embassy was about 18. That included the State Department, the Army and Navy, and a commercial attaché. We were responsible for everything: meeting incoming visitors and incoming ships, the so-called spy work, intelligence, protocol, and that was it. I don't know how many people are on the embassy in London nowadays, but I'd say probably 200 or 250. So I sometimes kid some of them and say, "We were able to do it with about 18 in those days."

Q: Did you file regular reports back to the Office of Naval Intelligence?

Admiral Strauss: Yes. One of the things that I came across was when I went up to the Vickers Works and was looking at the beginnings of the turrets for the new battleships. And I asked a question about the breech blocks, whether they would drop or swing to the side. And I was told, "Oh, there are two rights and two lefts." And that's the first time we realized that the British were building their new battleships with four-gun turrets.

Q: That must have been the King George V class.*

Admiral Strauss: Yes.

Q: Speaking of King George, what do you recall specifically about that funeral procession?

Admiral Strauss: The funeral took place in very cold weather, and, of course, it had representation of the heads of state. Then it had representation of the services. Captain W. S. Anderson, the naval attaché, represented the

---

*The King George V was laid down at Vickers-Armstrongs in January 1937, launched in February 1939, and completed in December 1940. The later ships in the class were the Prince of Wales, Duke of York, Howe, and Anson.

U.S. Navy.* Captain Furer, who was the naval constructor attaché in our embassy, represented the naval attachés.** And then, of course, just the plain assistant attachés came after that.

Naturally they had the Royal Navy, the brigade of guards, and other regiments. It was quite a very impressive procession. The casket was on a gun carriage that was towed by sailors and accompanied by the King's sons on foot. The casket had been in Westminster Abbey five days or something like that. And the King's sons took turns standing at the head and foot of the casket, leaning on swords with their heads bowed. I think it was a two-hour watch. They would rotate doing that. Many years afterwards, at Lord Mountbatten's funeral, I think it was quite as impressive and it was done in beautiful weather, so it would be hard to compare them.*** I think they were certainly equal.

Q: Did you wear your full dress regalia with the cocked hat and epaulets?

Admiral Strauss: Cocked hat, epaulets, trousers with the

---
*Captain Walter Stratton Anderson, USN. The oral history of Anderson, who retired as a vice admiral, is in the Columbia University collection.
**Captain Julius A. Furer, Construction Corps, USN.
***Admiral of the Fleet Louis Mountbatten, 1st Earl Mountbatten of Burma (1900-1979), who held many high-ranking posts, including First Sea Lord and Chief of Defence Staff.

stripes down the sides, yes.

Q: What was the national mood at that time?

Admiral Strauss: Well, I think the death of the King was a personal loss to the populace. The day after he died, there was a hush all over, and the shops had crepe on objects in the front windows and so forth. And I remember that the evening before he died, I went to the moving picture with some friends. Always then at any public performance, theater, movies, the last thing they did was to play the first bars of "God Save the King". And they played it very softly following that evening. When I left, there was a bulletin that said, "The King's life is peacefully drawing to its close." And then that night he died. The next morning I know that there was a hushed, funereal feeling over London.

A bit of sartorial information that I had not known is that normally when people wore tailcoat with a white tie, they wore a white waistcoat. But a white waistcoat is a "fancy" waistcoat, so that during the time of mourning one wore a black waistcoat with a tailcoat. So that you looked very much like a waiter during all that time. That was it.

Q: Quite in contrast, of course, was the coronation of George VI.* What do you recall of that?

Admiral Strauss: The main thing I recall of that is that I was pursued by people who seemed to feel I could get them suitable seats to see the procession. And I had to disillusion all of them. My boss was the then-Captain Walter Anderson. He had the same difficulty.

Q: I met him before he died some years ago.

Admiral Strauss: I used to go and see him out here at the Wisconsin Avenue Nursing Home in Georgetown. And I tried to go once a week. I didn't make it. I'd go every two, maybe three weeks. But he was in Bethesda for his 100th birthday, and I was there. Two people brought in cakes, and the head of the hospital came around to see him. He was very shaky by then. And his birthday was on the fourth of October.

Q: In 1981.

Admiral Strauss: And then he died on the 24th of October that same year. And I, of course, went to his funeral.

Q: I met him up in New York when he lived on Lexington

---
*George VI (1895-1952) was King of Great Britain and Northern Ireland from 1936 to 1952.

Avenue.

Admiral Strauss: Yes, I stayed with him up there once. My wife and I stayed with him.

Q: He was still very much the admiral.

Admiral Strauss: Yes. He was a very good tennis player. He had national ranking. Not high--I mean, 100th or something like that. Maybe more than that, but he played until he was 80.

Q: I'd be interested in your impressions of him. He went up very fast, and it's surprising he didn't play more of a role in World War II.

Admiral Strauss: You see, he was Commander Battleships at the time of Pearl Harbor. Well, you can't be Commander Battleships and--whether it's your fault or not--lose five battleships and then go on from there. He was Commander Caribbean Sea Frontier, and we have his album. One of the things in it was a personal letter from King Edward VIII, who was then the Duke of Windsor and the Governor General of the Bahamas.* He wrote to Admiral Anderson and said, "I'm leaving this job, but I want to thank you for your cooperation and help during all the time that we've been colleagues." Something like that.

Q: Do you think Anderson was something of a scapegoat as Admiral Kimmel was?**

Admiral Strauss: I don't say he was a scapegoat, because I don't think anything was ever alleged about him. But you just can't be commander of the biggest--you see, I used to think Commander Battleships was the really finest job--combat ships and lose, perhaps through no fault of yours, half of them, or whatever the number was, and come out of it. And the way the hierarchy of the Navy's set up, when you're in command of something and something happens under you, whether you directly deal with it or not, you are responsible. And it'd be pretty hard to give him a big job. They'd say, "Oh, there's the man who lost all the battleships at Pearl Harbor."

---
*Edward VIII was King from his father's death on 20 January 1936 until his abdication on 11 December of the same year to marry the American divorcée Wallis Warfield Simpson. He was governor of the Bahama Islands from August 1940 to March 1945.
**Admiral Husband E. Kimmel, USN, was Commander in Chief U.S. Pacific Fleet from February 1941 to December 1941. He was relieved a few weeks after the attack on Pearl Harbor and was retired in early 1942.

Strauss #2 - 132

Q: Well, I think it was partly political, too, in that the political aim was to indicate that the blame belonged in Hawaii. Admiral Kelly Turner, you would think, deserved some censure as Chief of War Plans, but he went on to a good wartime career.*

Admiral Strauss: Look, don't get me started on Admiral Kelly Turner. Have you ever read his life that Dyer wrote?**

Q: I've read portions of it, yes.

Admiral Strauss: I contributed a few things in that biography. Among the remarks about Admiral Turner I sent Admiral Dyer was an incident when Turner was made an honorary member of the prestigious Athenaeum Club, while we were in London after the war. It was at a time when officers were allowed to wear the grey uniform shirts with blue uniforms, to save laundry. I suggested to Admiral Turner that for our visit to the club we should wear white shirts. He changed but afterwards complained that, "Strauss made me change my shirt."

---

*Rear Admiral Richmond Kelly Turner, USN, was director of the War Plans Division of OpNav in December 1941 and later went on to hold a number of amphibious commands during World War II. He retired as a four-star admiral.
**Vice Admiral George C. Dyer, USN (Ret.), <u>The Amphibians Came to Conquer: The Story of Admiral Richmond Kelly Turner</u>, two volumes (Washington, D.C.: U.S. Government Printing Office, 1972.)

After lunch at the club, he put two pounds under his plate for a tip. I explained that at London clubs it was customary to give gratuities to the hall porter to be added to the servants' Christmas fund. Admiral Turner said, "I know what I am doing," and left the money. In light of after events, I should have kept my big mouth closed, because he probably put it down as another black mark against me. I had a lot of bosses in the Navy during my career, and I think Turner is the only one I didn't get along with.

Later, Admiral Turner was invited to come to the Admiralty to be awarded Commandership in the Order of the Bath. He went there on the designated morning with a few of his staff. On arrival it was clear that he had given away to his weakness for drink, to the surprise of the British officers present and to the embarrassment of his staff.

But when I went with Admiral Anderson in 1935, somebody here in Washington said, "You'll get along with him if you know how to handle him." And the naval air attaché, Leslie Stevens, who went on to be naval attaché in Moscow, said, "I wish I could get a boss that I didn't 'have to handle.'"*

But I found I got along beautifully with Admiral

_____
*Lieutenant Commander Leslie C. Stevens, Construction Corps, USN.

Anderson. And I had two things that helped me. One of them was that he'd served with my father, and the second thing was that his son got into the Foreign Service, and my family were very good friends of Wilbur Carr, who was the administrative assistant secretary in the State Department.* They introduced him to Wilbur Carr, so that sort of eased things up a bit.

Let me tell you what I mean by "handling" Anderson. For example, I might say, "Captain, have you got a minute?"

"No, no, my boy. I'm very busy. I've got to see the First Sea Lord in 20 minutes." And then that was that.

But if I'd say, "Captain, I know you are busy and you are on your way out, but sometime when you've got a minute, I'd like to talk to you."

"Oh, no. You sit down and tell me what it's all about."

Q: It's how you phrase things.

Admiral Strauss: Yes, and how you present things. I remember I got in bad once with him, and that was my fault. A new class of ship was coming to Portsmouth. The only reference book I had there was Jane's, and I looked up its draft in Jane's, and gave that as its draft.** Well,

---
*Wilbur J. Carr, Assistant Secretary of State.
**<u>Jane's Fighting Ships</u>, an annual warship compendium published since 1898.

Jane's was wrong, and when the ship came in, it was of a different draft. No harm resulted, but the fact that I'd got it wrong--that was the difficulty. I should have checked with Washington and made sure what her draft was.

Q: Jane's had a pretty high reputation.

Admiral Strauss: Yes, but it was wrong, and I suppose I should have got a more authoritative check on it.

Q: I think you started to mention Anderson's role in the coronation of George VI.

Admiral Strauss: Both he and Mrs. Anderson were seated in the Abbey for the coronation ceremony.* The rest of us were assigned seats in the bleachers which had been erected along the line of march. It was cold weather, and as I was given the chance to see the procession with friends, from a window overlooking the line of march, I opted for that. The exec from the New York, Commander James G. Ware, was in London at that time, so I gave my seat to him and saw the procession from the window, with refreshments handy.

Q: What are your recollections of it?

_____
*Westminster Abbey was the site of the coronation, which took place on 12 May 1937.

Admiral Strauss: It took place in the rain, which perhaps dampened some of the pomp, but it was still most impressive. Besides the units from the United Kingdom services, the dominions and many of the colonies were represented. In those days, uniforms were showy, so a parade with men in that assortment of uniforms was something to see.

One of the highlights was Queen Salote of Tonga, who rode in the parade in an open carriage in the rain, waving and saluting on all sides. She was a large woman physically, and at her side was a diminutive aide-de-camp. Someone asked who the little man by her side was, and the reply came, "That's her lunch."

Later, there was a naval review, and we were given places in a merchant ship from which to see it. The merchant ship kept clear of the review but kept close enough to give the spectators the best view.

Q: I've seen pictures of that naval review, and it appeared to be a very dramatic, impressive show.

Admiral Strauss: Well, it was. And at night they had searchlights. Most of the navies sent their very latest ships, but because the New York had been with the Sixth Battle Squadron during the war and Rodman was the division commander, they gave Rodman permission to fly his four-star flag in the New York and sent the New York over.* Well, the day that all the ships hoisted their dressing lines, damned if the dressing line in the New York didn't break. You see, that wasn't a very good opening gambit for the ship. There was a commentator, a retired British naval officer called Woodroff, and there was a great joke, because he was on the radio broadcasting the night display. And he said, "The fleet's all lit up. It's all lit up." And, of course, he was so obviously drunk, you see. And it used to be that people would go round saying, "Well, the fleet's all lit up."

Q: Woodroff was lit up, too.

Admiral Strauss: Yes. And they say he lost his job and got it back later on because he was such a good reporter when sober.

Q: Sending the New York certainly was a sentimental gesture.

Admiral Strauss: Yes, that's right. A number of people

---
*Admiral Hugh Rodman, USN (Ret.), represented the United States. He had been a rear admiral when he took the five U.S. battleships to join the British Home Fleet in December 1917.

Strauss #2 - 138

said we ought to have sent our latest, but I think that the New York was perfectly appropriate.

Q: Germany, for example, sent the Graf Spee, the new pocket battleship.

Admiral Strauss: I'd forgotten that.

Q: Did you have a hand in the arrangements for this?

Admiral Strauss: Oh, yes, indeed. I got a medal. Actually, they gave coronation medals, just distributed them around, and I got one of those. But I always claimed I got it for seating a dinner party, because we had the job with the Admiralty of deciding how this dinner for the Navy would be done. And you had people like the active First Sea Lord, but there would be a retired officer who was years ahead of him on the seniority list. You'd have a naval officer who had become a peer. You had a lot of them who had become knights. The question was, do you seat the people on their present jobs above the retired people? A peer would normally rate ahead of a full admiral. Do you do that? How do you do it? Well, we decided that we would seat the table completely on the rank and date of commission of everybody, without any regard to whether they were on the active list or the retired list or whether they were peers, or whether they were knights or anything like that. So we got off with that.

Q: If you said what the rules were, they would know, and they could go along.

Was there a special entertainment arranged for the crew of the U.S. ship?

Admiral Strauss: I don't remember. I don't know whether they were there long enough for any authorities to do anything about them. There were so many of them, you see.

Q: Where did you live while you were in London?

Admiral Strauss: I lived in three different houses. People used to say, "Why don't you pay your rent and you can stay still?" I lived first up north of the park in a house in Oxford Terrace, and then I lived in West Halkin Street, and finally in Great College Street. And that was a very nice house. We had a maid and a butler who came with the house. It belonged to an M.P. who was abroad for a while, J. P. L. Thomas.* The last place was just outside the courtyard of the Westminster School, very near the houses of Parliament.

---
*M.P.--Member of Parliament.

Q: Did you have a commissary in the embassy, or did you live off the British economy?

Admiral Strauss: We lived off the British economy. Later on, when I was back there during the war and also while at the IDC, I used the commissary, but I thought that really we didn't need it.* If there's anyplace on earth that you can get everything you want, it's London. And the only exception I remember is that Leslie Stevens, the naval air attaché, sent home for a particular kind of Stetson hat. Of course, the pound was $5.00 then. Things were expensive.

Q: Did you make friends with British civilians?

Admiral Strauss: Yes, yes. And this was the first time I'd ever heard of Mountbatten. I hadn't met him, but he was quite a figure. Besides his being a well-known naval officer, he and Lady Louis were part of the jeunesse doree about London. Mountbatten told me later that at that time he had been blackballed for membership in the Royal Yacht Squadron, because the governors thought that Lord Louis was too much of a playboy. However, during the war the Royal Yacht Squadron became his headquarters for a while. He took wry pride in that.

---
*IDC--Imperial Defence College.

Strauss #2 - 141

In 1937 Mountbatten became a captain. He was 37. I remarked to a Royal Navy officer that I supposed his early promotion was due to his royal connections. The officer said, "Perhaps, but he would have been promoted at the next six month group on his own merits." In those days, to be promoted to captain at 37 was phenomenal. Nowadays, I don't know. The rank structure, certainly in the U.S. Navy, has been so altered that I don't know at what ages officers are promoted anymore.

Q: How would you evaluate Anderson as the attaché?

Admiral Strauss: He was superb. He was first class. He was very intelligent and personable and was a good attaché.

He was relieved by Russell Willson, who is one of the greats, in my book.* I was with Willson only a comparatively short time, but we became very good friends. He would have been either commander in chief of the fleet or Chief of Naval Operations or something like that if he hadn't developed a bad heart. When he came up to be a rear admiral, they found out that something was wrong with his heart. They held him up a long time. I went to see him in the hospital, and I said, "Captain, everybody knows you've been selected for rear admiral. They know you are a fine officer. Why do you fight this thing?"

---
*Captain Russell Willson, USN.

And he said, "I'd rather be dead rear admiral than a live captain." Well, he became a rear admiral and was the commander of Battleship Division One.* But he couldn't stay at sea, and he became one of the members of the Joint Strategic Survey Committee, which really recommended the strategy of the war to the President. When the war was over, the President named a dozen men whom he considered the "war leaders." Among these were the members of the Joint Strategic Survey Committee. These were General Embick (father-in-law of General Wedemeyer), General Fairchild, and Admiral Willson.**

Q: Do you think it was his health, then, that held him back from wartime combat command?

Admiral Strauss: Oh, yes, oh, yes. His health was all that kept him from high command, in my opinion.

Q: He came ashore to the Naval Academy after he had the battleship division. He was Superintendent.

---
*Rear Admiral Willson commanded Battleship Division One, flying his flag in the USS Arizona (BB-39), from 1939 to 1941. He became Superintendent of the Naval Academy 1 February 1941.
**Lieutenant General Stanley D. Embick, USA, became chief of the Army's War Plans Division in 1939; Major General Albert C. Wedemeyer, USA, was appointed in October 1943 as deputy chief of staff in Mountbatten's Southeast Asia Command; Major General Muir S. Fairchild, USA, was eventually Vice Chief of Staff of the Air Force.

Strauss #2 - 143

Admiral Strauss: Yes, he was Superintendent. He wanted that job. I remember that before being appointed, he asked if my father might suggest him for the appointment.

Q: He was on Admiral King's staff after that.*

Admiral Strauss: Yes. Later, I was out at Bethesda one time when my father was sick. Actually, he died from there.** Someone came in and said, "Admiral Willson just died." (I think I remember it was on the golf course.) I thought it was Henry B. Wilson--a much older admiral, you see--but it was Russell. He was 64.

Q: What qualities in him did you so admire?

Admiral Strauss: He was very intelligent. I think he had one of the best minds I've ever been associated with. And he was likable, certainly as far as I was concerned. Helpful. I just think he was a good officer and a good man.

---
*To Willson's disappointment, he became chief of staff to Admiral Ernest J. King, USN, when the U.S. Fleet (CominCh) staff was established in late 1941. See Thomas B. Buell, Master of Sea Power: A Biography of Fleet Admiral Ernest J. King (Boston: Little, Brown, 1980), pages 155-156.
**Admiral Joseph Strauss, USN (Ret.), died 30 December 1948 at the age of 87. Vice Admiral Russell Willson, USN (Ret.), died 6 June 1948 at the age of 64.

Q: It's interesting about differing perceptions, because I interviewed an officer out of the class of '24, and his view of Russell Willson is almost the opposite of yours. He had served under him when Willson commanded the Pennsylvania. This officer thought Willson was a poor seaman and a poor leader and a few other things.

Admiral Strauss: Well, I don't know about him as a seaman, because I never was at sea with him, but no, I thought his decisions were well thought out. In fact, I'm surprised at that opinion, because I'm a great admirer of Russell Willson.

Q: Do you remember anything about Willson specifically as the attaché?

Admiral Strauss: I was with him a shorter time. He wasn't as flamboyant as Anderson, but he was very sound. One time he said, "You write a clear letter, but you use too many words. Then he told me about an author, perhaps Thackeray, who wrote to a friend, "Please forgive the length of this letter. If I had more time, I would have written a shorter one." I have used this often with my young officers.

Q: Speaking of flamboyance, Anderson had a very high opinion of himself.

Strauss #2 - 145

Admiral Strauss: Yes, he did.

Q: Did you have much dealing with the ambassador's family?

Admiral Strauss: Well, we were such a small group that we did. I don't know that I was ever invited with my wife separately over there, but we saw them as part of the group at embassy parties and gatherings. Then Helen Jacobs, the tennis player, was a part of the ambassadorial family.* I don't think she was related, but she lived with them. I used to play tennis at a covered court out in Kew, and occasionally Helen Jacobs would be there, although she was quite a different class than the rest of us as far as tennis was concerned. So I would say I saw her perhaps more than either Ambassador Bingham or Mrs. Bingham, except at entertainments, parties and gatherings of that sort.**

Q: Were the Kennedys there when you were there?

Admiral Strauss: No. The only time I saw Ambassador Kennedy was later.*** I came back with Admiral Johnson,

---
*Helen Hull Jacobs several times won the women's singles title in America and in 1936 won the women's singles championship at Wimbledon in England.
**Robert W. Bingham was appointed ambassador to Great Britain in March 1933 and held that post until his death in December 1937.
***Joseph P. Kennedy, father of John F. Kennedy, was appointed ambassador in January 1938, following the death of Ambassador Bingham.

when I was his flag lieutenant.* He took the midshipman cruise to Portsmouth, and at that time I attended a reception in the embassy given by Kennedy. I saw there Barbara Hutton and Court Reventlow.** They were still married, and I thought they were a very handsome couple. Reventlow was subsequently married to a cousin of my wife's, Peggy Drayton. He and Peggy were married for a number of years until he died.

Q: Could you give me any other memories of the British experience? Did you go to any receptions when you met the royal family?

Admiral Strauss: Yes. I went to the only court given by Edward VIII while he was King and the only levee given by him. Presentation at court is for women. The husbands just stand around and watch. The levee is attended by men and is for the diplomatic corps only. I remember going through the line. The German delegation was ahead of us, and when they came before the then King Edward VIII, Ribbentrop said, "Heil Hitler."*** He gave the stiff-arm

---
*Rear Admiral Alfred W. Johnson, USN, Commander Training Detachment, U.S. Fleet.
**Barbara Hutton was the wealthy heiress of the Woolworth chain stores founded by her grandfather. Danish Count Court Haugwitz-Reventlow was one of her several husbands; another was Cary Grant. As a pair, she and Grant were known as "Cash and Cary."
***Joachim von Ribbentrop was German ambassador to Great Britain, 1936-38, and minister of foreign affairs, 1938-45.

salute, and the King just nodded his head.

Q: Well, interestingly, as Duke of Windsor he was accused of having some Nazi sympathies.

Admiral Strauss: Well, he certainly didn't return that salute. But the levee was quite a show because of the uniforms. The Hungarians, you know, had caricul capes hung over their shoulders and the Indians had plumes, and it was a show. It might be said that the less important countries had the gaudier uniforms.

To get to the court presentation, for some reason you couldn't use your own car, and it was sort of bumper to bumper waiting to get in. The crowds were watching the whole thing, and some peer pulled down the car curtain and charged a sixpence to look at his wife and then he would raise the curtain. This was a joke.

Q: What are your memories of the abdication crisis?

Admiral Strauss: Well, I was in the lobby of the House of Commons when King Edward made his abdication speech. The curious thing was, for months beforehand, people knew of the impending crisis. The "monde" knew he was keeping company with Mrs. Simpson, but the man in the street didn't know anything about it. I remember at a house where I was staying, the host had a gardener who, when the Bishop of Bradford broke the news to the public in a sermon, said to my friend, "Do you mean to say that our King has really been carrying on with an American lady?"

Q: The British press was very restrained on that.

Admiral Strauss: Our press, of course, played it up a great deal, and why more of it didn't get back to England, I don't know. I mean, you went to lunch or a dinner party, and the people would talk about it. I'd never met his future wife at that time, but I remember going to a garden party at the palace, and she and Lady Louis Mountbatten were standing together and someone pointed out, "That's Mrs. Simpson." At the time of the crisis, the British Government asked the press lords to keep the news out of the papers, and these complied very well until the Bishop of Bradford broke the silence.

Q: In 1936 you were a delegate to an assembly on geodesy and geophysics. Do you have any special memories of that?

Admiral Strauss: Yes. I went up to Edinburgh and the big shots there were explorers. There was a Norwegian explorer called Helland Hansen, who'd lost his fingers.* They'd been frozen off. Everybody kowtowed to him. He was the big man. I had a paper from the Hydrographic Office, and many attendees had papers presented. They weren't going to present mine. I think I was too far down the totem pole. But I thought that having been assigned there and having the paper, that I should. So I insisted then and did get to read the paper on the work of the Navy Hydrographic Office before a subcommittee, for what it was worth.

Q: Acting as a representative of the United States.

Admiral Strauss: Yes. Of the Hydrographic Office, really.

Q: Was the purpose just to get it on the record?

Admiral Strauss: Well, it was to have the Navy take a part in this meeting, to be represented at the Union of Geodesy and Geophysics. I still have a nameplate pin that held the Union seal with a world on it.

Q: Any more recollections of England before we get you back to your next sea duty? If you can add any further specifics on the intelligence aspects of the job, those recollections would certainly be useful. Historians would

---
*Professor Helland Hansen was involved in exploration of Antarctica soon after the turn of the 20th century.

probably be more interested in that aspect of the duty than any other part.

Admiral Strauss: Well, the job was to try to get into places of naval interest and to report on them. I went with Captain Furer to see a new cruiser, HMS Aurora. The visit showed how strict the class lines are. When we finished the inspection, the captain took Furer to his cabin for tea. I was sent down to the junior officers' quarters for my tea. I was only a lieutenant.

Both the German naval attaché, Captain Erwin Wassner, and the German air attaché had been submarine commanders during the war. Both had received Pour la Merite, a German decoration which is equivalent to our Medal of Honor. The air attaché had been sunk but had escaped from his submarine. Wassner was promoted to rear admiral while on the job. He wasn't very tactful, because on the wall of his drawing room in London was mounted the steering wheel of a British merchantman his submarine had sunk.

One of the principal duties of any military or naval attaché is intelligence gathering. In Great Britain at that time, the British were very relaxed about letting Americans in on many of their naval activities. In addition to the visit to the new HMS Aurora, which I've mentioned, I visited the Vickers works in the north (where we learned about the four-gun turrets on the new battleships), the naval engineering college at Keyham, a communications activity at Portsmouth. At the latter I was shown new radio equipment which, alas, I did not have the expertise to take advantage of.

I had talks with Hadfield executives about their heavier shells. Very often, much could be learned from off-the-cuff remarks, such as the four-gun turrets. Inspecting the Aurora, I was shown the gas-tight hatch gaskets. I asked my guide if the Royal Navy would use gas shells. He said, "What's the use of gassing someone when you can blow him up?" The Navy Department asked us to find out any measures the Royal Navy was taking to suppress noise being transmitted through the steel decks. I found my way to the experimental facility at Teddington. There they had artificial heels tapping on a deck mock-up. I was told that their latest data on this subject had been obtained from our Bureau of Standards in Washington. Apparently the Navy Department had not touched in there.

After the Royal Navy's "Navy Day," where visitors are allowed aboard navy ships, a Royal Navy officer told me that they had apprehended a visitor who had penetrated a part of the ship not open to visitors. He turned out to be a naval officer. I asked, "From what country?"

My companion said, "I can't tell you, but if it had been you, you could have got away with it.

Strauss #2 - 152

Part of the daily duty was to scan all of the newspapers for items of naval interest. The more cogent ones were sent back to the Department. Like our press, many "secrets" are revealed through ordinary press reporting.

Q: How did your job with Admiral Johnson come about?

Admiral Strauss: When my tour over there was over, I came back to the United States. Jack Kane told me that Admiral Johnson was looking for a flag lieutenant.* Jack also told Admiral Johnson that I was free, and I was "hired." At the same time, Admiral Train needed a flag lieutenant.** And I was suggested for that job by Bob Campbell who had relieved me in London, but I'd signed up already with Admiral Johnson.***

Q: Had you known Admiral Johnson at all?

Admiral Strauss: Admiral Johnson was the son of a naval officer and a grandson of Eastman Johnson, the artist. The story runs that his father, while naval attaché to Chile, rounded a building in Santiago on a windy day. He had his

---
*Lieutenant Commander John D. H. Kane, USN, who was then serving in the Bureau of Navigation, which controlled officer assignments.
**Rear Admiral Charles R. Train, USN, who was Commander Battleship Division Two.
***Lieutenant Robert L. Campbell, Jr., USN.

Strauss #2 - 153

head down and knocked over a young Chilean lady. This lady became Alfred Johnson's mother. Alfred was fluent in Spanish since birth, and this fluency was responsible for some of his naval assignments.

My family had been longtime friends of the Johnsons. As a midshipman, I often invited Caroline, their oldest daughter, to Naval Academy events. She later became the wife of a Foreign Service officer and consul general, James E. Brown. Their second daughter, Elvira, married C. Burke Elbrick, who while ambassador to Brazil, was the first of the series of American ambassadors to be kidnaped.* He afterwards attained the rank of career ambassador, which was a rare achievement. So I knew the family, and my mother and father knew them quite well.

Q: This probably helped a good bit in your getting the job.

Admiral Strauss: Oh, I think so. When I was suggested to Admiral Johnson, he certainly knew who I was. And I enjoyed my time with him.

Q: What are your recollections of him as a naval officer?

---

*Charles Burke Elbrick was U.S. ambassador to Brazil, 1969-70. He was kidnaped by Brazilian revolutionaries in Rio de Janeiro on 4 September 1969, then released on 7 September after Brazil's government yielded to the captors' demands.

Admiral Strauss: Well, he was a very dedicated, patriotic, fine officer. When he took over the command, I believe he would have preferred an assignment connected with the naval aviation establishment. He had been on the fringes of aviation, but the hierarchy decided otherwise.

Alfred Johnson did not have the intellectual capacity of flag officers such as Walter Anderson or Russell Willson, but he had common sense, was a guardian of naval custom and tradition, and paid attention to the seagoing aspects of the Navy. I remember that he insisted that officers wear hats coming aboard ship. Otherwise, they had no way of saluting the quarterdeck. I don't know how this would work in today's military establishment, where officers in uniform go about in public holding their headgear in their hands or, if with forage caps, in their pockets.

Admiral Johnson was a good seaman. He was keen on pulling boats and encouraged boat competitions. He took great interest in the amphibious exercises we were engaged in off Culebra in the winter of 1937-38. An officer who had been on his staff, when Johnson was assigned to supervise the Nicaraguan elections, told me about some of the ploys needed to make sure that the game was clean-- letters steamed open and the like. This is one example of

Admiral Johnson's assignments because of his Spanish.

He respesented the Navy well in any international contact. I was always proud to have him in that capacity. On the midshipman cruise, we went to Portsmouth, and the Commander in Chief of Portsmouth was Admiral of the Fleet Lord Cork and Orrery.* He had a dinner for Admiral Johnson. By then I was his acting chief of staff as the senior person on his staff, although I was a lieutenant commander.

Q: It must have been a small staff.

Admiral Strauss: When I joined Admiral Johnson in the autumn of 1937, the senior member of his staff was Lieutenant Commander Campbell H. Minckler. Minckler had been one of Admiral Wilson Brown's "boys" and left to go with him when Brown became Superintendent of the Naval Academy.** Minckler had a quick mind; he could dictate at talking speed without having to change a word in the first draft. But he had drink, money, woman, and horse race trouble. Admiral Johnson, who was in a way a puritan, used to remark, "How can a man that bright have his habits?"

The admiral could be irascible. I remember that on one occasion he was due to go ashore with Minckler to

---
*The Earl of Cork and Orrery had previously been the principal naval aide-de-camp to the King.
**Rear Admiral Wilson Brown, USN, was Superintendent of the Naval Academy from February 1938 to February 1941.

accompany him. When the boat was alongside, there was no Minckler. I went below and found Mink, somewhat the worse for wear, was still asleep. I gave him the word and returned on deck to tell the admiral that Minckler would be there "in a minute." He would have none of it. In vigorous terms he expressed his ideas about Minckler and left without him. In spite of Campbell Minckler's ability, I don't think Admiral Johnson regretted his departure from the staff.

As a postscript, Admiral Brown was warned as to Minckler's disabilities but was alleged to have said, "I would rather have Minckler drunk than anyone else sober." Brown made a mistake; Minckler got into trouble in Annapolis and had to be let go.

The rest of the staff was Bill Marshall, Benny Katz, George Carmichael, and a Marine officer.* This was the core of the staff. For a while, we had Worthy Bitler and Chet Wood. Dave Nutter arrived, and since Minckler, the flag secretary, had left, I asked Admiral Johnson if I could not take his slot and have Nutter become flag lieutenant. This was done.

Q: What were the duties of this training squadron that he commanded?

---
*Lieutenant William J. Marshall, USN; Lieutenant Benjamin Katz, USN; Lieutenant George K. Carmichael, USN.

Admiral Strauss: Maneuvers, drills, and also they did a number of landing exercises. We had one quite extensive landing exercise on Culebra in the winter of 1938, and the Army commander was General Short.* Brigadier General Short, who was afterwards the man at Pearl Harbor when it was attacked. And we had a Marine contingent that went along. General Williams was in command of that.** He was a brigadier general. Our staff didn't think much of Short. But they had a major with the troops called Handy.*** We thought Handy was a wonderful soldier. He'd have to be to get to be Deputy Chief of Staff of the Army, and he was commander of the American forces in Europe. But for some reason or other, we thought this Major Handy was going to go a long way. We didn't think too much of General Short.

Q: What was it like as a staff on board the New York? Was that a comfortable flagship?

Admiral Strauss: Yes, oh, yes. And Admiral Johnson messed alone. He didn't have any of his staff with him. Admiral

---
*Brigadier General Walter C. Short, USA, Commander Second Infantry Brigade. In December 1941, as a lieutenant general, Short was commander of the Army's Hawaiian Department. He was relieved shortly after the Japanese attack on Pearl Harbor.
**Brigadier General Richard P. Williams, USMC, commanding the 1st Marine Brigade, Fleet Marine Force.
***Major Thomas T. Handy, USA, a 1936 graduate of the Naval War College.

Johnson finally asked for a chief of staff, and Captain Farquhar became his chief of staff, and he did mess with the admiral.*

My first contact with the battleship New York was in 1918. My mother and I were at the old Chamberlin Hotel at Fort Monroe. The Atlantic Fleet, under Admiral Hugh Rodman, were in Hampton Roads, preparatory to going to Annapolis for June Week, I believe. Admiral Rodman asked if I would like to make the trip with him in New York. As a Naval Academy candidate, I was ecstatic. The captain of the New York was William V. Pratt, afterwards CNO.** The flag lieutenant was Lieutenant Commander Jonas Ingram, a four-star admiral in World War II.***

At the time Admiral Johnson hoisted his flag in New York, the captain was G. E. Davis.**** I don't remember much about him. He was relieved by Captain Robert M. Griffin, son of a former Chief of the Bureau of Engineering who became a flag officer.***** Captain Griffin guarded his prerogatives as the captain of the ship, even with a flag on board.

---
*Captain Allan S. Farquhar, USN.
**Captain William V. Pratt, USN. As a four-star admiral, he was Chief of Naval Operations from 1930 to 1933.
***Lieutenant Commander Jonas H. Ingram, USN, who was Commander South Atlantic Force and later Commander in Chief Atlantic Fleet during World War II.
****Captain Guy E. Davis, USN.
*****Rear Admiral Robert S. Griffin, USN, was Chief of the Bureau of Engineering from 1913 to 1921.

Strauss #2 - 159

Q: What were your specific duties? I know what a flag lieutenant does in general, but are there any incidents that especially stand out in your mind?

Admiral Strauss: Because of the possible trouble with Japan, the U.S. Fleet, which was booked to be in New York for the World's Fair, remained in the Pacific. As a result, Admiral Johnson became the senior naval officer at the fair in 1939. And so every place he went, we had motorcycle riders with sirens out in front. The person who was in charge of Navy entertainment was Mrs. William Randolph Hearst.* I was told off to be her man Friday, and this was quite an experience. So pretty well every place that Mrs. Hearst went, I went too. There was a great deal of entertainment. There was entertainment for the men, too. There was a series of events. One time I accompanied her to an official dinner given by Winthrop Aldrich.** I went in full uniform, epaulets and trousers, and so forth. After dinner she said, "Let's go; there's a new night club opened up." And it wasn't the Stork Club, but it was one very much like it. "Let's go down there."

Q: Duty calls.

---
*William Randolph Hearst was one of the best-known newspaper tycoons of the era. He and his wife were estranged by 1939, and Hearst himself lived in California.
**Winthrop Aldrich was chairman of the board of Chase National Bank of New York.

Admiral Strauss: So we went along and had a sandwich and a bottle of something, and I knew I had about $8.00 in my pocket book. I thought, "My God, how am I going to do this?" When it came time to go, I started reaching, and Mrs. Hearst just waved her hand at the head waiter. And he said, "Yes, Mrs. Hearst." And we went out, so I was off the hook there.

On another occasion, we went in her chauffeur-driven car to an office building near the Battery. We went to an upper floor in the elevator and entered a darkened room, where could be dimly seen rows of seats and, at the end of the room, a movie screen. I was led to a seat and I found a glass of champagne in my hand. This was repeatedly filled. The picture was a preview of Lost Horizon. When the lights came on, I saw a dozen, perhaps 15 people in the room. I didn't know any of them but recognized the chairman of the National City Bank and others of that ilk among the group.

Q: Why was it up to the Navy to provide a companion for Mrs. Hearst?

Admiral Strauss: Because she was in charge of the Navy's part in the World's Fair, you see. They had a committee to do all these different things, decorations and so forth,

Strauss #2 - 161

and her job was being in charge of the entertainment and liaison with the Navy.

Q: It was really anticlimactic when the Navy didn't come in as large as numbers as they expected.

Admiral Strauss: I suppose so, yes.

Q: Was New York Navy Yard essentially your home base in that ship?

Admiral Strauss: No, Norfolk was.

Q: Oh, I see. How much time did you spend at sea?

Admiral Strauss: Quite a bit. It was not the kind of duty where one said, "I'm going to sea, keep dinner hot." No, we spent the winter down in the Caribbean. We did midshipmen's summer cruises. Individual ships we designated for individual tasks. We had our share of seagoing.

Q: What sorts of things did you personally do when the ship was at sea?

Admiral Strauss: Well, I was signal officer for the

admiral and often tactical officer for exercises. For instance, we would get an order from the Navy Department to send a ship to a flower show at Boston or something like that, and then we'd have to decide which ship to send and write its orders to dispatch it and so forth. On one occasion I was with Dave Nutter, who was flag lieutenant.* We were sitting in the flag office after dinner one night, and we had to send two ships someplace. We were arguing about which was the best. And finally we wrote up the dispatch telling these ships where to go. Mrs. Nutter, who had heard our discussion, said, "Is _that_ how battleships get sent around?"

Q: It seemed awfully casual to her.

Admiral Strauss: Yes.

Q: What foreign liberty ports did you hit?

Admiral Strauss: With the midshipman's cruise, we went to Portsmouth, Le Havre, Copenhagen. And Copenhagen, we really had a bang-up time there. Admiral Johnson gave a

---
*Lieutenant David L. Nutter, USN.

dinner for Prince Knud and his wife.* That was a protocol affair. They assigned a Danish lieutenant commander called Niels Bramer to work with me in setting this dinner up. And it was very amusing. I've used this expression since. We'd draw a diagram of the table and put someone here and there. Bramer would say, "Who is finer, the wife of the consul general or the executive officer's wife?" And it was always, "Who is finer?" You see, meaning, "Who is senior?" And I've used that since, "Who is finer?"

Q: It sounds as if you got a fair amount of protocol duty.

Admiral Strauss: Oh, there was plenty of it on that cruise. I have a picture of myself and Prince Knud someplace around here, taken at the dinner. Well, on that type of cruise you do. At sea the ships square off and hold gunnery drill on each other. But that's about all you can do.

Q: Was Admiral Johnson commander of the training squadron for that cruise?

---

*Prince Knud (1900-1976) was a naval officer who eventually reached the rank of rear admiral. In a 1953 Danish plebiscite that changed the country's constitution by allowing a female monarch, he was removed from direct succession to the throne. Thus when Prince Knud's brother, King Frederik IX, died in 1972, he was succeeded by his daughter Margrethe rather than Knud.

Admiral Strauss: Yes, Jack Kane, who was afterwards chief of naval history, was a first class midshipman on that cruise.*

Allen Blow Cook, a man who is dead now, had been graduated two classes ahead of me. He had to retire because he had TB, so he became a civilian professor.** And he was very good. He taught the midshipmen a great deal. For instance, he'd teach them about calling cards and how they should be made and he'd teach them naval history and the history of the different ports we visited. Allen Blow Cook gave the midshipmen some of the cultural background they would receive in a liberal arts college.

Q. He was in the English Department.

Admiral Strauss: Yes.

Q: Did it make a difference to your status being upgraded from training detachment to the Atlantic Squadron?

Admiral Strauss: It's a more prestigious title. I think that Admiral Johnson was irked at being in command of only a training squadron and wanted to have a title that sounded

---
*Midshipman John D. H. Kane, Jr., USN, who was graduated in the Naval Academy's class of 1942.
**TB--tuberculosis.

as though he was a part of a fleet, you see. He made two strong requests that the title be changed and that he get a chief of staff. And both of those things were done.

Q: Was the number of ships assigned to this squadron building during the time you were there?

Admiral Strauss: No.

Q: There were a number of the new-construction ships--the Brooklyn-class cruisers and the gold-platers. Were they going directly to the Pacific?

Admiral Strauss: We didn't have anything to do with them. You're right. Later on, the operational training command took new ships through, because when I had the Fresno I had to report to a training commander for the ship's shakedown, to get the ship readied and so forth.

Q: But that wasn't part of your function in the late 1930s?

Admiral Strauss: No.

Q: It sounds as if mostly what you were doing was just representing the Navy in the Atlantic.

Admiral Strauss: Yes, and then, of course, engaging in these amphibious exercises, we did quite a lot of work aimed at upgrading the ability to land on a shore. We found that the motor launches were unsuitable for this business and made recommendations for a different kind of fire support and a different kind of landing craft, different tactics. So I think the work done in connection with amphibious landings was useful in arriving at subsequent amphibious policy.

Q: Did you do any work involving submarines?

Admiral Strauss: No.

Q: Anything with the new aircraft carriers that were coming out?

Admiral Strauss: No.

Q: I guess the real buildup in the Atlantic came later than that.

Admiral Strauss: Yes, yes.

Strauss #2 - 167

Q: From there you went to your first command. That must have been a very satisfying experience.

Admiral Strauss: Yes. From there I put the Brooks in commission.* It had been laid up and was one of the destroyers that they were putting back into commission. And our first job was on neutrality patrol. We went up off of Nova Scotia, and as merchant ships came by we asked them to identify themselves. We never had any trouble with that. But it was hard duty.

We went through the winter, and we would get so much ice on the ship that it would have a lazy roll, because it got so much topside weight. I have some pictures showing how the ice went up the guys. And also the guns would get covered with ice. I decided we had to keep one gun that was able to shoot or we'd be in sort of bad shape. So I had a steam hose rigged to it, and we'd steam the ice off every so often. And I wrote a report of this duty, because the ships had been so used to being in Newport in the summer and the Caribbean in the winter that they'd never been under that kind of conditions.

We found out a lot of things that needed changing. For instance, the vegetables were stowed in an above-deck stowage space. Well, the potatoes would freeze and become

---

*After having been put out of commission in reserve at Philadelphia on 2 September 1938, the destroyer Brooks (DD-232) was recommissioned 25 April 1939.

inedible. The fuel oil wouldn't run from the tank down to the galley, so we had to put a can of oil on the stove itself and feed it into the burners. We found that the fire mains would freeze. We found that in the chiefs' quarters a layer of ice would form from the sweat under the deck and would leak down onto the men. And, of course, this business of the stability when you get all this ice topside. So those were several things that people hadn't thought of before operating in that type of weather.

Q: Were you sent there deliberately as an experiment, or was this knowledge a by-product?

Admiral Strauss: No, it wasn't an experiment. For some reason or other, people in the Navy Department thought that, to ensure our neutrality, we ought to keep a patrol out there, in case anything did happen.

Then, having spent the winter up there, we were sent to Panama for the summer. And we spent two weeks on the Atlantic side, stopping ships that were going through the canal and then two weeks on the Pacific side doing exercises. There were four destroyers altogether; the whole division was there. We fired torpedoes and then held maneuvers. But that duty was quite interesting. The Panama U.S. port authorities would put the Coast Guard on board to inspect the incoming ships' papers. Once, one of the waiting merchant ships, at anchor, was dragging down on the <u>Brooks</u>. It was broad daylight, but we had great difficulty in arousing anyone in the merchant ship. We finally did, but it made me realize that many merchantmen have scant crews.

Q: The war had started in Europe.

Admiral Strauss: That's right.

Q: Did this make a difference in the need for the U.S. Navy? Did you have a feeling that we would get into it?

Admiral Strauss: At that early time, I don't think we knew how long it was going to go on. Like a lot of people, even in Europe, we had the feeling, "The war'll be over by Christmas," or something like that. So I don't think that at that time we felt particularly that we were going to get into it.

Q: Did you have any encounters with German ships on your neutrality patrol?

Admiral Strauss: I don't think we saw any. Of course, British ships came in to different ports, Norfolk and New York, and so forth. A while afterwards, when I was in the

Nashville, we were in New York, and we were sort of host to a British cruiser that had been knocked about in the Mediterranean. And a young British officer said he was going uptown to the theater, and he said, "I hear there's an awful lot of holdups and so forth. Do you think it's all right to go?"

I said "Oh, it happens every now and then, but you won't have any trouble." Next day he came back. He was just outside the Navy yard gate when somebody shoved a pistol in his waist. So I wasn't a very good prophet on that one.

Q: You'd think that that would be one of the safer places, too.

Admiral Strauss: Yes.

Q: What were the satisfactions of command after this long training period you'd gone through as an officer?

Admiral Strauss: Oh. That was a terrific change; of course, I loved that. I think anybody who gets a command loves it. It was being your own boss and having a ship to yourself. It was very gratifying, yes. And the ship was very active on the neutrality patrols, both up north and in Panama, and then we went to the West Coast. We went up to

Everett, Washington. They took off one of the 5-inch guns up there, which made us sort of lopsided.

Q: What was the purpose of that?

Admiral Strauss: They wanted the guns for merchant ships.

Q: I hadn't heard of that sort of cannibalization. Did that affect your stability?

Admiral Strauss: No, no, not really.

Q: Did you have a gain in confidence in shiphandling by then?

Admiral Strauss: Yes, oh, yes. Those ships were very hard to handle. They had a big turning circle, and I never minded the current very much, but they blew badly. For some reason or other, their wind surface was troublesome, in making landings and so forth. If you had wind, you had to come in pretty fast. Otherwise you'd get either blown on or blown off.

Q: Did you have a capable wardroom?

Admiral Strauss: Yes. I had a good exec, William R.

Lefavour.* I had good officers. There was one officer named Cease that I'd seen as a midshipman.** And he'd taken part in a happy hour. He was rather fat, and he had some sort of musical instrument, and he clowned it. He didn't particularly prepossess me. And I found that this officer, when he graduated, was coming to the Brooks. And before he got on board, some issues arrived of the magazine called The Downbeat, which was for jazz aficionados. Well, this didn't endear him to me. And when he came on board he had a mustache. That didn't endear him to me. We nicknamed him "Count Basie," and yet I found out he was a splendid officer. He was a very fine pistol shot. And he took the men ashore, trained them in firing .45 pistols. As a matter of fact, I went ashore with him and he trained me and improved my shooting. So he showed that my prejudices were very ridiculous.

Q: Superficial.

Admiral Strauss: Yes.

Q: You went around to the West Coast. Did you have any operations with the Pacific Fleet?

---
*Lieutenant William R. Lefavour, USN.
**Ensign John M. Cease, Jr., USN, the destroyer's gunnery officer.

Strauss #2 - 173

Admiral Strauss: No. No. I did with some other destroyers, that's all. And then we had the overhaul at Everett, where they took the gun off. One thing that struck me about the civilian yards is how much quicker they did things than the Navy yards.

Q: Do you have any explanation for that?

Admiral Strauss: I think that time was money to them, much more than it was to a Navy yard.

Q: What other experiences do you remember from the Brooks?

Admiral Strauss: Well, I remember mostly times in the northern neutrality patrol and then the neutrality patrol down in Panama--off Panama on both sides--firing torpedoes and, of course, vetting the ships that came through. In Puget Sound, before radar, when fog set in, navigating there was a memorable experience.

Q: From there you went to the Nashville, which must have been very pleasant. She was a brand-new ship.*

---

*The Brooklyn-class light cruiser Nashville (CL-43) was commissioned 6 June 1938. Standard displacement: 9,475 tons; length: 608 feet, 4 inches; beam: 61 feet, 8 inches; draft: 19 feet, 2 inches; top speed: 32.5 knots. She was armed with 15 6-inch guns and eight 5-inch guns.

Strauss #2 - 174

Admiral Strauss: Yes. I was ordered as navigator of the Nashville. She was in the Pacific. By then, the Brooks was back on the East Coast, so I had to fly out to Hawaii. And to me it was a letdown, going from being a commanding officer to being a navigator. The captain was R. S. Wentworth, and we became friends and we served together afterwards in London during the war.* He was a very fine man, a very able man. He was a good shiphandler. He was quite evidently devoted to his wife. He once said he couldn't understand why men pursued a lot of women--just becoming fully acquainted with one took a lifetime.

Q: A real gentleman, from what I've heard.

Admiral Strauss: Oh, he was one of the finest. The only time I ever heard him swear was when he got his orders to leave the ship. He opened them up and said, "Goddamnit." Because he loved that job.

Q: Did you grow to like your job after you'd been there a while?

Admiral Strauss: Yes. I enjoyed being navigator.

Q: I gather there was a good deal of talent on board also,

---
*Captain Ralph S. Wentworth, USN.

in a new ship.

Admiral Strauss: One of the Fullinwiders, Simon Fullinwider, was exec.* One of the nice things was neither the captain, Fullinwider, nor I smoked. And usually the charthouse is just a fog. But the fact that none of us smoked, people were afraid to smoke in there, so we had a smoke-free charthouse. Of course, we worked with the fleet out of Hawaii, mostly.

Wentworth was the captain most of the time I was on board, but Frank Craven became captain.** And he was very professionally minded. He was always, quite rightly, doing different types of exercises and doing different types of training. He was preparing for war. And I always thought he would go a long way in the Navy. But during the actual war, he expended a great deal of ammunition shooting at what was supposed to be a Japanese fishing boat that he thought might have torpedoes on board.

Q: That was during the Doolittle raid, wasn't it?***

Admiral Strauss: It may have been. They saw this boat. They kept on shooting at it and didn't hit it. Of course,

---
*Commander Simon P. Fullinwider, Jr., USN. His father, a retired commander, was on active duty at the time in the Bureau of Ordnance in Washington, D.C.
**Captain Francis S. Craven, USN.
***See Edward P. Stafford, The Big E: The Story of the USS Enterprise (New York: Random House, 1962), page 64.

it would be an awful hard job with 6-inch guns to hit a single boat, but the Nashville expended a lot of ammunition, and I think that counted against Captain Craven. But he was very professional, very earnest in his business of training and preparing himself. So it was too bad.

In the spring of 1941, when we were in Pearl Harbor, we got orders without any notice to join up with a task force and go to sea. I owned half of a car which was on the dock, and I just had to abandon it. But the man that owned the other half, I think, took it. I was single then, but the people who had families and so forth couldn't tell them. They just disappeared. And we went through the canal along with the Mississippi, the battleship, and several destroyers and another cruiser. We picked up transports, and we went to Iceland to relieve the British garrison there. We took over the occupation. And we arrived just before the Fourth of July. It was decided that we shouldn't go in the Fourth of July, so we waited until the fifth of July and then entered Hvalfjordur.

Q: What was the significance of landing on the fifth? Was that just to avoid embarrassing the British?

Admiral Strauss: Yes, it would have sounded a little bit

overdone to land on the fourth.

Q: What was the Nashville's role in that expedition?

Admiral Strauss: It was just there in case of any trouble. The whole task group really was for that, in case there'd been any opposition, which was a pretty remote idea. But the fact that we were actually carrying troops in to relieve people who were at war might have caused some unpleasantness. I remember that I looked over the side once while we were lying out there, and I saw two dead bodies. And it's the first time I'd seen that in the war. It made me realize that it really was a war, to see casualties. They must have come from some torpedoed ship, or something like that.

Q: How was the weather on the trip?

Admiral Strauss: The weather was superb. And, of course, it being that time of the year, it never got really dark. And you never could get the bluejackets to go to bed. At 10:00 o'clock at night, it'd be light, and they'd be sitting on the bitts reading a newspaper.

Q: How did that ship ride?

Strauss #2 - 178

Admiral Strauss: It was a good ship at sea.

Q: Well, you'd been in the Concord, another type of light cruiser, earlier. How would you compare those?

Admiral Strauss: The Concord was a 7,500-ton, ten beam ship; the Nashville, a nominal 10,000 tons but probably 12,000 and with a proportionally broader beam, was a steadier ship. I don't know their respective turning circles, but it seemed to me that the Nashville could maneuver in less space than the Concord.

Q: Was there anything remarkable in the navigation realm during your time in that ship?

Admiral Strauss: No. I found out how to sight Mars and cross it with the sun during the daytime. If you did it at the right time, then you wouldn't have to take any star sights, because you had a pretty good fix there. Although I always did take star sights. But I remember Captain Craven once called me in, and he said, "Could you cross Mars, the sun, and the moon?"

And I said, "Yes, I think I could."

And he asked me if I had ever seen the movie The Time of Your Life. I said I had. He said there was a character, when asked to do something, said his heart was

not in it. He said, "I can see your heart isn't in it."
Well, it wasn't.

Q: What was your desire to avoid star sights--so you didn't have to get up so early?

Admiral Strauss: Well, you'd have to get up early, because one couldn't get the cross at twilight. But one could thus omit the evening star sights. It wasn't so much to avoid them as to have a backup, because sometimes you couldn't get them, you know. You'd at least have a fix that way.

Q: Was there any time spent on tactical development? These ships had those remarkable rapid-fire guns. Was there work on how those would be used?

Admiral Strauss: I don't think specifically on that. As I remember, we had short-range battle practice at one time during my time aboard and did very well on it, off of Hawaii. We had an excellent score on a night target practice.

Q: Those guns must have been something to behold.

Admiral Strauss: Of course, they weren't as rapid fire as the guns in the Fresno, the 5-inch dual purpose. I remember someone in the war said that they had an antiaircraft cruiser beside them firing at some airplanes, and said it looked as though the ship was on fire.

Q: I've heard that comparison on other ships. Well, you must have spent a lot of time on the bridge and gotten to know both captains pretty well because of your duties.

Admiral Strauss: Oh, I did, yes. Then Craven decided that besides the officer of the deck that a head of department had to be on deck all the time, really stand watch with him. You didn't have to do it four hours on and four hours off. You could stay six hours, or the whole morning or anything you wanted to, but anyway, it had to be a line head of department up there all the time.

Q: That gets pretty onerous if you have to do your star sights also.

Admiral Strauss: Yes. The rotation consisted of the gunnery officer, the first lieutenant, and myself, really.

Q: Not the engineer?

Admiral Strauss: I can't remember that he did.

Q: You must have had much more feeling about the imminence of the war at that point.

Admiral Strauss: Yes, yes. We did, because, of course, it was really an overt act, I suppose, taking those people into Iceland. Of course, the Reuben James was sunk somewhat later.* My sister christened the Reuben James so she always said they sank her ship.**

Q: That's interesting.

There was much to-do made about that sinking, because obviously that was the first one.

Admiral Strauss: Yes. It was an overt act. Reuben James was a bluejacket and had no relatives.*** Admiral Leigh was in the Bureau of Navigation, and he nominated my sister to christen her.****

---
*On the morning of 31 October 1941, while escorting a convoy to Iceland, the four-stack destroyer Reuben James (DD-245) was torpedoed by the German submarine U-562. The destroyer sank quickly; 115 crew members died, and 44 survived.
**Miss Helen Strauss was the sponsor when the Reuben James was launched at the New York Shipbuilding Corporation, Camden, New Jersey, on 4 October 1919.
***Reuben James was a boatswain's mate who served in a number of U. S. warships in the early 19th century. He accompanied Stephen Decatur in the burning of the Philadelphia at Tripoli in 1804 and was credited by some with taking a sword blow intended for Decatur.
****Captain Richard H. Leigh, USN, Assistant Chief of the Bureau of Navigation. As a rear admiral, he was later chief of the bureau himself from 1927 to 1930.

Q: James supposedly had been involved in saving Stephen Decatur's life from the Barbary pirates.

Admiral Strauss: Yes.

Q: So then it was back to England for you. How did that set of orders come about?

Admiral Strauss: I'd been my time at sea and rather more. On the fitness report you put what duty you would prefer. And I said that I would like to be a special naval observer with the British fleet. I'd talked to some of them. A classmate of mine, Ken Hartman, had been a special naval observer aboard an aircraft carrier in the Mediterranean that got very badly hit.* And he came back to the United States and had a very frustrating time. Because he'd been through all of this, and he'd go to someplace in the Navy Department and say, "You know, one of the things they found when the ship was torpedoed or hit a mine, that people sitting on the head were thrown up against the overhead and cracked their skulls." Or he would say, "They found out that even the electric backup lights got smashed

---

*Lieutenant Commander Kenneth P. Hartman, USN, was an observer on board HMS Illustrious. On 10 January 1941, the carrier was part of the escort for a convoy from Alexandria to Malta. She was attacked by the Luftwaffe and damaged by six bombs. She proceeded to Malta for temporary repairs.

and didn't work, so that people had to have hand torches and so forth." He said every place he'd go, he'd tell them these things that really they found out in battle.

And they'd say, "Kenneth, nice to see you. We'll have to have lunch sometime." He said people wouldn't pay any attention to him, though his information was firsthand.

Q: That's surprising, because that's very useful information.

Admiral Strauss: Oh, yes. He'd been through it and found out all these things that occurred that you probably wouldn't have thought of. So I thought that would be an interesting job, up near the front. And so I was assigned to be a special naval observer, and I flew from New York in one of the Pan American flying boats. We stopped at Bermuda, the Azores and Lisbon. And this man whom I mentioned, Burke Elbrick, was first secretary at the embassy in Lisbon. He came back later and was ambassador there, but he and his wife Elvira took me in. I stayed with them, waiting for transportation to go up to England. I was there three days, I guess. They took me around. It was rather interesting, because Lisbon was neutral, and it would have on the same airfield British and German planes. And we waited at the casino and, they'd say, "See that lady? She's supposed to be the German military attaché's mistress." And I'd get the lowdown on what was going on in Lisbon.

Q: I take it you traveled in civilian clothes?

Admiral Strauss: Yes. We were supposed not to be there, you see. You're quite right. And I had my uniform in my suitcase, but it wasn't bothered. Then, at the end of about three days, I got passage in a plane from Lisbon to England. The airport wasn't in London. I had to take a train ride back to London. I, for the first time, saw barrage balloons, which they had near the airport, and took the train down to London and there was a U.S. naval officer who'd come up from Lisbon with me. I think he was a lieutenant. And we landed in the blackout. It was raining hard, and I said, "I know a restaurant here in the middle of London that used to be good. Let's try it." It was called L'Aperatif and was on in Jermyn Street. We went in, pushed the curtains aside, and blinked at the light. The headwaiter said, "Good evening, Lieutenant Strauss. You haven't been here for a long time."

Q: That must have impressed your companion.

Admiral Strauss: Well, that man was my friend from then

on. So we had dinner, and then I reported to Admiral Ghormley, who was the special naval observer.* I had a lot of notes that I'd brought from Washington with me.

Q: Had you gone through briefings in OpNav?**

Admiral Strauss: Oh, yes, all over and had notes from different people there.

And so it was only a few days in London. I was getting my kit ready to go down to the Mediterranean. And one evening, I went to Quaglinos in civilian clothes and was dancing with a lovely. Someone tapped me on the shoulder and said, "You'd better get up to Grosvenor Square.*** The Japanese have just bombed Pearl Harbor." So I went right away, of course, and all the other officers in London were collected there. And the next morning all over London everybody blossomed out in uniform. So that was the end of my going to be an observer.

Q: What memories do you have of the blitz?

---

*Rear Admiral Robert L. Ghormley, USN, reported to London in August 1940 and was given the title special naval observer while working with the British on ways of cooperating in the war then in progress. He was promoted to vice admiral in September 1941.
**OpNav refers to the large, extended staff of the Chief of Naval Operations.
***Grosvenor Square was the site of the U.S. Embassy in London.

Admiral Strauss: Of course, the big blitz was over then. The little blitz came a few months later, and I remember well the sound of houses coming down. Very often a house that had been hit would stand there for some days, and all of a sudden, it would collapse, you see. Vibrations or something like that. I heard about a lady who was buried up to her neck and apparently the language she used, "Goddamn you, get me out of this, you so-and-so."

In early 1942, Ghormley was relieved, and Admiral Stark came over there and was commander of U.S. naval forces in Europe.* At the time of my arrival in London, Captain Paul Bastedo was chief of staff to Admiral Ghormley.** Captain Ralph Wentworth, who had arrived from being CO of the Nashville, was junior to Bastedo and became deputy chief of staff. This arrangement persisted until Admiral Stark took over. Bastedo stayed on while Wentworth went to Iceland as commodore in command there. The position of chief of staff and deputy chief changed under Stark's incumbency.

Q: Were you with Ghormley long enough to form impressions of him?

---

*In April 1942, Admiral Harold R. Stark, USN, who had been Chief of Naval Operations until shortly before, relieved Vice Admiral Ghormley and was given the title Commander U.S. Naval Forces in Europe.
**Captain Paul H. Bastedo, USN.

Admiral Strauss: Yes. Though it is difficult to evaluate a superior whom you only see from time to time in an office, I thought he was up and coming. My father had been captain of the Ohio at the time of the Mexican trouble. And Ghormley was his first lieutenant. And my father said that, "If I was going to send a landing party ashore, I would have put Ghormley in charge of it because I thought he was the most capable officer I had."

Q: That's interesting.

Admiral Strauss: Because, of course, Ghormley had a hard time. If you're going to be in a war, don't get in it at the beginning if you're a citizen of a democracy. Because you never have enough to work with and you can't shine, you see. It's all those people that come later, after things build up, and they learn their way around and have plenty of forces. But I always felt that Ghormley got shortchanged out there in the South Pacific, that he was unlucky that he was early in the war.* It's like Weygand in France and Gort in England.**

---
*Following his relief in London, Ghormley became Commander South Pacific Force. He was relieved by Vice Admiral William F. Halsey, Jr., USN, after U.S. naval forces suffered a number of reverses around Guadalcanal in the autumn of 1942.
**General Maxime Weygand was Allied ground commander in Chief when France fell to the Germans in the spring of 1940; at that same time, the 6th Viscount Gort, a general, was commander in chief of the British Expeditionary Force in France.

Q: Or even like Anderson, whom we were discussing.

Admiral Strauss: Yes. But later on, when things get going well and the commander has adequate forces, the job gets easier. For example, Montgomery had everything his way.* He had all the troops he could use, and the British Navy had sunk the munitions going to Rommel.** The time to come into a war was to come in later, if you can. I mean, Ghormley impressed me, what little I saw of him, very favorably. But I remembered that story of my father's, who thought he was terrific back in 1914 at Veracruz.

Q: What were your specific duties in that period before the war started?

Admiral Strauss: I was a planner. I was a planner in a little group that consisted of Captain Wentworth, Colonel Hart, a Marine, and the then Lieutenant Colonel Bolte who was afterwards the deputy chief of the Army, and also commander of the U.S. forces in Europe.*** He's 90 now. I

---

*Lieutenant General Bernard Law Montgomery took command of the British Eighth Army in North Africa and scored a series of victories that eventually led to promotion to field marshal and command of troops advancing on Germany itself.
**Field Marshal Erwin Rommel commanded Germany's Afrika Korps and dominated the North African theater until late 1942. He was one of Germany's most popular war heroes.
***Colonel Franklin A. Hart, USMC; Lieutenant Colonel Charles L. Bolte, USA.

see him. But he used to come in in the morning and give us a "navel salute," because the rest of us, you see, were Navy.

Q: That gesture didn't show up on the tape, so maybe you could describe that. He would bring his hand up to his midsection.

Admiral Strauss: Up to his navel and give a horizontal salute. And that was the navel salute that he would greet us with every morning. Well, we were very close-knit and it was a very close association, that little group there.

One of the people who came over to England was a man of about 60, called Paul Hammond, who was known worldwide. He worked in the financial world in New York, but his main claim to fame was that he was an international yachtsman and there's no greater fraternity than the international yachtsmen. And he won the race to Santander one time. And he had been reared up the Hudson with Franklin Roosevelt. He got commissioned and was a lieutenant commander, but he was able to sort of kick open the door and say, "Franklin, we ought to do so and so."

And Ernie King said, "Get that man out of Washington." So they sent him over to London.*

---
*Admiral Ernest J. King, USN, was Chief of Naval Operations and Commander in Chief U.S. Fleet.

And Paul knew everybody, and among his friends were the Mountbattens. And one time he said to me, "Dickie and Edwina, I'm having them to dinner tonight. You come along." So I did and we had dinner in the Berkeley Buttery. It was the first time I had met either of them.

Q: Was Mountbatten already a celebrity by that time?

Admiral Strauss: Yes. He had just become Chief of Combined Operations. He'd been ordered as captain of the aircraft carrier <u>Illustrious</u>, and he very much hated being taken out of her, because he liked the job. And, as you know, in the British Navy you can be a captain of an aircraft carrier without being an aviator, which he wasn't. And Churchill got him out. His predecessor as Chief of Combined Operations was Admiral of the Fleet Lord Keyes of Zebrugge fame. But Keyes was an old man, and I think he was getting tired on the job.*

Well, Churchill felt that this business of inter-service work, especially amphibious operation, was very important. And although Mountbatten's substantive rank was still captain, he was made a vice admiral, a lieutenant general, and an air marshal, all at the same time. And a little later he asked Stark to have a U.S. naval officer attached to his staff. Stark assigned me, and Mountbatten

---
*In late 1941, the 41-year-old Mountbatten relieved 68-year-old Admiral of the Fleet Roger Keyes, Royal Navy.

was kind enough to say, "I was hoping maybe I'd get you." Well, that was fine. So I was the first American officer on his staff after he became Chief of Combined Operations.

My immediate boss was a captain called Hughes-Hallett, who came to a certain distinction afterwards for several reasons.* I expected to be a sort of liaison officer, but I found out that I was completely integrated into the staff and as other American officers came on, they were, too. We were given just the same jobs as the British officers were in planning raids and that type of thing. So it was a fascinating assignment. I had the designation "USNO," U.S. naval officer.

To head up his staff, Mountbatten had three officers called respectively vice chief, deputy chief, and assistant chief. These spots were filled by an Army major general, Royal Marine major general, and a Royal Navy captain. I, alas, cannot recall the correct sequence of these three. The general was Charles Hayden. Major General G. E. Wildman-Lushington was the Marine. As an aside, Admiral Mountbatten once told me that he considered a Royal Navy captain the equivalent of a major general.

Mountbatten was accused of being a little bit like OSS. You know they always said OSS stood for "oh so social". And there were a number of people you might say were social celebrities, but they were all able. They

---
*Captain John "Jock" Hughes-Hallett, Royal Navy.

weren't chosen for their blue eyes or anything like that. One of the people he had on his staff was dressed as a major general. He was Sir Harold Wernher, one of the richest men in England, heir to a South African diamond fortune and married to Lady Zia Wernher, daughter of the Russian Grand Duke Torbay. They owned the great estate Luton Hoo. Wernher was particularly valuable because if you needed anything in large quantities, like 10,000 tons of cement, or so many iron girders, he could always get it for you. But it was a hard-working staff, and as I think everybody knows, that the commandos who were especially constructed battalions were a part of Lord Louis's command. They were organized and trained to do particular types of actions.

I shared a desk for awhile with a commander called Red Ryder.* He was R. E. D. Ryder, and he was the man who took the Campbeltown, which was one of the converted U.S. 50 destroyers we gave England, into Saint Nazaire and blew it up and then got out of there and got back to England.** And, as I say, I shared a desk with him for a while. From knowing him and two other bona fide heroes, Captain Appleyard and Major Hasler, RM, I decided that these are

---
*Commander Robert Edward Dudley Ryder, Royal Navy.
**On the night of 27-28 March 1942, HMS Campbeltown, loaded with explosives, was rammed into the caisson of a huge dry dock at Saint-Nazaire, France, a port on the Bay of Biscay. Delayed explosives later increased damage to the dry dock, thus precluding its use for the German battleship Tirpitz.

irreplaceable men but must be "oddballs" to do their exploits. Ryder, in spite of being a hero, was not promoted to captain. He retired and was elected to Parliament. He had earlier won the Arctic Medal; he had floated on a block of ice until rescued.

Q: How much contact did you have with Admiral Stark?

Admiral Strauss: He remained my official boss. He didn't bother me at all, but I saw him quite frequently.

Q: How much personal contact did you have with Admiral Mountbatten?

Admiral Strauss: A good deal. Because he used his staff, and knew all about them and he wasn't a sort of a boss who had little contact with those people down below. I saw quite a lot of him, officially and socially. I was there with him for about 18 months until he left to go to India, and he asked me if I'd like to go also. But I hadn't had any sea duty during the war, and I couldn't look people in the face. So I had to decline, although that would have been an interesting job. But I kept up with him through the years, and I would say that we really became friends. He was godfather to my youngest son. And back in about

1973 he once said to me, "Elliott, you're coming to my funeral."

I said, "It's quite possible that mine might occur first." But, sure enough, when he did die, I was one of the four U.S. military officers who had been designated by him to attend his funeral, which I did in due course.*

Q: Why were you included in that select few, do you think?

Admiral Strauss: Because we were friends and we kept up. I saw him a number of times, both in England and in this country. As a matter of fact, he's been here to my house briefly. He came here before we went to a luncheon at the Alibi Club one time. He was an impressive man; he dominated any gathering just by the force of his personality. He was particularly good with troops, with enlisted men. He knew just how to handle them, how to bring them forward, had that knack, that gift.

During his time in Combined Operations, they often thought of the invasion. The project of the invasion of Normandy came up increasingly, and he arranged a conference called Rattle at Largs in Scotland, at which the people who very possibly might have been the commanders of an invasion took part, to make an initial plan. As it worked out, none

---
*Mountbatten was killed 27 August 1979 by Irish terrorists who planted a bomb in his boat.

of the senior people who were there did end up in the invasion command. There was Admiral Sir Charles Little, Air Marshal Dalbiac, and General Morgan. Not the Freddy Morgan who was chief of staff of COSSAC later on, but another Morgan, known as Monkey Morgan.* And the idea was where the invasion should go, when and how it should be done. And my boss, Captain Hughes-Hallett, was there. He had a personality trait that when he talked he rubbed a pencil back and forth between his hands, and I can remember him when somebody said, "We should go to the area near Cherbourg, but there are no harbors there."

And he said, "Then if there are no harbors, we shall have to build one." And that was the origin of the idea of the artificial harbor, which was actually done for the invasion of Normandy.

Admiral Mountbatten was assigned as a personal flagship a yacht called the Sister Ann. And it was the property of Daisy Fellowes, who was a rich, rather fashionable lady. And the captain was a RNVR lieutenant commander called Teacher. And when we went on board to be taken up to Largs, Colonel Hart was with me. And I'd been on board the Sister Ann before, and when he came on board I introduced Lieutenant Commander Teacher to him. Frank Hart was very polite and said, "How do you do," and was going to pass on.

---
*General Sir Frederick Morgan; COSSAC--Chief of Staff to the Supreme Allied Commander.

And I said, "You know, he's the Teacher of Teacher's Highland Cream."

And Colonel Hart said, "How do you do! How do you do!" He'd warmed up considerably to the young man when he found out his connection with Teacher's Highland Cream. Well, the conference at Largs, as I have said, was really the nucleus of a plan for the invasion of Normandy. And it went through a great many vicissitudes.

Q: It went through a great many delays, also.

Admiral Strauss: Yes.

Q: Lord Mountbatten was a man of great enthusiasms. Did his staff have to restrain him on some of those?

Admiral Strauss: Yes. I think that's true, that because of his enthusiasm and his go-ahead, I'm not sure that his decisions were invariably the best ones. This had shown up in some of his handling of his destroyer squadron. The man I went to afterwards, who was the naval commander in chief of the Allied invasion of Normandy, Admiral Sir Bertie Ramsay, was less flamboyant and less colorful, but I think probably his decisions were, on the whole, more thought out than those of Mountbatten.*

---

*Admiral Sir Bertram H. Ramsay, Royal Navy.

Q: Did the staff try to rein Mountbatten back if they thought he went too far?

Admiral Strauss: I can't remember any particular instance of that, but I'm sure that the senior people on his staff would advise him, would give him counsel on these things. I don't think he had to be restrained from wild ideas, which sometimes occurred to Churchill, for example, "Habbakuk," an antiaircraft platform on a harnessed iceberg.

How would you like me to go from here--the Dieppe raid?

Q: Surely, yes.

Admiral Strauss: I've made some notes. The Dieppe raid was on the 19th of August.* Prime Minister Churchill had decided that some fairly large effort should be made. The war had become so stagnant by then he felt that some activity was due, and it was decided that an operation which would give them some information should take place. Another thought was that the Canadians had been in England for some time and were restless. And so a plan was conceived to land on Dieppe and to try to take prisoners,

---
*For an excellent overall account of the 1942 operation, see Terence Robertson, <u>Dieppe: The Shame and the Glory</u> (Boston: Little, Brown and Company, 1962).

destroy the batteries, and test the ability to land on an enemy coast. A subsidiary aim was to try to capture a German radar.

A plan was made in Combined Operations, but then the Canadians were called in, the actual landing force, because it was a principle that the people who did the operation would make the plan that obtained. Combined Operations felt that to go in directly across the beach was probably not feasible. They should attack from the flanks. But the Canadians felt that they could do a direct assault. And a compromise was made that was a combination of a flanking movement and a direct assault.

The Canadian brigade was commanded by a Major General Roberts, and there were assorted units from other parts of the British Empire which took part in it.* It took place on the 19th of August of '42. And the surprise element was a combination of landing ships, which carried landing craft and craft which went directly across from the Portsmouth area. The support was seven "Hunt"-class destroyers and one Polish destroyer. A "Hunt"-class destroyer wouldn't qualify as a DE today in our Navy. It had 4-inch guns with step-by-step fire control. And the units arrived there on time for the most part--there were two that didn't--and effected surprise. So for the first hour or so, there were no German planes up.

―――――――――
*Major General John Hamlton Roberts, Commander Second Canadian Division.

I was in the "Hunt"-class destroyer called the Bleasdale, which was to give fire support, make smoke. The landings started. The Canadian troops started ashore. They had a hard time, because some of them landed in too deep water and when the tanks got ashore, the beach was shingle and the tracks rotated on the shingle, and they had a difficulty in getting off the beach. Then eventually, in an hour or so, the German planes started coming over, and the British planes came over from England, but the fighters could only stay a very short time, so they had to come over in waves, really.

From a naval standpoint, the raid, I think you could say, was a success. The air battle was a success, considering the limitation of the numbers available and the flying range of the planes. From the military side it was almost a fiasco, because a great many of the Canadian troops were killed and many more were captured. One of the few successes was on the one flank. A commando under Lieutenant Colonel Lord Lovat got up and silenced one of the 5.9-inch guns.* The other one was never silenced. Captain Hughes-Hallett was the naval commander for the operation, and I heard him afterwards say that he had read in accounts of battles that the decks ran with blood. And he said, "I never expected actually to see that, but on

---

*Lieutenant Colonel Lord Lovat was commander of Number 4 Commando.

this raid I did. The decks were running with blood."

We took on board a great many people: troops who had escaped from the beaches and some aviators who were shot down. And I saw one Spitfire shot down by our own antiaircraft fire in the latter's enthusiasm.* This is not a rare occurrence at all. I sometimes thought of trying for a doctorate on the amount of casualties that in any war one inflicts on its own side. I mean, at a wild, uninformed guess this would run between 10 and 15%.

One of the "Hunt"-class destroyers, the Berkeley, got a direct bomb hit and was broken in two and had to be sunk by torpedo fire from one of the other destroyers. An American colonel called Hillsinger was on Mountbatten's staff; he was in the Berkeley and he lost a foot in the action.** He later wound up having several operations and lost more and more of the leg each time. The destroyers got in so close to the beach that one of my main worries was that we would go aground because the ship didn't pay too much attention to soundings. There were no leadsmen, and the depth finder in the Bleasdale went out very early in the game. And they were in so close that they were subject to gun and rifle fire from the shore.

Q: What was your personal reaction while all this was

---
*The Spitfire was a British fighter plane that won fame in the Battle of Britain. It was faster and more maneuverable than the German Messerschmitt ME 109.
**Colonel Loren B. Hillsinger, USA.

going on? You spoke of the captain who saw the decks running with blood; what were your reactions as the thing unfolded?

Admiral Strauss: Well, anybody who said that he was not frightened--I don't believe him. So what was my reaction? Well, I was, of course, hoping it would be a success. We were sent off when it was decided that some German E-boats were getting into the fight. Three of the destroyers were sent off to try to find them and deal with the E-boats. We never found them.

Q: What were your specific duties as this thing went on?

Admiral Strauss: I was an observer for Combined Operations.

Q: Perhaps it would have been better to have had a specific job that more busily engaged you. As an observer you have time to think about all the bad things that go on.

Admiral Strauss: Yes, I certainly did.

In 1977, while on a holiday visit to London, I received a telephone call from Lord Mountbatten, inviting my wife and me to lunch at Broadlands.* When we arrived,

_____
*Broadlands was the Mountbatten family estate in Hampshire.

we were introduced to a young Canadian who was a representative of Radio Quebec. He had come to England to persuade Admiral Mountbatten to take part in a program conducted by Radio Quebec. This program was an ongoing one called "Aux Yeux du Present." The series covered battles and campaigns from Actium, through Waterloo, and down to World Wars I and II. The battle was presented in detail, and then a jury would decide whether the battle was really necessary and whether it was well conducted. The representative of Radio Quebec wanted Mountbatten to take part in the presentation of the raid on Dieppe, in which the Canadians had the major part, and which was set up by the Chief of Combined Operations.

Mountbatten said that he was unable to go to Canada at that time but said, "Elliott Strauss was there. Why don't you get him?" So, in due course, I went to Quebec, was powdered up for the TV camera, along with other participants in the raid. Among them was a Canadian major general, who had been a lieutenant colonel, second in command at the time of the raid. He was in remarkably good shape physically, but, alas, was senile and could contribute little. However, another general, who was a major in 1942, added a great deal to the proceedings. There were former enlisted ratings, all of whom took part in a two-hour review of the battle. The final reel of the film which emerged was one of Lord Mountbatten, recorded by him in England. This was, to me, the most interesting part of the recording.

The jury was asked two questions: should the action have taken place, and should the Canadians have been the troops employed? It decided that the raid was worthwhile but that the Canadians had not yet had the experience required to carry out this particularly concentrated action.

Radio Quebec gave me a copy of the tape, which I have not yet had the opportunity to screen.

Q: How soon did it become apparent that the raid was a fiasco ashore?

Admiral Strauss: I think when Hughes-Hallett got word that a part of the Canadians had surrendered. And when they had to abandon the tanks, I think it was pretty well known that that part of it was not gaining its objectives and would have to be called off.

The naval commander of the Dieppe raid was Captain John Hughes-Hallett, Royal Navy. He afterwards became a vice admiral and when he retired became a member of Parliament. He was known as "Hughes-Hitler," which I think was rather unfair, although he was very austere and he never married. And I remember someone else on the staff, a British lieutenant commander named Costobadie.* Hallett got ahold of him and said, "Costobadie, I want you to make me an outline plan for so and so and have it ready by 4:00 o'clock this afternoon."

And Costobadie said, "Captain, I'll try to do it," but he said, "Commander So-and-so had me up up until 4:00 o'clock this morning and I'm not in very good shape."

And Hallett said, "Costobadie, I don't care how you spend your evenings. I want that report by 4:00 o'clock in the afternoon," which was, I'm afraid, rather typical of him. But I liked him and kept up with him. He had a stroke later on. We still exchange letters. His brother, also a vice admiral, was head of the British military delegation here in Washington after the war.**

One of the things he did while he was still a naval officer, he wondered how they handled the men in the transports. And he put on a private's uniform and went aboard a transport to check on this. It's sort of the initiative he had; I've forgotten whether he was a captain or a rear admiral at that time. In other words, he wanted to know firsthand, and I give him full marks for that. When I was at the IDC, we were taken aboard the Illustrious

---

*Lieutenant Commander Ackroyd Norman Palliser Costobadie, Royal Navy.
**His brother was Admiral Sir Charles Hughes-Hallett, Royal Navy.

to witness an exercise at sea.* Hughes-Hallett was commanding officer. He lent me his cabin for the night while he slept in his sea cabin.

Q: Well, we're right at the end of the tape. That's a good one to end on.

---

*IDC--Imperial Defence College, which Strauss attended in the late 1940s; HMS Illustrious was an aircraft carrier.

Strauss #3 - 206

Interview Number 3 with Rear Admiral Elliott B. Strauss,
U.S. Navy (Retired)

Place: Admiral Strauss's home in Washington, D.C.

Date: Monday, 10 November 1986

Interviewer: Paul Stillwell

Q: Admiral, just to backtrack a bit, I think you wanted to explain why your job as assistant naval attaché in England was established.

Admiral Strauss: Yes. The Chief of Naval Intelligence, who was Captain W. D. Puleston, decided--either himself or in concert with others--that it would be a good idea to keep track of Japanese merchant ships.* The idea was that before the Japanese would make an overt act towards war, they would call in their merchant ships from a lot of the ports around the world. And the Navy Department knew that Lloyd's got notice of the movement of ships immediately.** And in those days the telephone communication wasn't all that satisfactory, so ONI set up an additional assistant naval attaché to keep track of the movements of the Japanese merchant ships.***

When I got to London, I set up a board on the wall

---
*Captain William D. Puleston, USN, Director of Naval Intelligence.
**Lloyd's of London is a large firm that insures a great many commercial ships.
***ONI--Office of Naval Intelligence.

with a curtain that could be pulled over it, and little mock ships with drawing pins.* And every day I would get the daily Lloyd's list of the movement of the merchant ships around the world. Lloyd's listed all merchant ships, Japanese among them, and I would post these latter on the board to see whether there were any marked changes, or any dramatic moves. And during the period of somewhat over two years that I was there, I never saw any, but we kept the board up. One of my difficulties, at first, was finding the location of some of the ports that the Lloyd's list gave, for instance Mormagao, and places like that that I'd never heard of.

Q: Where is Mormagao?

Admiral Strauss: It's in Japan, someplace in Japan.

Q: It's interesting that this would be established in London as a precaution against war with Japan.

Admiral Strauss: Yes, yes. Well the idea was that ONI felt that it could get the information so much more quickly. For instance, they might get a one- or two-day jump on it if the move was dramatic.

---
*Drawing pin is the British term for an item known to Americans as a thumbtack.

Q: Was there a means of transmitting information back to Washington from this on a regular basis?

Admiral Strauss: Well, of course, we had telegraph and radio, and, of course, we did have telephone communication, but you didn't just pick up the phone the way you do nowadays. You may have had to have several hours' delay, or it may be that the circuits were down. But, of course, you could get it back. But if they'd done it in Washington, they would have had to wait for the Lloyd's list or the information from the Lloyd's list to get there--for several hundred ships.

Q: Did you report regularly on this plot, or was the idea that you would notify them if something dramatic happened.

Admiral Strauss: Yes. That was it. I didn't report regularly on it.

Q: So it was a lot of work for which you didn't ever realize the desired benefits.

Admiral Strauss: No, it's true that at the end there was a question whether it was really worthwhile, but since that was the job we kept it up all the time.

Q: Did you have any direct contact with Captain Puleston?

Admiral Strauss: Yes. I saw him before I went over, and he was then writing the life of Mahan.* He charged me to get information from a number of people in England who had had relationships of some sort or another with Mahan. One of them was a retired major general called Sir Ivor Maxse, who apparently had been quite a friend of Mahan's. And I did call on General Maxse and got a few letters from him. When I first got there, I was so busy that I didn't start out trying to get in touch with these people right away, and Captain Puleston wrote to my boss and said he hadn't heard from me, and was I able to do what he had requested. Well, my boss, Captain Anderson, took it rather as a joke, but I did get Puleston a certain amount of information.**

There were others besides General Maxse. And Maxse was very good. He lent me the actual letters from Mahan on the understanding that they'd be sent back. But I think that Admiral Puleston's main interest was in the book he was writing, and that was rather more important than other things. You may remember, he was a very good historian. He wrote one of the first, and one of the best, accounts of

---
*Captain William D. Puleston, USN, author of a number of books, including <u>Mahan: The Life and Work of Captain Alfred Thayer Mahan</u> (New Haven, Connecticut: Yale University Press, 1939).
**Captain Walter S. Anderson, USN, U.S. naval attaché in Great Britain.

the Dardanelles Campaign and then he did write a life of Mahan.* And my father said that was very difficult, because he said it's difficult to write about somebody who has only written and hasn't done very much besides.

Q: Puleston's book was really the standard biography of Mahan for at least a generation.

Admiral Strauss: Yes. Then he wrote a book, which I have a copy that I've referred to a number of times. It's about the influence of force on history.** He showed that movements in history have taken place because of diplomacy. But even when you charged it to diplomacy, it succeeded because there has been enough force behind it, either to use it or to threaten to use it, to back up the diplomacy. And I think some of these people that always urge negotiations don't realize that just talk without something behind it usually doesn't result in very much.

Q: Well, that well bears out the famous Theodore Roosevelt dictum, "Speak softly, but carry a big stick."***

---

*William D. Puleston, The Dardanelles Expedition: A Condensed Study (Annapolis, Maryland: U.S. Naval Institute, 1927).
**William D. Puleston, The Influence of Force in Foreign Relations (New York: Van Nostrand, 1955).
***Theodore Roosevelt, President of the United States, 1901-09, was a strong advocate of a powerful Navy.

Admiral Strauss: ". . . big stick." Exactly, yes.

Q: We got up last time to the raid on Dieppe, and I wondered what was the immediate fallout from that? Were there recriminations over the number of losses and prisoners?

Admiral Strauss: No, I don't believe so. I think it was taken that the effort was worthwhile. That I question, because I think that some of the lessons we learned from it were wrong lessons. I may have mentioned that one of the lessons they thought they had learned was that you could keep attack transports off an enemy coast only long enough to drop one relay of boats, that you'd have to get the transports out of there. Well, of course, we learned in the Pacific that with adequate air support you keep a transport there all day, or even longer. So that that was supposedly a lesson we learned which was a false one. And there were others. One thing learned: bombardment by 4-inch guns is not heavy enough to make the defenders keep their heads down. In the Pacific and at Normandy major-caliber guns were used with more success.

There was a dispute afterwards, because Combined Operations in their outline plans had thought that the attack should be by two flanking motions, and the Canadians rather thought that they should go in directly. Of course, the actual assault was a combination of the two. So that all together the military side, the Army side of it, was a fiasco. The naval side went off as well as possible, although in the air cover, the fighters, on account of the distance, could stay over the action a very short time. I saw one Spitfire get shot down by our own forces.* It was a matter of too much zeal and airplanes flying around, and one battery started on the Spitfire. And then others joined in, and the pilot did come down in a parachute and, so far as I know, he was rescued.

Q: Did you file a report on your observations back to Washington?

Admiral Strauss: I submitted it to Admiral Stark.** As a matter of fact, I went into his office the next day, and he and some of the staff listened as I reported what had gone on.

Q: What are your impressions of Admiral Stark from that period?

Admiral Strauss: Admiral Stark was a very, I hate to use

---
*The Spitfire was a British fighter plane.
**Admiral Harold R. Stark, USN, Commander U.S. Naval Forces in Europe.

the term "nice man," but he was. He was good to me. He was good to his subordinates. Admiral Conolly once said that Chiefs of Naval Operations alternated between sailors and politicians.* And I think that Admiral Stark could be rated among the politician numbers that had had that job. He was, I think, a good diplomat, and he aspired to be ambassador to France after the war was over, and established, I think, a very good relationship with General de Gaulle.

I once came back into the headquarters at Grosvenor Square and saw this tall French officer standing up in front of the Marine's desk there. The tall general had an aide with him. The Marine was saying, "de Gaulle?** How do you spell it?" Well, I rushed in and took charge of him. At the same time, Lieutenant Williams, who was Admiral Stark's flag lieutenant, came rushing down the stairs, obviously very disturbed. The general wasn't amused, and Lieutenant Williams took charge of him and took him off to Admiral Stark's office.

Q: A useful point to be made is that we need both types. It was the politician Stark who got the forces for Admiral

---
*Admiral Richard L. Conolly, USN, who was Commander in Chief U.S. Naval Forces Eastern Atlantic and Mediterranean, 1946-50. Strauss was at the Imperial Defence College in England during that period.
**General Charles de Gaulle was head of the Free French forces in exile.

King to use to fight the war.*

Admiral Strauss: Yes, I suppose that's fair enough. I know that one of the things that Admiral Stark did, he would write birthday letters to the senior officers of his time. He always wrote my father a birthday letter, although I don't think he'd actually ever served directly with him.

Q: Did you have personal contact with him in reporting on the events you'd seen?

Admiral Strauss: Yes, I saw him quite often, almost constantly. I mean, there was no difficulty in getting in to see him and, as a matter of fact, he sent for his subordinates quite often. His first chief of staff was Captain Bastedo.** And he was succeeded by someone who had been his deputy, Commander Flanigan.*** Commander Flanigan was a remarkable person. He was a go-getter and a very able officer, but the story was that he had married the daughter of Senator Hiram Johnson.**** The rumor was

---
*Admiral Ernest J. King, USN, was Chief of Naval Operations and Commander in Chief U.S. Fleet during World War II.
**Captain Paul H. Bastedo, USN.
***Commander Howard A. Flanigan, USN (Ret.) Flanigan was recalled to active duty as a special naval observer in England.
****Hiram W. Johnson (1866-1945), governor of California, 1911-17, Progressive senator from California, 1917-45.

that he'd gotten her away from some other man to whom she was married and that Hiram Johnson said that he would keep after Commander Flanigan to see that he didn't get anyplace. So he retired as a commander.

He came back and was first on Admiral Ghormley's staff and then Admiral Stark's staff.* I was told once when I planned to do something, "If you do that, Commander Flanigan won't like it." And I thought, "Well, I really don't care whether a retired commander likes it or not." I was wrong. Commander Flanigan became a captain. He became a commodore. He became the deputy chief of staff to Admiral Stark, and his real chief of staff at that time was Rear Admiral George Barry Wilson. People would go right by Admiral Wilson's door to go to Commodore Flanigan's door, because Commodore Flanigan was able to get things done.

After he left London, he came back to Washington and was made a rear admiral and was in charge of transportation for the Navy. Paul Hammond, the man who introduced me to the Mountbattens, once said that Flanigan would either end up a millionaire or in jail.** Well, he ended up a millionaire, and afterwards he lived outside of Geneva. He had a string of race horses that he raced in Paris, and he

---
*Vice Admiral Robert L. Ghormley, USN, was special naval observer in England until relieved by Admiral Stark in April 1942.
**Lieutenant Commander Paul L. Hammond, USNR, was a special naval observer in London. Vice Admiral Louis Mountbatten, RN, was Chief of Combined Operations; his wife Edwina was active in Red Cross work.

became, I should think, a number of times a millionaire.

At the time of the invasion of Normandy, the operational naval part was under Admiral Kirk, who had previously been naval attaché, London, and who was sent back there to be the naval commander of the U.S. section of the naval invasion forces.* Under him was Captain Gordon Hutchins, who had most of the working members of the staff under him.** And Admiral Stark was restricted to mainly logistics support of the landing forces in England. And we were known as either Pat's boys or Hutch's boys, and there was quite a rift between the two, which, of course, in wartime is rather ridiculous. I was one of Hutch's boys, and Hutch got taken sick and had to be sent back to the United States, so this gave Pat's boys rather the ascendancy for a certain amount of time. Then Captain Lyman Thackrey was sent to replace Captain Hutchins, and he was my immediate boss all during the period of the invasion of Normandy.***

Q: Now, you've talked about Pat's boys. Was that Pat Flanigan?

Admiral Strauss: Yes. As an example of the relationship

---
*Rear Admiral Alan G. Kirk, USN, Commander Task Force 122 (Western Naval Task Force) for the Normandy invasion in June 1944.
**Captain Gordon Hutchins, USN.
***Captain Lyman A. Thackrey, USN.

between Commodore Flanigan and Captain Gordon Hutchins: one day a messenger brought a message from Pat to be cleared by Hutch. It ran something like this, "We are expecting the 20 landing craft to arrive in April and be off-loaded in Liverpool. We will be very happy to have them."

Hutch said, "No, there are 25, they will arrive in May, they will be off-loaded in Plymouth. That last statement is right."

Q: It sounds as if Flanigan was a very capable individual.

Admiral Strauss: Oh, he was a go-getter. I once asked another captain, "Why do you always sort of stick so close to Commodore Flanigan?"

He said, "Because he gets things done." The captain I was talking to was in charge of the construction of some of the artificial harbors for Normandy, and he said, "If I need a thousand tons of cement, I get the runaround if I talk to anyone else." He said, "If I ask Pat for it, I get it right away." I think his subsequent career in New York shows that he was a man who got things done. I think if he'd stayed in the line of the Navy, he undoubtedly would have gone very far.

Q: If he hadn't had to work against Senator Johnson's influence.

Did Stark seem to be still devastated by the Pearl Harbor experience, or had he gotten past that?*

Admiral Strauss: If he was bothered, he certainly didn't show it.

Q: Did he seem to have a pretty good grasp of the situation in Europe by the time you encountered him?

Admiral Strauss: I think so, yes. He was a very intelligent man, and I think a very capable man. He'd been captain of the West Virginia, but he didn't impress me as being a sailor man the way, for instance, Admiral Conolly did.**

Q: Well, interestingly, he had relieved Captain Anderson as skipper of the West Virginia. They were classmates, but Anderson had the ship first.***

Admiral Strauss: As I never served at sea with either Admiral Stark or Anderson, I really should not evaluate

---
*Admiral Stark had been Chief of Naval Operations at the time of the Japanese attack on Pearl Harbor in December 1941.
**As a captain, Stark commanded the battleship West Virginia (BB-48), 1933-34.
***Captain Walter S. Anderson, USN, who was Strauss's boss in London, had been in the Naval Academy class of 1903 with Stark. Anderson commanded the West Virginia from January 1932 to December 1933.

either as "sailors," but after having served ashore with both, if I had to go to sea under either, I'd choose Anderson.

Q: Well, you had had those lessons from Dieppe. Did you then get on with the planning for the North African operation?

Admiral Strauss: Yes. General Patton came over with a small staff to get the intelligence for the landings in North Africa.* A small team was formed, mostly from the people in Combined Operations and was headed by then Brigadier General Truscott.** I remember that Pierpont M. Hamilton was an Army lieutenant colonel. There was a Marine major, Campbell, and a couple of Army officers. And we were supposed to furnish General Patton and his staff with the intelligence for that part of North Africa.

For instance, we had pilots that had been into Casablanca. We had photographs of the beaches and postcards that showed that sort of thing, which was more available in Europe than in the U.S. The people who knew that part of the world--there were many more in Europe than there would be in the United States. After examining the weather on the Atlantic Coast of Algeria, we said that

---
*Major General George S. Patton, Jr., USA, commanded the Army's Western Task Force for the invasion of North Africa.
**Brigadier General Lucian K. Truscott, Jr., USA.

there were only four or five days a month where you could really do a proper landing there because the sea was too heavy. And Patton said, "Well, suppose that the sea is too heavy, what happens?

And we said, "Well the landing craft would probably get overturned."

And he said, "Well you know what happens when things get overturned. They get washed ashore." And he said, "If that happens, well, the men will get washed ashore, and then they'll be there ready to fight." Well, I thought this was one of the most silly conversations I'd ever heard. And my opinion of Patton from that short time with him, I thought he was rather a blowhard. He had a squeaky voice and he was rather a poseur and I'm afraid my opinion of him wasn't very high. Well, of course, I was completely wrong, as subsequent events turned.

Before he left, he in a way apologized for this. He said, "I realize you people have given me what you found as scientific observers, and I have to be guided by that." As one of Napoleon's edicts had it, Patton was lucky, because the day that the actual landing took place, you could practically walk ashore, and his landing was a great success. Lieutenant Colonel Hamilton, incidentally, was Pierpont Morgan Hamilton; he was a direct descendant of Alexander Hamilton, and, what is probably more practical, a grandson of J. Pierpont Morgan. When he went ashore at

Arzeu to deliver a message to some commander inland, it was with a colonel who was, of course, his superior. The colonel was shot from ambush, and Hamilton went on and delivered the message and received a Congressional Medal of Honor for it.*

Q: Were you thinking in terms of using carriers for air cover, since you couldn't use fighter planes out of England, as you had at Dieppe?

Admiral Strauss: I think the idea was that the enemy air power wasn't enough to bother too much about down there. I can't remember whether there were carriers or not. It just doesn't stick in my mind that there were.

Q: Well, you had the Ranger there and I think one or two of the new jeep carriers.

Admiral Strauss: Did they?

Q: Mountbatten, of course, had been promoted over the heads of a good many senior people to this Combined Operations job. Was there resentment on some of the seniors he had to deal with?

---

*The incident occurred 8 November 1942 near Port Lyautey, French Morocco, when Hamilton was accompanying Colonel Demas Craw.

Admiral Strauss: Yes. The Navy in particular, and the other services also, felt that he was taking forces and material away from them that they could better use. I don't think at that stage that they took the lessons that Combined Operations was trying to learn and the equipment that they were trying to construct, seriously enough. It's understandable that some old-time fleet commander would think that this comparatively young man, who was taking men away, taking landing craft away, was a usurper.

Mountbatten had the utmost in charm, but he could be tough. And one time I remember his having a meeting of a lot of, I suppose, 20 or 30 other officers of the Navy, Air Force, and the Army, and they had a meeting place that had a big O-shaped table. But it could be broken up into bits. And he came into the room with these people and he said, "Gentlemen, something seems to have gone wrong in our housekeeping arrangements." The table wasn't round the way he meant it; it was in bits. There was a young lieutenant who was responsible for this. Mountbatten said to him out of the corner of his mouth, "Give me by 12:00 o'clock your reasons in writing why this table isn't properly fixed." Then he said, "We'll deal with it very quickly." And he told me afterward, "You only ask somebody for their reasons in writing when they haven't any." (Laughter)

I realized from that tour of duty that the great have

to watch their P's and Q's. One afternoon in the early autumn of 1942, just after I joined the Combined Operations staff, I was going to the moving pictures with then Lady Louis, and Mountbatten was joining us. And they each had a Riley runabout car. And, of course, gasoline was very short at the time, and they had an allowance. They both turned up, she first and he, and they said, "Oh, my heavens. We've got to get one of these away from here. The people see two of us with two Riley cars, it's the sort of thing that the papers can get on to: 'Mountbatten's wasting gasoline.'" But you realize that you never get to where you are safe from attack.

A few days after the invasion of Normandy, Lady Louis was then at Broadlands, which wasn't very far away from Southwick Park, which was their place. She invited me to luncheon and asked me to bring someone with me, an officer friend. So I asked this brigadier who'd just been over to Normandy to come with me. And, they were, of course, very interested in hearing what was going on on the other side. The other guest was the chairman of CBS, William Paley. I didn't know who he was even at that time, but I sat next to him. And they said, "Well, tell us about what happened over in Normandy."

And he said, "I had a beefsteak in Bayeux." There was no red meat very much in England at that time, so the first chance he got, he talked about what he ate. He went on and told them, though, about his experiences. But that was his first impression, "I had a beefsteak in Bayeux."

In the 1950s, when I was in Tunisia, two British destroyers came in there, and the skippers' wives came to Tunisia at the same time, of course, quite separately. Both of these wives had been WRNS in the Navy at the time of the invasion.* And in my living room I had a picture of Admiral Ramsay and a picture of Admiral Mountbatten.** The two captains were men whom I'd known as fairly junior officers back then. They and their wives said, "Ramsay, oh what a marvelous man. Wasn't it a tragedy he was killed?" and "He was one of the greatest men . . ." Then I showed them the picture of Mountbatten and they said, "Oh, yes. That's very nice," but I could see that their admiration was really for Ramsay and not for Mountbatten.

Q: What was your personal role in the latter part of 1942?

Admiral Strauss: After I left Combined Operations, at the time that Admiral Mountbatten left, I was transferred to the planning staff of Admiral Little, who was a potential naval commander for the invasion of Normandy.*** He was detached and was sent down to the Mediterranean before the

---
*WRNS--Women's Royal Naval Service.
**Admiral Sir Bertram H. Ramsay, RN, was the top naval planner for the British phase of the North Africa invasion and served as deputy to Admiral Sir Andrew Cunningham, RN, the Allied Naval Commander for the invasion.
***Admiral Sir Charles Little, RN.

invasion, but at that time General Sir Frederick Morgan was assigned as COSSAC, which stood for Chief of Staff of the Supreme Allied Commander. And he was in charge of the planning for the invasion of Normandy, and his whole setup was directed to that end.

His headquarters was in Norfolk House in London, and my little group under Thackrey was the U.S. component of the naval staff for the invasion of Normandy. We spent our time there doing very much what we had done, only in a larger way for Normandy as the little group which did the intelligence for North Africa. This involved forces planning, for instance, things like ambulance LSTs and beach gradients, force composition.* It was really the forerunner of Neptune, which was a code name, of course, for the naval part of the invasion of Normandy, and it was to write some of the detailed plans and the overall plans for that operation.

Before the invasion, the staffs moved to Southwick Park, which was just north of Portsmouth. The Norfolk House phase was, of course, before Eisenhower was even appointed. The discussion then was whether General Marshall or General Eisenhower would be the supreme allied

---

*LSTs--tank landing ships, which were designed to carry tanks and put them ashore by means of ramps lowered from the bow.

commander for the invasion.* The British naval commander was Vice Admiral Sir Philip Vian, and the American section was commanded by Rear Admiral Alan Kirk.

At Southwick Park the planning went on really as before. The thought then was that Admiral Sir Frederick Morgan would be the chief of staff to whoever was appointed supreme allied commander, and, as it turned out, General Eisenhower wanted General Bedell Smith for his chief of staff.** It was successful, but in some ways I feel that it might have been a mistake. It would have been logical to have an American as supreme allied commander and a British chief of staff. I asked General Morgan if, when the invasion came, he would get command of an Army corps and take it over. He said, "No, they're going to keep me here as a hostage because if the plans go all right, well, I'll be all right. If something goes wrong, they want me right here to put the blame on." And he was kept on as deputy chief of staff to the supreme allied commander. I think that General Morgan has never got sufficient credit for the part he played in the invasion. Later on, when we were in Southwick Park, and actually just before I was detached to go back to the United States and get an assignment at sea, I went to see him and said, "I'm

---
*General George C. Marshall, USA, Army Chief of Staff; General Dwight D. Eisenhower, USA, Supreme Allied Commander.
**Lieutenant General Walter Bedell Smith, USA, chief of staff at the Supreme Headquarters Allied Expeditionary Forces, 1944-45.

leaving, General, and I'd like to call on you and pay my respects."

He was living in a tent in Southwick Park. And he said, "Don't bother about the respects. I have just been given a bottle of whiskey. You come down this evening, and we'll see what we can do about killing it." So I had a long session with him in his tent, and I must have been very naive because he said, "You know, this war will be over pretty soon." And he said, "The young fellows can go back and raise families and get jobs. We middle-aged ones, for the rest of our lives we're going to be wound up in trying to do something about the threat of Russia. That's going to be our job. They will be trying to take over the world, and we've got to do something about it." Well, I thought these were our gallant allies, and it had never occurred to me in my, perhaps, ignorance that what he said was true. But General Morgan was one of the first people to be aware of that and to try to tell people what was going to happen.

Q: Did you go to the scene of the invasion in North Africa?

Admiral Strauss: No, I was still, at that time, on Combined Operations staff, and it was a number of months started. So, no, I didn't go. This answer is truthful, but not complete, because I almost went.

Who on the naval staff of the North African force put the request in, I've forgotten, but there was one for Captain John Huse, an EDO officer attached to Naval Forces Europe, and me to visit North Africa.* We both went to Redruth in Cornwall to get a British military flight to Algiers. Also waiting there was Captain Guy Russell, RN, later a four-star admiral and a commandant of the IDC.** It rained buckets, and the plane could not take off. As I remember it, this continued for a week. By then, Huse and I would be late for our regular assignments, and we returned to London. Jack Huse, Captain Jerauld Wright, and I were sharing a flat at 25 Berkeley Square.*** Jack was an inveterate cigar smoker, and our flat often gave evidence of it. He somehow had access to Romeo and Juliet cigars, unobtainable in England. Mountbatten loved these, and Jack Huse was able to furnish them to him.

Once, a shipment of babbitt-lined bearings for landing craft arrived, so badly packed that the babbitt was dented. Admiral Mountbatten said, in exasperation, to Huse, "Why is it that our RN engineer officers are not up to yours?"

Jack said, "They never will be until you give them social equality."

---
*Captain John O. Huse, USN; EDO--engineering duty officer.
**IDC--Imperial Defence College.
***Captain Jerauld Wright, who later became a four-star admiral and served as Commander in Chief Atlantic Fleet in the 1950s.

Lord Louis: "What do you mean? They _are_ equal."

Jack Huse pointed out that in spite of all the effort of Admiral Beatty's regime to effect this, a Royal Navy commander (E) had about the status and prestige of an executive branch lieutenant.*

During the war, a Naval Reserve lieutenant, John Schiff, a partner in the merchant banking house Kuhn Loeb, was originally in the Supply Corps, but he found that the line was more prestigious and shifted to the line.** He asked to join the three of us, regular naval officers, who occupied the apartment at 25 Berkeley Square. Huse was a former submarine commander who had developed arthritis and became an EDO. John Schiff joined us, and he and I became good friends. After the war, while I was putting the _Fresno_ in commission and before the ship became habitable, I rented the top floor of Schiff's triplex apartment on upper Fifth Avenue in New York.

It was from 25 Berkeley Square that Captain Wright told our maid, "Don't bother for dinner for me or breakfast until I tell you again." He left. We did not know where he was going, but this was the start of the expedition to North Africa, led by General Mark Clark and Ambassador Robert Murphy.*** Jerry was nominally in command of the

---
*Admiral of the Fleet Sir David Beatty, RN, First Sea Lord, 1919-27.
**Lieutenant John M. Schiff, USNR.
***Major General Mark W. Clark, USA; Robert D. Murphy, counselor of the U. S. Embassy in Vichy, France.

British submarine which transported them, because, with the memory of Alexandria and Dakar, it was believed that the French would accept an American naval officer better than a British one.

We had two Hungarian maids; being enemy aliens, they couldn't be in the armed services or work in a factory. We were among the very few households in London with domestics. Mrs. Wright wrote an account of her war back in the U.S. and was rather bitter about scrubbing floors in Washington while her husband lived in luxury with two maids. Jerry said that though these girls spoke no English but "Yes, yes," nothing untoward ever happened to them.

Before General Morgan came on board as COSSAC, there was a lull in the invasion planning. In anticipation of the buildup of landing craft from the U.S., a skeleton Amphibious Force Europe was instituted. Its main function prior to the arrival of the new craft was to help the British increase the serviceability of their landing craft. To this end, the Navy had recruited technicians from the automobile companies, Chrysler, etcetera. These men were not in the military but wore a designating brassard and had an official standing. One of their functions was the provision of spare parts for the crafts.

Commander Huse was designated Commander Amphibious Force Europe. With his engineering background, he was eminently fitted for the job at this stage. When his designation reached Washington, the Navy Department said, Huse cannot command a force; he is an EDO." So I was given the job, and Jack Huse was returned to Washington to be the czar of spare part procurement.

Among the group I inherited was a reserve lieutenant who was whiz at repairing and refitting landing craft. One day I was summoned to the chief of staff's office. Captain Bastedo said, "Read this." "This" was a letter from BuPers saying that my lieutenant had claimed that he was a college graduate, which he was not, that he had married an English girl while married to a first wife, and that he owed some terrific sum to creditors.* When the lieutenant returned from the field, I faced him with the letter. He said that he had attended the college, but did not understand that he had to be a graduate, that he had a certified divorce from his first wife before marrying the second, and that the debts were his wife's, not his.

I asked him how many times he had been married and was nonplussed when he replied, "Five times." I returned to Captain Bastedo with this tale, and advised that this man, an excellent and valuable worker, was not really a lieutenant, just a mechanic which someone had hung two stripes on. And I suggested that we smooth over BuPers.

Paul Bastedo said, "Elliott, to an adult, marriage is

---

*BuPers--Bureau of Naval Personnel.

a serious business, and if you keep that lieutenant, you will have trouble." So he was allowed to resign for the good of the service and was shortly rehired as a technician, where he continued his work with the landing craft.

As craft started to arrive from the U. S., an officer from the class of '22 was assigned as the force commander, with the rank of commodore, and I reverted to planning.

Q: To whom did you report on the planning for Normandy? For example, there would be obviously a number of naval requirements for U.S. forces to be involved. Who was to make sure that those were provided?

Admiral Strauss: It was between Stark and Kirk. I'd known Admiral Kirk since he was a lieutenant commander. As a matter of fact, his mother-in-law had introduced my mother and father to one another. His father-in-law was Captain Frederick L. Chapin, who died on the active list of the Navy. And Kirk told me that his appointment as the naval commander for the U.S. section of the invasion was made rather against Admiral King's wishes. There was enough political power behind it so that he got the job--I believe Dean Acheson was his backer--but he was in the position that if his foot slipped at all, he might well be taken out of it.* He walked much more tenderly than he would have if it had been a clear-cut appointment.

He was kept a rear admiral the whole time, as I remember, and his opposite number, Philip Vian, was a vice admiral. When I left Mountbatten's staff, I was assigned to Admiral Kirk's staff, but really had no function because I was almost immediately transferred to Admiral Sir Bertram Ramsay's staff. I was the plans officer under Thackrey, who was the chief of our little group. Thackrey's staff consisted of Lieutenant Colonel Robert Bare, USMC, a communicator, Caruthers, he was a commander. I'm trying to remember--a lieutenant commander named Finn, and that was it.** We had people attached from time to time--outsiders who came and went, but we did the naval planning.

Of course, the actual operational planning was done by the force commander, that is, Kirk. And we just did the part that depended on the Allied Naval Commander in Chief himself. One time, for instance, the lines of demarcation between the beaches were laid out east and west. And Admiral Kirk sent for me and said that the U.S. Navy planners would like to have the lines made normal to the beach, because they felt that the craft would have to cross from one sector to the other with these east and west lines. I went to see Admiral Vian and his staff, which I

---
*Dean G. Acheson was U. S. Secretary of State, 1949-53.
**Lieutenant Colonel Robert L. Bare, USMC; Commander William R. Caruthers, USN; Lieutenant Commander William S. Finn, USN.

think was still in Norfolk House, and I said, "Admiral Kirk thinks it might be better to have these lines normal to the beach," and told him why.

And he said, "You Yanks want everything." He said, "No, I won't do it. They're going to stay where they are." Well, that was the answer. Why, I don't know, but that was the sort of thing, among the many things, that we had to do.

Q: You were really planning for the invasion to take place sooner than it actually did, weren't you?

Admiral Strauss: No, no. It may have been shifted a matter of days. When they were trying to decide the best time to have it, very early, the story is that Churchill had a group around him and said, "Does anybody here know when the Norman invasion, William the Conquerer's, when that took place?"*

And some idiot said, "1066." But the answer was that it was in September. But early on they decided to do it within very close limits of factors such as moonlight and tides. Of course, the big decisions were things like the artificial harbors, how to construct them, how to take them over, doing away with the beach obstacles and then the

---
*Winston S. Churchill was Great Britain's Prime Minister, 1940-45.

logistics afterwards. For instance, they had laid an oil pipeline between the coast of England and the beaches, a small pipeline to start out with.

As everyone knows, the date of the actual invasion was touch and go on account of the weather, and General Eisenhower had a lot of courage when he decided to go ahead with it. After the first landings, of course, we were very anxious for news in the headquarters at Southwick Park. The first reports that came back were encouraging, because our Utah Beach went very smoothly. There were very few casualties, and the three British beaches went very well. The real fighting was on Omaha Beach. And some of the British members of Ramsay's staff more or less asked, "What's holding you Yanks up? Why can't you go? Everybody else has gone inland." The answer was that the whole fighting was taking place on Omaha Beach.

On D+2, I went over to Omaha and Utah, where the troops had pretty much moved inland, and the only threat was from dropped mines.* They would hold up all movement of sea traffic from time to time until they found out where the mines were and what could be done about them. And there were some German aircraft coming along the beaches, and there was antiaircraft fire trying to stop them. But, otherwise, it was pretty quiet. During the time we lay off

---

*D+2 was 8 June 1944, two days after the D-Day invasion on the sixth.

the beach, Eugene Carusi, one of the beachmasters, received .30-caliber bullet through the top of one lung.* Gene was a friend from Washington. He was a Naval Academy graduate, had resigned, but came back as a reserve for the war.

We came over in a small Coast Guard cutter, the <u>Long Island</u>, which ferried people back and forth. Cross-channel communications had by then been established, and there was a naval officer who was going to go over in one of the cross-channel steamers. A transport officer said, "Would you mind if a Marine Captain So-and-so shared your cabin?" And the naval officer said, "I make it an invariable rule never to share a cabin with a stranger of my own sex. No, I want to go alone."

Q: What were your observations when you got over to Normandy?

Admiral Strauss: Well, I think it was General Foch said that a battle is won with remnants, and one of the things I did was to go on board an abandoned British cruiser that had an American naval officer on board, who had some logistics job, and there was no electricity.** The lights in the cruiser were all oil lights. It was cold, and he

---
*Commander Eugene C. Carusi, USNR.
**Marshal Ferdinand Foch was supreme allied commander in France during World War I.

was doing the best he could there. I don't say that was typical of the whole operation, but you realize how it isn't like the pictures of soldiers marching in a straight line right through the enemy; it's pretty much hit and miss. Of course, as I say, the actual invasion had gone inland by that time. There was only the logistic elements and the security elements on the beaches.

Q: Did you get ashore?

Admiral Strauss: Oh, yes. My observations of both beaches were done from the shore. I was impressed. On Utah Beach they had miniature tanks loaded with explosives. When I say miniature I mean two or three feet long. They were supposed to be controlled by wires from inland and launched against landing craft. Most of them were still in their holes in the wall. They never got them out.

Q: Yes, I've seen a picture of one of those in Admiral Morison's history.* It's striking how small they were.

Admiral Strauss: Yes.

Q: Did the situation seem pretty well under control ashore--supplies flowing and so forth?

---

*See Samuel Eliot Morison, The Invasion of France and Germany, 1944-1945 (Boston: Little, Brown and Company, 1957).

Admiral Strauss: Yes. It was later--I think it was D+12, that the big storm came along and destroyed a number of the artificial harbors and also the causeways, which had been erected so that the landing craft could discharge some distance out from the shore. And that was quite a setback, as everybody knows. It wasn't fatal, but it held them up for a while in getting steadily the amount of provisions ashore that they had planned.

Q: Had you had any contact with Admiral Deyo, who commanded the bombardment force?*

Admiral Strauss: Yes. I knew Admiral Deyo very well. Actually, at that time, I don't think I saw him. I went on board Admiral Kirk's flagship.

Q: That was the Augusta.

Admiral Strauss: No, it was a communications ship.

Q: I see.

Admiral Strauss: It was a communications ship; I'm trying to remember the name of it. And I saw Admiral Moon, who

---
*Rear Admiral Morton L. Deyo, USN.

Strauss #3 - 239

afterwards committed suicide, and nobody quite knows why.* But that understandably upset Admiral Kirk very much. And then, of course, Admiral Hall was the other commander afloat.** I remember Admiral Moon as a rather taciturn officer; I only saw him a few times and those briefly.

Q: Had your planning included the bombardment forces that were under Deyo?

Admiral Strauss: That was more Kirk than it would be us. Ramsay had to put his stamp on it, but whatever the Americans wanted within reason, that was their job. And it's the same way that Vian did the British half of it.

Q: I've gotten the impression that Admiral Moon was a real worrier, and that he just seemed to be overwhelmed by his concerns.

Admiral Strauss: I think that's all anybody could get out of it. I don't think I saw Admiral Deyo at that time. I knew Admiral Deyo very well. I'd known him when I was in Newport at the War College. He and his wife were good

---
*Rear Admiral Don P. Moon, USN, was Commander Task Force 125, the assault force for Utah Beach. He shot himself on 5 August 1944, on the eve of the invasion of southern France.
**Rear Admiral John L. Hall, USN, Commander Task Force 124, the assualt force for Omaha Beach.

Strauss #3 - 240

friends, and I saw him after the war. But at that particular time I don't think I came in contact with him.

Q: What are your recollections of him from the other periods? What sort of man was Deyo?

Admiral Strauss: He was what the French call <u>grand seigneur</u>, a great gentleman. And I remember Admiral Kelly Turner once said that, "You know, someone who has a pleasant personality, I always suspect him."* And he said, "It took me some time to realize that Admiral Deyo was as good, if not a better, commander than Admiral Wilkinson."** Because Deyo was so smooth and gentlemanly that Admiral Turner didn't go for him at all.

Q: Wilkinson was very highly regarded also.

Admiral Strauss: Oh, yes. Oh, yes. He was an outstanding officer. I'm getting ahead of myself, but, after the war I was assigned to something called the Joint Postwar Committee that was supposed to decide the best of way of winding down from the war. Admiral Wilkinson was a member. We were having a meeting one afternoon, and Admiral

---
*Admiral Richmond Kelly Turner, USN, on whose staff Strauss served following World War II.
**Vice Admiral Theodore S. Wilkinson, USN, was Commander Third Amphibious Force, Pacific Fleet, during World War II.

Wilkinson said, "I've got to get out of here. I've got to catch the afternoon boat to Norfolk." And so he left the meeting.

The next morning when I went to the office someone said, "Did you hear? Admiral Wilkinson was killed."

And I said, "Oh, that's ridiculous. I saw him at 3:00 o'clock yesterday afternoon." But, of course, that's exactly what happened. He was drowned leaving the Norfolk boat, in his car, which fell between the boat and the slip.* He managed to push Mrs. Wilkinson clear. (Vide Teddy Kennedy.)**

Q: It can happen that quickly.

Admiral Strauss: Yes.

Q: Are there any other thoughts to wrap up the experience in Europe before you got assigned to command the Charles Carroll?

Admiral Strauss: Well, of course, Admiral Ramsay and his staff stayed in Southwick Park following the invasion, because they had some responsibility for the flow of

---
*Admiral Wilkinson died 21 February 1946.
**In 1969 Senator Edward M. Kennedy (Democrat--Massachusetts) drove off a bridge at Chappaquiddick, Massachusetts. He managed to escape from the car, but the woman with him drowned.

supplies and follow-up men over to the beaches. But gradually this started to phase out. That is, members of the staff started leaving. After I left, Admiral Ramsay and Rowell, his planning officer, were flying from someplace in France to Belgium, and the plane came down, and they were both killed.* A number of senior officers were lost in the war by airplane accidents. The number was very high, indeed.

I don't know whether I mentioned that Commander Rowell was very clever, an outstanding officer. At these planning meetings, I once asked him, "Does it worry you as a commander that your Army number is Lieutenant Colonel, Acting Major General, temporary Lieutenant General, and your Air Force opposite number is a Wing Commander or Group Captain So-and-so, Acting Air Marshal, Acting Air Vice Marshal, Temporary Air Marshal?"

And he said, "Not at all." He said, "I've been in the service as long as they have. I've had as much responsibility." And he said, "Furthermore, I speak for the Allied Naval Commander in Chief." And I thought how sensible that was, that this business of ratcheting up rank so that your man has got more power than the next man is so foolish.

The reason the Royal Navy did that came out of World

---

*Admiral Bertram H. Ramsay, RN, was killed on 2 January 1945 in a plane crash, along with Commander G. W. Rowell, RN.

War I, when they had a great many temporary promotions. When the end of the war came, they had to axe many of these people. They weren't going to go through that again, because it ruined the Navy for a while. The Royal Navy had to do it so quickly that it couldn't be done according to who was the best officer. They'd say, "Lieutenant Commander Jones--oh, he's got a rich wife. Let him go. Lieutenant Commander Smith can--well, he's in China. We'd have to bring him back. Let's keep him." And so it was done that way, and so they weren't going to go through that again.

The line in the logistic flow to Normandy was known as the red ball. Things that had to get there suddenly, quickly, that were required in sort of an emergency. There was a provision for getting those over by a very special means of transport.

Q: Did you have any contact with Douglas Fairbanks while you were over there?*

Admiral Strauss: I certainly did. Because his father and stepmother, Mary Pickford, had received the Mountbattens on their honeymoon out there in Hollywood, his relationship

---
*Lieutenant Douglas E. Fairbanks, Jr., USNR, was a noted movie actor of the era, as well as being the son of a famous actor.

Strauss #3 - 244

with the family went back for a long time.* And he wanted to come to Britain and was ordered there to Mountbatten's staff. Because I, as a commander, was the senior American officer, he was ordered to report to me. But don't get any idea that I was his boss, because he once said, "You know, every time I go anyplace I have to get a set of orders." He said, "I'd like to have a set of orders that allows me to go wherever I'm needed."

And I said, "I've been trying for that for 25 years, and I never made it. So I don't think that you can go do that." Well, he did go down to the Mediterranean with Captain Charles L. Andrews and worked on this deception.** They used records that would play the sounds of ships coming to anchor or troops landing, and so forth, to deceive. He did work on that.

One day, a WRN officer came into my office and said, "Commander Strauss, we WRNS are having a little party on Thursday, and we'd like very much for you to come."

And I said, "Oh, thank you very much. I'd be delighted to come."

And she said, "By the way, don't you know Lieutenant Fairbanks?"

And I said, "Yes."

And she said, "Could you invite him?" Well, we both

---
*Mary Pickford was a famous actress from the era of silent films.
**Captain Charles L. Andrews, Jr., USN.

Strauss #3 - 245

went, but I realized that they weren't inviting me for my blue eyes.

Q: Was he a capable Naval Reserve officer?

Admiral Strauss: I don't really know anything about his performance. He was an actor. He, of course, got quite a number of medals and so forth, which you can manage to do, I think, if you're an actor. I saw quite a lot of him after the war, because he lived temporarily in a house next door to my family's house on Massachusetts Avenue, and we used to walk down to work together. And not so long ago, he had lunch with us here. He was in a play, and I got hold of him; he came out to luncheon.

Q: You haven't really discussed Ramsay. How much contact did you have with him?

Admiral Strauss: Oh, a good deal, because staffs, even staffs for something like the invasion of Normandy, were not as large as they are now. I don't know how they did it, but the admirals in that era had comparatively small, compact staffs. And they didn't have much rank on them. Ramsay's chief of staff was Captain Creasy, later an admiral of the fleet.* The answer is I saw him a great deal and had the utmost respect for him. He was thoughtful, and I think his decisions were wise ones. He wasn't bonhomous particularly. He was polite and friendly, but not one of the boys at all. You know how he got the job.

Q: No, I don't.

Admiral Strauss: Well, he was chief of staff to the commander in chief of the Mediterranean Fleet, Admiral Backhouse, and apparently Admiral Backhouse was not only his own commander in chief, he was his own chief of staff.** And Ramsay once said to him, "It's no good my being your chief of staff; you never use me." And Backhouse apparently got very cross with him. I don't know whether he fired him from that or not. But, anyway, Ramsay retired from the Navy and was one of the few officers, like Admiral Somerville, who was brought back from the retired list, and he was put as the commander of Dover.***

Dover was shelled from the French coast, but Ramsay's

---
*Captain George E. Creasy, RN. On 14 August 1951, Admiral Sir George Creasy was appointed Commander in Chief of the Home Fleet.
**Admiral Sir Roger Backhouse, RN.
***Vice Admiral Sir James Somerville, RN, was retired in 1939 because of tuberculosis. After recovering, he assisted Ramsay during the evacuation of Dunkirk in 1940, moved to other assignments, and was formally restored to the active list in 1944.

handling of Dover was so exemplary that when the time came they gave him this job. And if he had not been killed, he would have been either a viscount or an earl, which the other senior commanders all were. They were all given peerages.

Q: I gather that you had very high regard for him as a naval commander.

Admiral Strauss: Oh, I did, yes. I did.

Q: How were you treated on these staffs? You'd been over there so long, were you not regarded as an outsider anymore?

Admiral Strauss: Well, one of the things that I think I may have mentioned, on Mountbatten's staff I really expected to be sort of a liaison officer, and it wasn't that way at all. I became an integral part, so that if CCO needed the planning on a raid he would say, "You and you do it," and it might be one British and an American.* We were completely integrated there. Of course, on Ramsay's staff we were a little staff within a staff, but we were used as a regular part.

---
*CCO--Chief of Combined Operations.

Q: Well, if it was not liaison, though, didn't the British lose some of the advantage of having an American in that spot?

Admiral Strauss: No, because you give your American point of view. You say, "This is the way we would do it." For instance, the British did most things by meetings, whereas we do most things by the commander getting the staff opinions and then making the decision. I don't know whether I've expressed that well, but they depend more on meetings, and we depend more on staff representations, leading to decisions. Mind you, the British decision will be made at the top, but it's more integrated down below.

Q: Did they have operation orders similar to the American style in the British staffs?

Admiral Strauss: Yes. One of the things that impressed me was the power and the influence of a secretary, with the British as compared to us. With us a secretary was usually the man who put around the tablets and the paper clips. With them, the secretary had a great influence on shaping a paper, which, after all, represented the result of the meeting.

Therefore, their secretaries were usually higher in rank than ours. A brigadier might well be the secretary for an important meeting. I once got into some degree of trouble by remarking that if I were going over a pile of papers, mixed American and British, if I could read one of them without making my lips move, the chances were that it was written by a Britisher. On the whole, they seemed to be more literate.

On this subject, attached to Thackrey's group we almost constantly had reserve officer talent: lawyers, real estate men, businessmen, what have you. Red Thackrey said to me one time, "Why, when we have to have a report or a dispatch written, is it always one of us stupid naval officers who ends up doing it? Why can't these high-priced 'tycoons' write them?"

Q: Any other comparisons you would draw between the different staff systems?

Admiral Strauss: I think that British meetings were more important, and there were more of them. On the American side, if it was a communication matter, our commanders would get the communication officer and maybe someone who was tied into it. They would get their opinion, and then go ahead from there, rather than having the whole group sit in and get in on it.

Q: The Atlantic was not as important a focus for the U.S.

Navy as the Pacific was. How much were you able to keep up with the Pacific campaign from England?

Admiral Strauss: Very little. Very little. Oh, I mean, for instance, a British captain gave a dinner for us. This was while we were still in London. It was a victory dinner for Midway.* We learned of the main operations and the general progress, but as for following them--no.

Q: Just the highlights.

Admiral Strauss: Yes.

Q: You'd been away from a seagoing job since before the war. Were you anxious to get back to sea?

Admiral Strauss: Very anxious to get back to sea. Of course, I hadn't been away all that time, because, you see, I was flag lieutenant to Admiral Johnson, and then I had the destroyer.** Then I was navigator of the Nashville. You see, I left the Nashville to go to London to be an observer with the British Fleet just a couple weeks before Pearl Harbor. So, I hadn't been away all that time.
_____
*In early June 1942, at the Battle of Midway, a force built around three U. S. aircraft carriers, sank all four Japanese aircraft carriers committed to the battle.
**In the late 1930s, Strauss served on the staff of Rear Admiral Alfred W. Johnson, USN, Commander Atlantic Squadron, U.S. Fleet.

Q: Well, it was really about three years, though, away from a U.S. Navy ship.

Admiral Strauss: Yes, yes. That's true, and I felt very strongly about that. As a matter of fact, I told Thackrey that I wanted to get out there and get back to sea, and he said, "Don't worry. You've got to stay here until after the invasion." And so as soon as the invasion of Normandy was over, I got ordered back, and I was assigned to take over the Charles Carroll.

The commanding officer that had had the Charles Carroll previous to my taking over as commander was Harold Biesemeier.* I took over from an interim commander that had it a short time, but Biesemeier was a character in the Navy. He told me once that he would never be a captain. He said, "I have it on the highest authority. Admiral King said to me, 'Biesemeier, you'll never be a captain.'" Finally, of course, he was a captain and retired as a rear admiral.

After the war, I ran into Biesemeier and mentioned to him that I had had to get rid of his exec who was a "queer." Biesemeier said, "I thought something was wrong with him, but we were in the middle of a war and I was too busy to bother with it."

---
*Captain Harold Biesemeier, USN.

When I got the orders to the ship, I had a time finding out where she was. I flew to England and found out that she was in Naples. So I flew to Naples and took over command there just as the invasion of the south of France was ending. The ship was filled up with North African goums, black Moroccan troops with a French lieutenant colonel in command of them. I was to take them to Algiers, which I did. I took them to Oran. And on the way over the paymaster came in and said, "I was lucky." He said, "In Naples I got a whole load of fresh pork for dinner today."

And the French lieutenant colonel who was messing with me said, "My men won't eat it. They're Mohammedans, you see." So he had to get to work and dish up something else. I don't know what they did, but anyway he was able to feed them.

Q: What kind of shape, material condition, was the ship in?

Admiral Strauss: It was very good, yes. She had been the _Del Uruguay_ of the Delta line before she was taken over by the Navy, and had been through the landings in North Africa, and then the landings in the south of France.

Q: So she was an attack transport, not just a point-to-point transport.

Admiral Strauss: You're right. I think it had something like 20 boats, you know.

Q: What kind of officer talent and enlisted crew did you have compared with some of the combatants you'd been in before?

Admiral Strauss: I had one Naval Academy officer, and he was on board because he got seasick in small ships. My exec was a regular merchant marine officer. I'll tell you more about him later on. Well, after discharging the troops in Oran, we went to Norfolk. My engineer was a reserve officer, and he said, "You're going out to the Pacific. All my friends are here on the East Coast, and I sort of live here. I'd like to get a job on the East Coast."

And I said, "Well, unfortunately, you're chief engineer of this ship, and you'll be going out to the Pacific." There was some school coming up, and he asked to be transferred to that school.

So I called up the Bureau of Naval Personnel, and I said, "I have an engineer on here that doesn't seem to like the job, and doesn't want to go out to the Pacific, and I'd like to get someone who does."

So they said, "All right, we'll fix you up when you

get out to the West Coast." We went through the canal and went around to San Francisco. We arrived in San Francisco just before New Year's Eve, 1944, and I got orders to transfer the engineer, and the new engineer came on board. He'd been captain of a PT boat, and he was somebody quite different.

I told the departing engineer, "I'm very sorry I can't give you a satisfactory fitness report on account of your attitude." The people down in the wardroom told me that he'd said, "You people are going to the Pacific. You'll all be dead and I'll be still all right." Well, they transferred him to one of the islands, Ulithi, or something like that. And Commodore Acuff saw me after the war, and he said, "Did that chap come off your ship?"*

And I said, "Yes."

He said, "Damn you." He said, "We had a hell of a time with him."

Q: Did you get a good engineer out of the deal?

Admiral Strauss: Yes, I got a very good engineer. On New Year's Day, 1945, I went to sleep about 10:00 o'clock at night. Two of the officers knocked on the door, came in my room, and said, "We don't think we should go out to the Western Pacific with an exec that makes passes at the

---
*Captain Jasper T. Acuff, USN, Commander At Sea Logistics Group Third Fleet.

sailors." This man was a very good seaman and rather tough, you see.

And I said, "I know he's tough. If you're doing this because he's tough, I'm going to saw you off at the ankles. But I want to know the truth of it." Well, they convinced me. So next day I went over to the 12th Naval District, where I saw a very nice man, a commodore named Davenport Browne, and I said, "We're going to sea day after tomorrow, and I've got to get a new exec. What shall I do with this man?"*

He said, "Transfer him to the sick list, and get him ashore. We'll take care of him." He said, "I'll get you an exec." Well, that afternoon this 50-year-old banker, who'd been hauled out of some cocktail party in Seattle, reported on board as the exec. His name was Jim Thwing.** Jim Thwing is now 92 years old, and I've kept up with him. We stayed in Seattle, and he took us around a couple of years ago. But he was assistant vice president of a bank up in Seattle, and was quite a long-time reserve officer. So I got the queer exec off the ship. The next day we sailed for the New Hebrides, Espiritu Santo.

Q: Did you have a load of troops on board?

---
*Commodore Davenport Browne, USN, Commandant of the 12th Naval District.
**Commander James G. Thwing, USNR.

Admiral Strauss: No. No, we had nobody on board at that time.

The commander at Espiritu Santo was a man I'd known in Newport, and he had become a commodore. There were three kinds of commodores in the war. There were bright, young commodores, like Arleigh Burke, who was promoted ahead of time.* There were consolation-prize commodores that had done very well, but weren't going anyplace. And then there were commodores that were made in order to have enough rank on the job so that they were senior to captains. Well, this officer, I think, was a consolation prize commodore. He was a very, very nice chap.

So then we went to Ulithi and then to the Russell Islands. And I remember there I was told to anchor in a depth of water that was just a little bit less than the length of the anchor chain. And I demurred, and the local people said, "All the anchorages are that depth, and that's it." So I did. Well, there was never a breath of wind, so that a ship could stay there. We didn't do very much. We were sort of waiting. We went to the Solomon Islands, just were sent down there to have a look around. There was nothing. The occupation was pretty much over. Then we went to Manus, and we didn't have any troops on board during any of this time.

---
*Commodore Arleigh A. Burke, USN, was chief of staff to Vice Admiral Marc A. Mitscher, USN, Commander Task Force 58.

Q: It sounds as if they were hard put to find something for you to do.

Admiral Strauss: Well, they were waiting for a push, you see; that was it. Then we got orders for Okinawa. And we loaded up with the headquarters company and some more of the 5th Marine Regiment. And just before sailing, Ernie Pyle came on board.*

Q: Where did you embark them?

Admiral Strauss: In the Russell Islands. And I remember the night before we left, the station had a party for the commanding officers of all the ships in the anchorage there. There was a small hospital, so the feminine contingent were the nurses from the hospital. They had quite a big dinner there with the commanding officers of ships and the nurses. After the dessert came, a truck backed up to the dining hall. An American chief petty officer got out, and about eight or ten woolly-looking Melanesians with musical instruments came out. And this chief petty officer sat them around in a circle, and they started playing "She'll Be Coming 'Round The Mountain When

---

*Ernest T. Pyle was a popular war correspondent for the Scripps-Howard newspaper chain. He specialized in reporting the personal side of the war.

She Comes." I said, "I have now seen everything." These Melanesians playing "She'll Be Coming 'Round The Mountain When She Comes." Well, that was the entertainment for the dinner.

Q: Was it a reasonable approximation?

Admiral Strauss: Yes, oh yes. He trained them pretty well. So the next day we started up for Okinawa.

Q: Where was Pyle? Did he have good quarters?

Admiral Strauss: Yes, he had one of the officers' quarters. I remember I asked him to dinner, and he said he couldn't come because he'd just accepted the chief petty officers' invitation to dinner.

Q: Well, that was his specialty.

Admiral Strauss: Oh, yes. He was the enlisted man's man, and he was very pleasant. He signed that picture you see on the wall. He went ashore at Okinawa and came back and wrote on the photo, "My gratitude for a happy voyage, upon a happy ship, with such a happy ending." Then the next day he went ashore and went over to Ie Shima, and that's where he was killed.*

Q: So he left from your ship to his fatal encounter.

Admiral Strauss: Yes.

Q: But he struck you as a good shipmate while he was on board.

Admiral Strauss: Yes, oh yes. And he was a heavy drinker, but, I mean, not, obviously, to me.

Q: He did so on board ship?

Admiral Strauss: If he did, I don't know about it.

Q: Was there rehearsal before you got to the invasion?

Admiral Strauss: Not really, no. We had to do things on the way out. We streamed paravanes for the first time, and luckily ours streamed all right.

Q: Had you had much chance to practice your craft as an amphibious skipper?

---

*On 18 April 1945 Pyle was killed by Japanese sniper fire on the small island of Ie Shima, near Okinawa.

Admiral Strauss: We'd done a number of things. For instance, we substituted DUKWs for some of the landing craft, and we had hoisted out the boats and the clamber nets and so forth.* We'd done all of that, but as far as any landings, no. There weren't any, because up to that point we didn't have many troops on board. We had transported Marines from one place to another. We went over to Guadalcanal and picked up a group, and I've forgotten where we took them. But I was impressed by how much better the Marines were as troops on board than the Army was. They were much more precise, and they didn't have the gambling troubles and so forth.

Q: Did you have a good group of boat officers to run the assault waves?

Admiral Strauss: Yes, yes. We had embarked our landing party, which was specially trained for that. I've got the roster and all the jobs and all up there in my files. We had three doctors and a dentist, and we were supposed to be a relief hospital ship if there were heavy casualties. And one doctor, a junior lieutenant, was assigned to remain on board during the Okinawa landing. And then we had a lieutenant surgeon, who was the doctor for the landing party. The latter came to me a couple of days before the

---

*The DUKW was a U.S. Army amphibious truck.

landing. He said, "You know, I'm a surgeon, and to have me ashore on the landing party would be a waste." He said, "I should be on board where I can do operations. And this junior officer could well be the landing party doctor."

Well, it sounded sensible to me, so I put this up to the division doctor. And he said, "Yes, I think that's the right thing to do." So I shifted them. Well, the young jaygee was very unhappy, but I told him that this was the best use of our talent. Damned if he wasn't killed by a sniper on the island. I felt very bad about that, because that was our main casualty. When they did land, he was with the landing party, and was killed. So I had to write to his wife and so forth. It was a difficult letter to write.

Q: I'm sure. How did Jim Thwing work out as the exec?

Admiral Strauss: Well, he was an awfully nice guy. I can see where he never got past being assistant vice president, because he wasn't a great brain at all. I used to get very cross at him from time to time. But he was always gung ho. I mean, he did everything that you asked him to do with a will. So, I think, on the whole, I was lucky, because this was a really a bunch of trained seals. But there was one reserve officer I remember who was a music major, and this didn't commend him to me as a naval officer. But when that man was on watch, I could sleep very contentedly. He was a very fine officer.

Q: Did you have some others with whom you didn't sleep so well when they were on watch?

Admiral Strauss: Oh, yes, several of those. They were a good group. The senior doctor came from New Orleans. He had been a friend of Dr. Weiss, who is the man who killed Huey Long.* He used to tell me about Dr. Weiss and describe the scene of the shooting.

At Okinawa we sent our troops ashore on D-Day.** We had a load of napalm on board. And I told the crew, "The sooner you get this napalm out of here, the sooner we can leave." We were there, I think, three days. And then with four of the other transports we were sent back to Hawaii. I saw one kamikaze shot down. I've often thought the Japanese were foolish not to go after the transports, rather than after the destroyer screen, because if they had actually sunk a couple of transports it would have interfered with the invasion force much more than sinking,

---
*Huey P. Long, demagogic governor of Louisiana, 1928-31, and Democratic senator from 1931 until his assassination on 8 September 1935 by Dr. Carl Austin Weiss, who was slain by Long's bodyguards.
**The USS Charles Carroll (APA-28) landed elements of the 1st Marines at Okinawa on 1 April 1945, remaining on station for four days.

say, or damaging a screen destroyer.

Q: How close to the beach did you get?

Admiral Strauss: Well, when we first landed, we were quite well out. I suppose I would say three or four miles, but after the troops got ashore, then we moved in quite close so that we could get things back and forth.

Q: To shorten the boat run.

Admiral Strauss: Yes.

Q: Did you feel any sense of peril on board the ship?

Admiral Strauss: Well, you never knew what was going to happen. You didn't know what the air cover was, or what would be the object of any Japanese attacks, either from Okinawa or from the mainland, or what naval forces were around. So that I was glad to get out of there.

Q: What was the purpose in going to Hawaii at that point?

Admiral Strauss: Well, that was really for recreation. And on the way back they asked us all what our best speed was, and mine was 14 1/2 knots, which I reported. And the

<u>Jefferson</u> was 14 1/2 knots. And then some of the others said that they could do 15, and so that we were on our own. We weren't in any formation. And gradually the <u>Jefferson</u> and I sailed past 15-knotters. Then we passed the 15 1/2-knotters. We were honest, but they thought they'd get some advantage by saying they were faster.

By that time I had a division commander on board. He was put on board just after the invasion, Duke O'Leary.* He had been explosives officer at the Torpedo Station. I relieved him. He was a submariner, but had not been used in the submarines. He had a transport flagship, and his flagship was sunk, so they put him on board the <u>Carroll</u> without any job. He just was a passenger. But it was pleasant having him on board, and when we got to Hawaii he said, "Let's go ashore and have a swim."

So we went to the Moana Hotel, which was a leave and recreation hotel, and we went to Waikiki Beach, which I hadn't been to since well before the war. The first time I went there was as a midshipman in 1921. And so we went swimming, and the first thing I knew a half grapefruit hit me in the face, and when I got out one foot was all covered with fuel oil. And so I wasn't as happy about the romantic Waikiki Beach as I'd been before.

Then we went from there back to San Francisco, and arrived just when the meeting for the U.N. was going on.**

---
*Captain Forrest M. O'Leary, USN.
**U.N.--United Nations.

We went ashore and went to the Fairmont Hotel, and thought we'd like to swim. But we were told that this place was reserved for the U.N. delegation, and that there was no place for heroes from Okinawa. While we were there, Claiborne Pell, who was a member of the delegation and whom I'd known as a child and knew his family very well--I saw him and invited him out to the ship for dinner. And he told me that Charles Carroll was one of his ancestors. So it was suitable that he'd come on board the ship.

Q: Carroll was one of the signers of the Declaration of Independence.

Admiral Strauss: Yes, that's right. Yes. And I think Claiborne was a direct descendant in some way.

Q: He was later a U.S. Senator, wasn't he?

Admiral Strauss: He's still a Senator.* As a matter of fact, he's probably going to be chairman of the Foreign Relations Committee. And I loved Claiborne dearly, and he's a gent first class, but I don't look forward to seeing him as chairman of the Foreign Relations Committee.

---

*Herbert Claiborne Pell, Jr., was a Coast Guard Reserve officer during World War II. In 1945 he was on loan to the State Department for the conference in San Francisco. He has been a U.S. Senator from Rhode Island since 1971.

Strauss #3 - 266

Q: What happened next with the Charles Carroll?

Admiral Strauss: They wanted me to take something like 30 or 40 officers to sea with me, because then they could claim that such a proportion of all officers had been to sea. I said no, that we've got just the right amount of room and to overcrowd ship, and, perhaps, have them mess at two sittings would be undesirable. I said, "I won't do it, just as a statistical gesture." So we went back to Manus. And I remember one time I had a decision that by zigzagging we wouldn't make Manus harbor by night, and by not zigzagging we would get in behind the booms. And once you're in they put the booms out and you were safe, you see.

Q: Were you escorted?

Admiral Strauss: No. So I said, "The hell with zigzagging; I want to get the ship in." Otherwise, you're out at night and zigzagging or not, you are still vulnerable. Well, it was a time that the Indianapolis was sunk.* And, of course, Captain McVay got hell for not zigzagging, though after the war the CO of the Japanese submarine stated that he was so close that zigzagging

---

*The heavy cruiser Indianapolis (CA-35) was torpedoed and sunk 29 July 1945 by the Japanese submarine I-58 while en route from Guam to the Philippines.

wouldn't have bothered him at all.*

Q: Sometimes it's as good to be lucky.

Admiral Strauss: Yes. But it's true. We got in and the ship was safe, and we could open up all the watertight doors and everything.

Q: Was it intended that your ship would be used in the invasion of Japan?

Admiral Strauss: I think yes. And I was surprised. You see, the atom bomb had gone while we were at sea and Roosevelt had died while we were at sea.** But then I was ordered to come back to the United States on leave, and go back to be chief of staff of Admiral George Murray, who was, I think, commander of the Gilberts and Carolines.***

After being relieved of command, I flew from Johnston Island back to Honolulu, and then from Honolulu to Washington. And flying over Olathe, Kansas, we got the word that the Japanese surrendered. The plane that took us from Hawaii was a Navy plane. It had WAVES on board, and I

---
*Captain Charles B. McVay III, USN, was commanding officer of the USS Indianapolis (CA-35) at the time of her sinking; CO--comanding officer.
**President Franklin D. Roosevelt died 12 April 1945. U.S. atomic bombs hit Hiroshima on 6 August and Nagasaki on 9 August.
***Vice Admiral George D. Murray, USN.

hadn't seen a WAVE up to that time.* I'd seen a lot of WRNS, but no WAVES.

So then we landed in Washington. I went on leave, and went in to see the detail officer. And he said, "You've either been at sea or away from the United States for ten years and the war is over. I don't see any use of you going back to the Pacific." So they assigned me to this joint postwar committee first. And Harold Train was the boss.**

Q: What was the object of this committee?

Admiral Strauss: It was to try to find the best way to wind down the war: what committees could be done away with, any restructuring of the armed forces. I was only there a short time. Russell Willson came along.*** He took over the United Nations planning. His group was relieved when the "alternate Joint Chiefs of Staff" were established. These were General Ridgway for the Army, Admiral Kelly Turner for the Navy, and General Kenney for the Army Air Forces.**** These officers were actually the deputies for the real chiefs of staff of the services. Russell Willson advised Kelly Turner to take me on, which

---
*WAVES--Women Accepted for Volunteer Emergency Service.
**Rear Admiral Harold C. Train, USN.
***Rear Admiral Russell Willson, USN.
****Lieutenant General Matthew B. Ridgway, USA; General George C. Kenney, USA.

he did. He did not know me, and I had never served with him. Before taking the job, I spoke with Admiral Art Davis, whom I knew quite well.* Davis said, "I wouldn't take this job."

And I said, "Why not?"

Davis said, "Well, he's cranky now, and he's a dipso." The job sounded so interesting to me that I foolishly disregarded Davis's wise counsel and took the job. Art Davis was regarded by everyone as a coming man. He was in the upper councils. For some reason he was never commander of a fleet or the CNO.

I was acting chief of staff to Turner at the outset, while he was awaiting a flag chief of staff.

Q: Well, this would really be the precursor to the United Nations permanent organization, wouldn't it?

Admiral Strauss: Yes. Our first assignment was to go to London, where the first General Assembly was scheduled to take place to "create" the United Nations. It took place in January 1946. General Ridgway's chief of staff was Major General John Deane, who had been the logistics man in Moscow for aid to the Russians, and Kenney's chief of staff was Brigadier General Pearre Cabell.** I was only a

---
*Rear Admiral Arthur C. Davis, USN.
**Brigadier General John R. Deane, USA. Brigadier General Charles Pearre Cabell, USA.

captain.

We embarked for the voyage to England in the <u>Queen Elizabeth</u>, which had just been decommissioned as a transport. The staterooms still had extra bunks, which had been used by the transport.

Well, the delegation that went over was very fashionable, indeed. We had Mrs. Roosevelt.* We had Senator Vandenburg.** We had Leo Pasvolsky, who was one of the assistant secretaries of state.*** We had Joseph E. Johnson, who was afterwards head of the Carnegie Foundation for Peace; James Reston; and last, but not least, Alger Hiss.****

Shortly before we were to start out, one of the justices of the Supreme Court, I think it was McReynolds, called me and said that Mrs. Roosevelt had a particular kind of seasick remedy which she found very efficacious.*****

---

*Eleanor Roosevelt, widow of President Franklin D. Roosevelt.
**Senator Arthur H. Vandenberg (Republican-Michigan).
***Leo Pasvolsky, Russian emigrant, author, and noted economist.
****Joseph Johnson, longtime trustee for the World Peace Foundation; James B. Reston, noted journalist in the Washington bureau of <u>The New York Times</u>; Alger Hiss was a high-ranking State Department official who was convicted of perjury after denying charges of passing secret documents. He was sentenced to five years in prison.
*****James C. McReynolds (1862-1946) was Attorney General of the United States, 1913-14, then served as an associate justice of the Supreme Court, 1914-41. He was one of the "nine old men" President Roosevelt railed against in the late 1930s because they were stymying his New Deal legislation.

He would send it to me, if I would be kind enough to deliver it to her on board. So in due course, a messenger with goggles and gauntlets arrived, and handed me a small package. And I had always been very suspicious of Mrs. Roosevelt, and wasn't kindly inclined to her. But when we got on board I sought her out, and gave her the seasick remedy, and I was never more charmed by anybody in my life. I became a devotee of Mrs. Roosevelt from then on, because she was perfectly delightful.

Q: Why had you felt cool toward Mrs. Roosevelt before that?

Admiral Strauss: I don't know. I just think I was one of the great number of people who were anti-Roosevelt in general, and accordingly Mrs. Roosevelt. I thought she was too much of a do-gooder and so forth. While we were there, the Pilgrims had a dinner, quite a showy dinner. The Earl of Derby was the chairman, and they had speeches. And there was no question about it, Mrs. Roosevelt's speech was way the best of any of these dignitaries who spoke. She was an accomplished speaker.

But, on the way over, we were all in uniform, and as everyone knew, my boss Kelly Turner drank much too much. And it was embarrassing, because one time when we were having pre-dinner drinks, it came time to go into the mess hall, and Turner said, "Help me up." Captain Denys Knoll was the secretary.* He and I had to sort of lift Turner by the arm, then take him into dinner. And that was noticed, I'm sure, by those around us.

General Kenney was very scornful of the ship. He said, "Isn't this a ridiculous way to cross the ocean? It's taking us six days. You could fly across in one day. You could cut this ship up into bits and we could fly it abroad."

And we said, "What would you do with the propellers, General?"

He said, "Strap them under the fuselage." General Kenney, in remarking on the Nuremberg trials, said, "It makes our profession less attractive."**

When we arrived in London, they started committee work for the different aspects of the U.N. I was on something called the trusteeship committee, and General Kenney was the military member. The State Department representative was Dulles, afterwards Secretary of State.*** There were probably not more than five of us in the room, and someone, maybe Dulles, suggested, "I think that we ought to give Okinawa right away for trusteeship."

---
*Captain Denys W. Knoll, USN. Knoll, who retired as a rear admiral, has been interviewed as part of the Naval Institute's oral history program.
**In 1945-46 top German military officers and civilian officials were tried for war crimes at Nuremberg, Germany. Several were executed, and others were imprisoned.
***John Foster Dulles was Secretary of State, 1953-59.

And Kenney said, "Well, let's take it easy. We spilled a lot of blood there, and we can relinquish it later. I don't think we should be in a hurry for it." That was about the extent of the conversation.

The next day there were headlines in the London paper, "Military and civil authorities disagree about the future of Okinawa." And Secretary Byrnes sent for the participants of the trusteeship meeting, and he also sent for Admiral Turner.* Well, Admiral Turner was sick and couldn't get up, so he designated me to go. And Secretary Byrnes sat us down. He said, "Admiral, sit over here." I was a captain, but I don't think Byrnes could tell the difference. And he said, "You know, you military people are used to talking out frankly in staff meetings and so forth." He said, "In civil life you can't do it. I've found in my long experience that someone will always tell the press."

Well, I didn't like to say, "How do you get anything done, if you're afraid someone in your midst is going to tell the press?" And today I don't know who did let this out, because the conversation was just about as I recounted it. But somebody tried to make, as people so often do, political capital by leaking it to the press. Well, that, of course, eventually blew over. And, as I think everybody knows, the original idea of the U.N. was that the Security

---

*James F. Byrnes, Secretary of State, 1945-47.

Council would be the strong arm, and the Military Staff Committee would be its military cutting edge, if military action were needed. The original members were the United States, England, China; of course, that was Nationalist China, Russia, and France. And these five were the members. They were the big powers. And the whole idea was that they would control since they were the dominant powers. The General Assembly, which was made up of delegates of all the other members, could get together once or twice a year and let off steam, and that was about it.

As it turned out, the Security Council became impotent because of the vetoes, and the General Assembly took over, but all they could do was resolve. And, as someone said, "Action is action, but a resolution is a bleat." And that's about how the thing stands today. And then the Security Council was emasculated, because other countries claimed that they should join, but the first five, with the substitution of Communist China for Taiwan China, still persists. There are additional members, which in rotation, can even take the chairmanship over.

The decisions were taken at the London meeting on trusteeship and on the location of the U.N. headquarters. There was some indecision for a while whether its headquarters would be in London or New York and New York won out. It was established first at Hunter College in New York. During my incumbency there, it was in Hunter

Strauss #3 - 275

College. Rear Admiral Ballentine joined as Admiral Turner's chief as staff, and then-Captain Jim Doyle, who was senior to me, also joined this staff.*

Q: Doyle had been with Turner in the South Pacific.

Admiral Strauss: That's right. He was afterwards a vice admiral. His son is a retired vice admiral here now, is on Naval Historical Foundation with me.**

Q: Did you have any contact with Alger Hiss during the course of this?

Admiral Strauss: Yes. Alger Hiss was to my mind the most impressive person I had to deal with. You would ask when such a meeting was going to be, and people would say, "Well, I think it's at half-past 3:00, but we'll have to get the list out." You would ask Alger Hiss, and he would say, "It's at half past 3:00 and in such-and-such room of the such-and-such building." He knew the answers to everything, and was quiet, forceful without being aggressive, and to my mind a very impressive man.

Q: Were you surprised when he came to the grief he did?

---
*Rear Admiral John J. Ballentine, USN; Captain James H. Doyle, USN.
**Vice Admiral James H. Doyle, Jr., USN (Ret.)

Strauss #3 - 276

Admiral Strauss: Yes. Yes.

Q: Was your own role diminished when Ballentine and Doyle came in?

Admiral Strauss: Oh, yes, very much. Even the Marine colonel was senior to me. I wrote up the weekly meetings of the military staff committee. I did that mainly for Captain Dennison, who was on the Military Diplomatic Committee of the Chief of Naval Operations Office in Washington.* They were the receiving end for whatever went on in the United Nations.

Kelly Turner was certainly an able man. He was, I think, the only boss that I didn't seem to be able to get along with. Our duties there were minimal, because the military staff committee really had no particular activities at that time. It never got into action. The Secretary General had a personal military officer on his staff that he wanted to attend our meetings. In my low level I opposed it, because I felt that we should be able to talk back and forth and come to some decision without being kibitzed.

There was even a motion to let the press sit in, and we very strongly opposed that, because as military people

_____
*Captain Robert L. Dennison, USN. Dennison's oral history is in the Naval Institute collection.

we got along with each other very well, even the Russians. And I don't think there would be any difficulty with our colleagues, except that our elders and betters controlled us. But as military people, we were able to talk things out. And I felt that you could very well in a meeting say to your British counterpart, "Oh, we can't do that old man; you're crazy." But if the press covered it, there'd be a headline: "American Accuses British of Insanity."

Q: There would probably also be a good deal of posturing for the benefit of the press.

Admiral Strauss: Oh, it just wouldn't work at all.

Q: Was that a sort of disappointing time for you?

Admiral Strauss: Yes, it was. It was frustrating first, because it was quite evident that Turner didn't like the cut of my jib. And he overloaded his staff. He got a Marine colonel on there and a Marine major. His staff was much larger than the staff of the others.

About that time, I was ordered to put the <u>Fresno</u> into commission. I must say that I felt that it was a much better choice of jobs than the one I was in, because I'd always wanted command of a major ship.

Q: How did that opportunity come about?

Admiral Strauss: Well, I'd applied for command of a cruiser, and this cruiser was going in commission. I guess they came down to my name and from there, that was it. She was being built in Kearny, New Jersey. While I was at the U.N., I lived in the Astor Hotel in New York, but, of course, when I left the U.N. my quarters in the Astor were no longer available.

Q: Where did you find a place to live when you got the cruiser?

Admiral Strauss: John Schiff, whom I'd known in my London days, was again back in New York, and he had a three-storied apartment on Fifth Avenue. He rented the top floor to me, and I used to have breakfast very early in his apartment down below. And this worked out very satisfactorily. We were supposed to be in uniform, but I had to catch the subway from upper Fifth Avenue down to the Battery, really, where a station wagon from Kearny would pick up officers living in Manhattan and take us over to the shipyard. But most of the people in the subway at that time of the morning were char ladies and so forth, and I didn't like to be hanging on to a strap with four stripes

Strauss #3 - 279

on my arm, so I used to go and have a civilian jacket and keep a uniform coat in our office in Kearny, New Jersey.

This is an interesting period, putting a ship in commission, accumulating the crew and the officers. And, as I think I've mentioned once before, that the naval constructor who was in charge of our construction, finishing it off, was Captain Leonard Kaplan, who was a very good officer and did a very good job, and was very helpful to us in the ship during that time.*

Q: How far along was the construction when you reported?

Admiral Strauss: Her construction was just about completed. Certain things still had to go on, for instance, radars and so forth. I reported to her in October 1946, and she was commissioned November 27.

Q: Did you have a good exec?

Admiral Strauss: Yes. My exec was John Roenigk.** He was a very able officer and unflappable. He was very chagrined that he'd never heard a gun go off in anger, and the reason was that he was a Japanese language student, and they'd kept him in Pearl Harbor the whole time because he

---
*Kaplan has been mentioned previously in this oral history because of the controversy concerning his class standing at the Naval Academy in 1922.
**Commander John G. Roenigk, USN.

was very valuable there. But he was good at sea, and I enjoyed my time with him.

Q: Did you have a capable wardroom? I would think more so than in the transport.

Admiral Strauss: Oh, they were all Naval Academy graduates, and the heads of departments were lieutenant commanders, most of whom had been out of the Naval Academy only about five years. And I found out that they knew their jobs--for instance, the gunnery officer, the navigator, and so forth. But what they lacked was a sea experience. You had no trouble about them learning the intricacies of the fire control system, but when a blow came up and you'd say, "Don't you think you ought to hoist in the boats," it was something they'd probably never thought about. Their knowledge of seagoing and of protocol probably left something to be desired. So that I think this seasoning people in their grade has a lot to recommend it.

Q: Did you have a good shakedown cruise?

Admiral Strauss: We were finishing off at the shipyard in through the first part of the winter, and I think it was in December or January that we started on our shakedown cruise. I reported both to Commander Destroyers Atlantic Fleet and to the head of the training command, because it was while we were under training that I had these two bosses. And we took the ship to Guantánamo. It was in very bad shape at that time as far as cleanliness was concerned, because in the winter it was very hard to do anything about cleaning it up.

The change into reasonably warm weather was fine, and the training group came on board and started putting us through our paces. We had to have gunnery drills. We did all sorts of things. The 8-inch gunned Toledo with Captain Detzer, a great friend of mine on board, was going through training at the same time.* We at 6,000 tons had to tow the 13,600-ton Toledo, and then she towed us, and we did all these necessary drills. And had final inspection.

But that came later, because while we were undergoing training, we were called off to be present at the inauguration of the new President of Uruguay. And, for this expedition they put on board Admiral Ernest Herman Von Heimburg.** And we had a very interesting cruise. We were in Montevideo for the inauguration with several other ships. There was an Argentine ship and a British ship, and the captain of the British ship and the admiral on board

---
*Captain August J. Detzer, Jr., USN, was the first commanding officer when the USS Toledo (CA-133) went into commission 27 October 1946 at the Philadelphia Naval Shipyard.
**Rear Admiral Ernest H. Von Heimburg, USN.

had been colleagues of mine during the time in London. So that was a very pleasant reunion. I think there was a French cruiser, and we had the usual parties and ceremonies. But it turned out that we did a bad job, because a month or so after we left, the new president died. On the way back we stopped at Rio, and Admiral Von Heimburg was so taken with Rio that he asked to be made the next head of our naval mission there, which he was shortly after this cruise.

One thing that struck me was at a factory in Brazil, which had been started up by our Bureau of Ordnance. They were making 5-inch/38-caliber guns, and I was told that they couldn't use the old machinists in this work because they were used to working with calipers and couldn't read drawings, so they had to get youngsters and train them right from scratch to do the job. But they turned out very good 5-inch guns there in the factory in Brazil.

Q: Did you see any evidence when you were in Montevideo of the Graf Spee that had been scuttled years earlier?*

Admiral Strauss: No, although there may have been a monument or something like that.

---

*The German pocket battleship Graf Spee was scuttled by her crew at Montevideo in December 1939 following a battle against three British cruisers.

Q: Perhaps you could discuss the capabilities of your own ship a bit more. This was one of the antiaircraft cruisers and very rapid fire, I would guess. Did you have a lot of towed sleeves to practice against?

Admiral Strauss: For our final drills at Guantánamo, where we had to do everything, they'd do things like clamp the whistle open so you couldn't hear yourself and you had to do something about that. And we fired at sleeves, and the first time we fired, we fired ahead of the sleeve, which was bad. And this was something in the predictor that had gone wrong, and we had to apologize to the towing plane. But we got that ironed out and finally, when we had our final battle problem, there was only one cruiser that had gone through that had a higher score than we did on gunnery. So we were very lucky on our first time, because it would have been possible to hit the plane.

So, now if I do say so, we had a very good passing out drill. I mean, both the physical inspection of the ship and then the going through a simulated battle experience. Beforehand, I was told to take this training very seriously. It was, of course, a relief going from this routine to the trip down to Montevideo and Brazil. I was told, "When you come back, make sure that you go through the rest of the shakedown and do it well." Because a previous cruiser with a very good commanding officer had sort of taken it easy, and he got a rather bad show out of the thing.

Q: Did the city of Fresno, California, show an interest in the ship?

Admiral Strauss: They gave us a cup or something. I don't think they could afford a real silver service the way the old battleships used to get punch bowls and goblets. They gave us a token cup or something of the sort.

Q: This, of course, was right after the period of great demobilization. Did that cause you a problem with the enlisted crew?

Admiral Strauss: No, it didn't. It caused us some trouble with material. For instance, our first lifelines were steel lifelines because they were the only sort available. Later on, we got rid of them and got copper lifelines and wormed and parcelled them.

Later on, I was present at the commissioning of the destroyer named after my father, and it was much grander than ours because ours was so recently after the war that a lot of the things were in short supply. When we were sent abroad, which we were shortly afterwards, I had to get better cabin silver and so forth, because the stuff they had given the Fresno was very poor. Because we were going abroad, I could say that we had to put our best foot forward there, so I was able to get some nicer things for the ship.

Q: The advantage of a copper lifeline being that it wouldn't rust?

Admiral Strauss: Yes. It didn't fray the same way either.

Q: Did you have a fairly stable crew, or was there a good deal of turnover?

Admiral Strauss: I would say from past experience it was about normal.

Q: Were you pleased with the job that the shipyard did in finishing her off?

Admiral Strauss: Yes. Shortly after our shakedown, when we went back to New York, the Little Rock, which was stationed in Northern Europe, had some difficulty, I think mechanical difficulty. And they sent her back from Europe and sent us to take her place. Well, I was delighted at this, but curiously enough some of the officers and crew weren't. I know my first lieutenant was very upset at this. And I told him, "I can remember back when they had the 40T squadron in the Mediterranean, people would pay their colleagues to exchange places with them and get there." It was considered a plum job. For instance, I got some Filipino mess boys in place of the colored, among the few that were left in the Navy, they gave me for the trip.

And we went from New York to Plymouth. We were really, I suppose, as much as anything based on Plymouth, although we weren't in there very much. We held a gunnery practice off of Torquay, which wasn't too far away. The British towed the sleeves for us. The great difficulty with it is that almost any place in the English Channel you were in danger of hitting something like fishing boats, and very often we'd start out and find the range fouled with fishing boats. We got some firing in.

We went to Rotterdam, and were the first American man-of-war in Holland after the war, and going up the river we passed a great big cage, with prisoners of war still in it. And they all ran to the front of the cage to watch the ship go by. And, when we got into Rotterdam, I found that the Dutch carrier, the <u>Karel Doorman</u>, was there, and the admiral was a very old friend of mine, Alfred de Booy, who'd been Dutch naval attaché in London when I was there as an assistant.*

---

*In the late 1930s, as a lieutenant commander, de Booy was Dutch naval attaché in London. By the late 1940s, he was a rear admiral. In the early 1950s he was Commander in Chief and Chief of Naval Staff for the Royal Netherlands Navy.

Q: Why had these prisoners not been repatriated?

Admiral Strauss: I don't know. Maybe that they were waiting for some reparations on the other end.

Q: They were Germans, I take it.

Admiral Strauss: Germans, yes.

Q: Why was your crew reluctant to go on that cruise?

Admiral Strauss: Well, the crew wasn't, but there were certain ones of them. They didn't want to leave home and mother and the usual thing. For instance, my first lieutenant, Bitterman, said, "Here we've been down there all winter, and now we're back and I've got to go away again."*

Q: Was the hospitality fairly good? I mean, those countries were still recovering from the war, so they couldn't be too generous.

Admiral Strauss: Well, they were good, though. In Rotterdam the main hospitality came from our own embassy. The ambassador was Herman Baruch, who was the brother of

---

*Lieutenant Commander Frank J. Bitterman, USN.

Bernie Baruch, and he had a ball for the officers, and I must say it was one of the nicest parties I've ever been to.* And I've heard some rather invidious things said about Herman Baruch, but in my opinion, certainly while we were there, he fulfilled my idea of an ambassador very well. He looked like one, and this ball was first class. But even before this ball, while we were at sea, the naval attaché, Captain Pete Brady, sent us a message saying that he would like to have a party for the bluejackets, half one night and half the next, at the zoo in Rotterdam.** Apparently that was a good place to give parties. And he asked whether he could serve hard liquor or whether they should stick to beer. Well, we talked that over and told him, "Please stick to beer." Captain Brady and his wife gave these two parties at their own expense. It was a very nice gesture on their part, and they furnished young women from the community both nights. And the ambassador's party was on another night for the officers alone.

Admiral Conolly made the trip over in the ship.

Q: You picked him up in England?

Admiral Strauss: Yes.

---

*Bernard M. Baruch was a well-known American businessman, statesman, and advisor to Presidents.
**Captain Parke H. Brady, USN.

Q: What recollections do you have of him?

Admiral Strauss: Well, to me Admiral Conolly was a really great naval officer in every way. And he would have made a superb Chief of Naval operations. I think he wanted to be Chief of Naval Operations. He was then Commander U.S. Naval Forces Eastern Atlantic and Mediterranean. I once told him, "To my mind you've got the best job in the Navy. You've got this command from here down to the Persian Gulf, and if you go back there, you're wrestling with Congress and so forth." But it just didn't work out. These very top jobs, it's a matter of timing and politics as much as anything else. But as a commander there in the Mediterranean, he was called "In-Close Conolly," and he and General Truscott were supposed to have been possibly the best amphibious landing team. No, I think he was a great man. I think it was a great tragedy when he was killed with his wife in that airplane accident.*

I don't think I persuaded him that being CinCNELM was a better job than CNO. Fresno became his flagship. He and his staff gave us an inspection in Greenwich. Conolly used to have dinner parties aboard for some of his friends, using the wardroom for these as the flag quarters in the AA cruisers were too small.** I saw him later when he was

---
*Admiral Conolly died 1 March 1962 at the age of 69.
**The Fresno was an antiaircraft (AA) cruiser, armed with 5-inch guns, and thus was smaller than cruisers with 6-inch or 8-inch guns.

president of the Naval War College, and after he retired and was president of Long Island University. He once wrote an unsolicited fitness report which gave me more than my due. I have a signed photograph of Admiral Conolly: "To the Captain of my Flagship."

Q: He got that nickname "Close In" because he was not one to stand off. He got right in with the action.

Admiral Strauss: Yes, yes, right in where he knew what the guns were doing and so forth.

Q: Did you have any operations with the Royal Navy or other navies during that cruise?

Admiral Strauss: No, I had two destroyers attached to me, and there was a repair ship, so that I was designated Task Force 21. I suppose it was the smallest force in the Navy, but it was a task force rather than a task group. As a force commander, I was the authority who could say whether officers or men who wanted to marry English girls could do so or not. And I solved this one, of course, by having the chaplain go ashore and interview the parents and the girls and check otherwise. I had to act on his recommendations. It only happened a very few times, two or three times we had that problem.

Q: What were the criteria for saying yes or no?

Admiral Strauss: It had to be a matter of judgment, you know, that you felt that this wasn't just a bit of a slap and tickle and whether the parents would agree and whether the man had a reputation as a steady customer and so forth. Also whether he would know or would admit whether his family would like it or not.

Q: This kind of authority isn't granted to naval officers for weddings in the States. Was it because of the international aspects?

Admiral Strauss: Yes, yes, because, you see, during World War II there were an awful lot of dustups with funny marriages.

Q: Well, obviously your concern was that it was a legitimate thing.

Admiral Strauss: Yes, yes. I suppose that if a lady was fairly far along in a pregnancy, you'd have to say yes, you see.

Q: There wouldn't have been that opportunity in the short time you'd been over there.

Admiral Strauss: No, not for our people. No, that's true, so that didn't arise. I remember that Admiral Stark's Royal Navy liaison officer was a four-star admiral who would have had a big job in the war except that he'd got a bad heart: Vice Admiral Sir Geoffrey Blake. And he had a WRN personal assistant who was called Miss Casement, and she was a niece or something of Roger Casement, you know, the Irish patriot who was executed. Obviously a lady. And she became enamored of a reserve chief petty officer who was a very nice young man.

They got married and Admiral Blake had to be best man, only he disapproved of this, and the last time I saw her she was out of uniform and very pregnant, and was going back to the United States with this chief petty officer. And I've often wondered how that thing came out. You see, in London he had an apartment, and the two of them could lead their own lives. When they returned to the United States, unless the young man had immediate demobilization, his wife would be thrown in with other bluejackets' wives. I wondered how that marriage would get along.

Q: Some of those lasted, no doubt, and some didn't.

Admiral Strauss: Yes.

Q: Were there any other stops during that cruise?

Admiral Strauss: Yes. We went to Le Havre, and we went to Rotterdam. I remember that we had receptions in both of those places on board, and that the ambassador didn't come to our reception in Rotterdam, but Phil Bonsal, who was the deputy chief of mission, who's here now and I see all the time, did--came on board to represent the ambassador.* In Le Havre I was rather cross, because the naval attaché, who was Henri Smith-Hutton, didn't come himself and he didn't send an officer.** In London, when a major ship came in, we always either went down ourselves or the naval attaché did, or he sent an assistant. He sent a clerk. I didn't like this too much.

We had a French captain who was our liaison officer, and he took a party of officers in a motor launch which he got ahold of to Torquay, the resort. And it was the first time that any of us had seen ladies on the beach with very brief bikinis and very brief brassieres. And the officers were enchanted. And when the French captain said, "I think

---
*Philip W. Bonsal, counselor of the U.S. embassy to The Hague in 1947-48, and ambassador to Colombia in the mid-1950s.
**Captain Henri H. Smith-Hutton, USN, was naval attaché to both France and Switzerland, from 1947-52. His two-volume oral history is in the Naval Institute collection.

we should go back," I said, "All right, boys," I said, "Let's go."

"Yes, Captain." And it was an awful job getting them away.

Q: Understandably.

Admiral Strauss: Yes.

Q: Well, that sounds like a pleasant cruise to take.

Admiral Strauss: Oh, it was. Oh, we went--this is interesting I think. We went up to Greenwich, and the president of the naval war college at Greenwich was Admiral Sir Patrick Brind, whom I'd known well in London.* And before anchoring I sent a message, "Permission to salute your flag upon anchoring." And I got a message back that the last salute that had been fired there had been by Sir Francis Drake, and he'd broken all the windows, and Queen Elizabeth had decreed that there would be no further salutes fired.** So I didn't fire. But I had Admiral Brind on board to luncheon, and I had a couple of ladies that I'd known in London who came down and he went all over

---

*Vice Admiral Sir Eric James Patrick Brind, RN, President of the Royal Naval College Greenwich.
**Sir Francis Drake (1540-1596), English navigator and privateer.

the ship. Another person I had on board was Admiral Anderson, who was working for the telephone company then.* He came on board for lunch once. But I'd always wanted to take a ship that near to London. The Thames was so dirty that you couldn't wash the decks down with the water from the river, and I was worried about it in the fire system; there was so much debris in it that it might have clogged the fire mains.

Q: Were you well satisfied by then with the condition of the ship that--that you'd brought her up to snuff after the winter in New Jersey?

Admiral Strauss: Oh, yes. By the time we got through training, she was in good shape.

Q: How long did that cruise last?

Admiral Strauss: Until the autumn of '47. Then I was relieved by Captain Michelet, who had been the head of the Department of Modern Languages at the Naval Academy.** And I was ordered to go to the IDC in London. But, because the IDC started on the fourth of January, they had to do something with me until then. I went to the National War

---
*Walter S. Anderson, for whom Strauss had worked in London in the mid-1930s, had retired as a vice admiral in 1946.
**Captain William G. Michelet, USN.

Strauss #3 - 296

College for a couple of months, just to park there, but it was very interesting because I was able to contrast the National War College and the Imperial Defence College.

Q: Sounds like an assignment that you had requested.

Admiral Strauss: I guess I did, but before I took it I asked to get out of it. I said I'd spent so much time in England I thought it might be harmful. Roland Smoot, who was the captain detailer, said the chief of Naval Operations had approved me for it.* And he said "No, anybody who graduates has a plus. I can't see that it would do you any harm." Well, I didn't have anything to say about it, and I wasn't sorry except that I just did not want to "have too much English duty."

Q: Did you have any sense of regret giving up the ship command?

Admiral Strauss: Oh, yes. Oh, yes. Oh, a single ship command, I think, of a real man-of-war is the best thing that the Navy has to offer. I have On a Destroyer's Bridge written by H. H. Frost.** He ends up the book by saying,

---
*Captain Roland N. Smoot, USN; Smoot's oral history is in the Naval Institute collection.
**Lieutenant Commander Holloway H. Frost, USN, was commanding officer of the USS Toucey (DD-282) when Strauss served in that ship in the late 1920s.

"The command of a destroyer is the finest job in the world--bar none." And I think he felt that way, and I still feel that way, because, for instance, when I had DesFlot 6 it was a fascinating job. But it isn't the same feeling, because each ship has her own commanding officer.

Q: You didn't have as much control.

Admiral Strauss: No.

Q: What are the satisfactions that come with a ship command?

Admiral Strauss: Well, it sinks or swims, it's good or bad because of you. It's like Napoleon said, "There are no such things as good and bad troops; there are only good and bad officers." No, I hated leaving it. But there were only seven cruisers in commission at that time, and one was very lucky to get a piece of one, especially one that's active.

Q: And you had a chance to put your stamp on the ship because as the first skipper you established a good deal of tradition and practice that would be followed.

Admiral Strauss: Well, I hope so. You see there were only

three captains. There was Michelet, and then another one, and then the ship was decommissioned. So only three commanding officers the whole time.

The commander in chief in Plymouth, where <u>Fresno</u> was "based," was Admiral Pridham-Wippell.* He was a very nice man and was very kind to me and took me under his wing. When we were in port I had a standing invitation to go to dinners on Sunday. You know, the city of London has these old guilds: the shoemakers, the tailors, and so forth. And they'd have these city dinners and if you've ever been to one of those, there are about nine courses. They start with oysters and terrapin and go on. He had me to a city dinner. They're all men who attend, and if you're in the services you wear your decorations and so forth, or you wear white tie.

Pridham-Wippell was a member of the Cordwainers; Cordovan leathers is where the name comes from. Also, while I was assistant naval attaché, I was taken to a dinner at the Naval College at Greenwich, and that was done bang-up. The waiters were in knee britches and stockings and powdered wigs, and they had two snuff boxes; one was given to the mess by Samuel Pepys and these boxes are

---

*Admiral Sir Henry Daniel Pridham-Wippell, RN, Commander in Chief Plymouth.

passed around the table and everybody'd take snuff.* The commander who was the mess president presided. For his grace he hits the table with the gavel and says, "Thank God." That's the grace. And then they start in from there. If you come as a guest, you wear white tie.

Q: Where did your change of command take place?

Admiral Strauss: I think probably in Plymouth. Then I came back to this country in the liner America.

Q: So then you spent some time at the U.S. National War College just briefly.

Admiral Strauss: Yes, yes. A couple of months.

Q: What were your impressions of that?

Admiral Strauss: I thought that it was very well done. I felt that in the American fashion, that if we had a spare 15 minutes in Washington, we had to do something with it. Whereas in London it was much more leisurely, but you came along, you realized that you were learning a lot just the same. With the discussions before luncheon and so forth,

---

*Samuel Pepys (1633-1703) was a British naval official and noted diarist who offered a candid account of his activities and opinions.

you got a lot. You see, we had students from the foreign office, the post office, and the customs besides the Army, Navy, and Air Force officers.

The lectures were superb. The people that they got in discussed all facets of life. We had a couple of Communists; one of them was a very tough Communist MP, and somebody asked him why the Russians put so many people in prisons.* And he said, "Because they disagree with the government." And he said, "When we're in power and any of you people disagree with the government, you'll end up in prison."

Then there was a very suave one who said "We're all men together." Mountbatten had just come back from India, and he spoke to us about the takeover there, and it was clear he favored the Indians over the Pakistanis. We also heard from politicians, industrialists. I think the lectures were really the most informative. Then we had problems about how would you do set problems, and had teams. One team would work it their way, and the other team would work it theirs. This would be followed by general discussion as to which solution seemed the better.

Q: What was the substance of the study? Was it mostly strategic concerns?

---
*MP--member of Parliament.

Admiral Strauss: Yes. For instance, the opening theme when we were there proved to us that the British Empire was now a drain on Great Britain, except for British Honduras and Malaysia. Britain got an income from those two, and every other dependency cost them money, you see. The politico-economic side of questions was discussed.

The college was still the IDC. We just had the British military and civil services, South Africa, Canada, Australia, New Zealand, plus three American military officers. They didn't have the State Department that year; one FSO came the following year.* Now the college is called "The Royal College of Defence Studies" ("Imperial" is frowned on), and the students come from all the NATO countries and even from outsiders.** Under the IDC the restricted student body were able to discuss certain confidential matters. With the existing setup, I do not see how this is possible. The Commandant my year was Air Marshal Sir John Slessor. He was later a Marshal of the Royal Air Force (five stars) and Chief of Air Staff.*** He had a wide reputation as a strategian.

Q: Were living conditions still relatively austere in England?

---
*FSO--foreign service officer.
**NATO--North Atlantic Treaty Organization.
***Slessor was Chief of Air Staff from 1950 to 1952.

Admiral Strauss: Yes. Gasoline was very short supply.

The college had the King to luncheon. And they asked me if I could get a ham and a turkey from the commissary, which I did. And that was sort of the piece de resistance at the luncheon for the King. And I had a short talk with him. He asked me where Admiral Kirk was now, and I told him he was ambassador to Belgium at that time.

Q: Was he a personable individual?

Admiral Strauss: Oh, yes. Oh, yes. He was not particularly dynamic, but you knew he was King.

Q: How would you describe it?

Admiral Strauss: Well, I don't know. I can't describe it. Having been born royal, though not in line to be King, must give an ingrained assurance.

Q: That was the time when there was the great unification squabble among the U.S. Armed Forces. Were you in touch with that problem?

Admiral Strauss: Yes, that was going on afterwards, when I came back to the CNO's office. Because that was a time

with the officers to see him off and cheer him.* And, as I think you know, what effect that had on Admiral Burke.** How he was held up, you know, because he'd been OP-23 dealing with this thing, purely from the standpoint of what the law was. Truman wanted to hit everybody who were parties to this dispute, so they held up his selection to rear admiral. I mean, you knew all that.

Q: He's talked about that at great length.***

Q: We're near the end of the tape. I wonder if there are any other things about that tour over in England that you wanted to put on the record. Do any of the lectures that you attended at the IDC especially stand out in your mind?

Admiral Strauss: Yes. I remember that we looked forward very much to Stafford Cripps's lecture, and he talked down to us as though we were a bunch of boy scouts.**** I was very disappointed. I thought here's a man who really

---
*Admiral Louis E. Denfeld, USN, left office as Chief of Naval Operations on 1 November 1949 after a term of nearly two years. He was not appointed to an additional two-year term because of his disagreements with civilian superiors.
**Captain Arleigh A. Burke, USN, was espousing the Navy position in the Navy-Air Force squabble. He aroused so much animosity that the Secretary of the Navy took his name off the list of officers selected for rear admiral. It was restored by President Harry Truman.
***Admiral Burke devoted considerable discussion to this topic in his own Naval Institute oral history.
****Sir Richard Stafford Cripps (1889-1952) served as president of the Board of Trade (1945-47) and Chancellor of the Exchequer (1947-50).

should have a very broad view of things.

Q: The Atlee government was then in power.* Did you see the drift toward Socialism?

Admiral Strauss: Not noticeably. The military people were conservative, probably to a man. There was a civil servant--town and country planning, as I remember it--who was pro-Labour. He was kidded quite a lot, because his government was in power.

Q: It's quite ironic that Churchill had presided over the war, and now Atlee had been elected when peace came.

Admiral Strauss: Yes, when you consider that they considered him in a way the savior of England and then to toss him out right at the end.

Q: Not to be able to enjoy the fruits of his victory.

Admiral Strauss: No. Of course, he came back, but it was an anticlimax, I think when he came back. Did you read Lord Morin's account of--Lord Morin was his doctor.**

---
*Clement Atlee was elected Prime Minister of Great Britain in 1945.
**Relman Morin, Churchill: Portrait of Greatness (Englewood Cliffs, New Jersey: Prentice Hall, 1965).

Q: I've heard of it; I haven't read it.

Admiral Strauss: Well, I think it was outrageous, because everything involving a patient and his doctor is supposed to be confidential. And he just told all; I didn't admire him for that.

Q: Do you have any final thoughts to complete the interview?

Admiral Strauss: I had one amusing experience while I was at the IDC. Air Commodore Bobby Sharp, who was a student there, had a friend who had been a lady-in-waiting to the Queen, and she was having a few friends in.* And the Queen and Princess Margaret were coming. It was in the Queen's honor, and Sharp asked me whether I would like to go with him, and he had me invited. And I suppose there were 15 people in the room, and when the Queen and Princess Margaret came in, they were led around us.

My friend stood next to me, and there was a man on my right, a young man with patent leather hair, tall and very handsome. And first Princess Margaret came through and shook everybody's hand. She kept looking at this man when she shook my hand; she was still looking at him, you see.

---
*Air Commodore A. C. H. Sharp, RAF.

Bobby Sharp was short and baldheaded. When she took him by the hand, she was still looking at this other fellow. So the next day, he said to me, "We didn't do very well there, did we?"

Well, then the Queen came through, and when the Queen shook my hand, I was the person she'd been waiting all of her life to meet; there was no question about it. Her training and so forth was perfect; you felt that she concentrated on you and was so pleased to meet you, whereas the daughter--as I say, this chap with the shiny hair got all of her attention.

Q: Well, that's a good note to wrap it up on, because we are right at the end of the tape.

Admiral Strauss: Sharp came over to the United States afterwards. He was very American-minded. I think that's why he asked me, and I think he became an American citizen. Then he died. He got to be an air vice marshal, which is equivalent to a rear admiral.

Strauss #4 - 307

Interview Number 4 with Rear Admiral Elliott B. Strauss,
U.S. Navy (Retired)

Place: Admiral Strauss's home in Washington, D.C.

Date: Monday, 17 November 1986

Interviewer: Paul Stillwell

Q: Admiral, last time we finished our discussion of the Imperial Defence College.

Admiral Strauss: Yes, after the Imperial Defence College I reported back to the Navy Department and was assigned to the Strategic Plans Division of the CNO's office, and I had one of the two branches. Captain Karl Hensel had the other branch.*

Q: He's a classmate of yours.

Admiral Strauss: Yes, he's a classmate, and he was relieved by Harry Sanders, also a classmate.** The director of Strategic Plans was first Admiral Freddy Boone, then Admiral Ingersoll.***

Q: What are your impressions of Admiral Boone?

---
*Captain Karl G. Hensel, USN.
**Captain Harry Sanders, USN.
***Rear Admiral Walter F. Boone, USN; Rear Admiral Stuart H. Ingersoll, USN.

Admiral Strauss: A very competent, hard-working, intelligent man. He's not particularly bonhomous, but he is fair to his staff, and I think did a fine job as director of Strategic Plans. Admiral Ingersoll had more ups and downs, he was more bonhomous. I think he had, perhaps, more evident sense of humor, although Admiral Boone certainly had his share. They were both fine officers.

Q: Did your planning take into account the desire of the Navy to get into the strategic bombing business?

Admiral Strauss: I can't remember that that obtruded itself at the time. There was still a certain jealousy among the services, and I remember when General Bradley made his statement that naval officers were mostly "fancy Dans."* I was coming down the corridor one morning with some other officers, and we passed Admiral Fechteler, who was Chief of Naval Operations, and he greeted us.** He said, "Good morning, Dans."

Q: He had a good sense of humor.

---
*General of the Army Omar N. Bradley, USA, Chairman of the Joint Chiefs of Staff, 1949-53.
**Admiral William M. Fechteler, USN, Chief of Naval Operations, 1951-53.

Admiral Strauss: Yes.

Q: What do you recall about the period when Admiral Denfeld was not reappointed.* Was that a traumatic time in the Navy Department?

Admiral Strauss: Yes, it was. When he finally left, I was among a great many officers who went down to the terrace in front of the Pentagon to cheer him and say goodbye. When Admiral Sherman took over, there was certain amount of resentment among officers in general because of the fact that he had replaced Admiral Denfeld.** Of course, he was possibly one of the best Chiefs of Naval Operations we've ever had. I would have been very pleased to see Admiral Forrest Sherman President of the United States. I thought he was of that caliber.

You may remember that at that time Captain Burke had been selected to be a rear admiral, but because of his connection with the dispute between the Navy and the Air

---

*Admiral Louis E. Denfeld, USN, served as Chief of Naval Operations from 15 December 1947 to 1 November 1949. He was expected to have a second two-year term but was fired by Secretary of the Navy Francis Matthews because of his support for naval aviation in the inter-service battle against the newly formed U.S. Air Force.
**Admiral Forrest P. Sherman, USN, became Chief of Naval Operations on 2 November 1949.

Force, President Truman held up his appointment.* Burke had no real part. All he did was to look up the laws governing the rights of each service in the naval aviation domain. The story was that when Admiral Sherman took over, the President asked him what he could do to restore the morale of the Navy. And Admiral Sherman told him that, "One of the first things you ought to do is to lift the hold on Captain Burke's appointment to be a rear admiral."

One other thing that Admiral Sherman did never came to any fruition because he died.** In his desk there were some uniform stars which had the inner points of the stars' rays connected, forming a little pentagon. And he had put white, red, orange colors in there to restore the old idea that paymasters wore white, doctors maroon, and so forth, which I think was a very good idea because the present leaves insignia, unless you're an expert you can't tell the difference between a civil engineer and a medical service corps officer. So this was a step in the right direction. I'm not sure it would have ever gone through, but I think if he'd lived he would have pushed it.

---

*In 1948-49, Captain Arleigh A. Burke, USN, was in charge of the Operational Research and Policy branch (OP-23), which spearheaded the Navy's battle against the Air Force over roles and missions of the two services. CNO Admiral Forrest Sherman pulled Burke from this controversial duty in early 1950, when he was assigned as Navy secretary to the Defense Department's Research and Development Board. Burke was promoted to rear admiral in September 1950.
**Admiral Sherman died 22 July 1951, less than two years after taking office as Chief of Naval Operations.

Strauss #4 - 311

Q: What problems was your division involved in?

Admiral Strauss: I thought that one of the difficulties of the Strategic Plans at that time was that the director of Strategic Plans and the staff had to be too concerned with minutiae of the Navy rather than their main job of concentrating on strategic plans. For instance, you couldn't make commission pennants longer because they might interfere with the gun sights. That all came up to the Chief of Naval Operations's office. I mean, that's a sort of ridiculous example, but it's the sort of thing that I'm talking about. I always felt that the chief was kept busy on these minutiae and putting out fires rather than the long-range planning.

Q: Did you get involved in any long-range planning cases along with the minutiae? For example, NATO was then coming into being.*

Admiral Strauss: Yes. I was occupied by trying to get a command structure for NATO. We examined the part the allies would take and the responsibilities of the different sections. And I did draw up a number of diagrams for that. And Admiral Sherman saw them, and in a way it may have been

---

*NATO, the North Atlantic Treaty Organization, was formally established in 1949.

a basis for the structure that eventually emerged.

Q: Was that the major thing that you were involved with during that tour of duty?

Admiral Strauss: Perhaps. The allocation of material, we had something to do with that. I would say those two things were, perhaps, the main concerns. However they were cutting back on the size of the services at that time, and Admiral Sherman wanted to keep one antiaircraft class cruiser in commission, although it was above the quota that had been assigned to the Navy. And one of the things I had to do was to write out a paper justifying the retention of this cruiser as a special class that they wanted to keep their eye on. And that went to the Joint Chiefs, and the Joint Chiefs did approve it. It was sort of this type of thing that came up all the time.

One other thing was at that time Air Marshal Slessor put out a paper which said in effect that it was not worthwhile concentrating on conventional weapons because the next war would be wholly a nuclear war. I may have overstated that a bit, but that was the thesis. And I was asked to write a paper combating this, which I did. Now that I remember, this came later during Admiral Burke's incumbency, because when he looked over the paper he said, "It's a good paper, but did you ever hear the story of the monkey who tried to get the nuts out of a jar. He took so many in his hand that he couldn't get his hand out of the jar." And he said, "I think you may have done that in this paper. Because whereas it states the case, it perhaps states it so strongly that it may be self-destructive."

Q: So, did you tone it down?

Admiral Strauss: Yes. Yes, I did.

Q: The Korean War broke out during that period. What effect did that have on your office?

Admiral Strauss: Really, very little. Both the basic planning, that amount which we could do, and the putting out of fires and the taking care of minutiae really went on pretty much as before.

Q: Was the bulk of that handled by operations rather than plans? You had a big buildup, for example, in forces.

Admiral Strauss: Yes, it was. It was handled by operations--ship movements and so forth.

Q: Well, you talked about getting into the detail of how many cruisers you would have, for example. There was a dramatic increase in force levels, reactivations and so forth.

Admiral Strauss: Yes, yes. There certainly was. Another thing I noticed was that a lot of the facilities in Washington were taken away to serve. For example, if you had a doctor out at Bethesda, the next time you looked he'd gone out to the Pacific. And that was true, of course, of a great many line officers and staff officers.

Q: At the time of his death, Admiral Sherman was negotiating the bases deal with Spain.

Admiral Strauss: Yes.

Q: Would that be the sort of thing that would come under your office, looking for bases?

Admiral Strauss: Yes, yes, and I remember foreign naval officers and officials of foreign countries came over wanting things, one I remember was the Turks wanted some motor torpedo boats. And when we looked over the inventory, we found that there were practically none left. They'd all been decommissioned. The South Americans came up and wanted bigger ships. It seems to me it was about that time that the Nashville class of cruisers, a couple of them, were given to Chile.*

Q: Argentina and Brazil got some also.

Admiral Strauss: Yes.

Q: In fact, one was recently sunk during the Falklands War. She had been the old Phoenix.**

Admiral Strauss: The Phoenix.

Q: And the St. Louis I know went down there; and the Brooklyn.*** What was our general naval strategic policy concerning South America at that point?

Admiral Strauss: I think that we tried to build them up and we cooperated with them. My impression of South Americans, both from that tour and from others, was that the Chileans were real sailors. The rest of them, I'm sure they were competent naval officers, but I never felt that South Americans as such were what I would call sailors,

---
*The ex-USS Nashville (CL-43) and the ex-USS Brooklyn (CL-40), decommissioned light cruisers, were sold to the Chilean Navy in 1951.
**The ex-USS Phoenix (CL-46) was transferred to Argentina in April 1951. In 1956 she was renamed General Belgrano, and was sunk by the British on 2 May 1982 during the Falklands War.
***The ex-USS St. Louis (CL-49) was transferred to the Brazilian Navy in January 1951 and renamed Almirante Tamandare.

with the exception of Chile, who were certainly seagoing and very capable mariners.

Q: Did you have a chance to go to sea with them? What did you base that assessment on?

Admiral Strauss: No, I've never been to sea with them, but I've known a great many of them. And I've watched them in the dockyard and watched them recommissioning a ship and so forth. I knew the Spanish naval attaché in London. He'd been there a long time, and I hadn't any particular regard for him. He was a nice man, but as a sailor he seemed a "fuddy duddy." I think he was a diplomatic type rather than a seagoer, and I could go on multiplying that for some of the other naval officers from South America that I met.

Q: So the Chileans had the sort of seasoning that you wish your officers in the Fresno had had?

Admiral Strauss: I think that's true. Of course, I suppose the explanation is that the country's practically all coast, and so they have to be capable sailors.

Q: Now, building up an alliance in NATO, did you have to mesh U.S. strategic plans with those of foreign nations such as Britain for example?

Admiral Strauss: Yes. One of the things, for instance, that we talked about was convoying, where they would break off, like the mid-ocean meeting point in World War II. It's where we'd take over from the British or the Canadians and so forth. That came up at that time.

Q: I would imagine that your recent experience at the Imperial Defence College was quite useful in that billet.

Admiral Strauss: It was useful, perhaps knowing something of the psychology and feelings of our British allies. Of course, the broadest subjects that we took up--strategic subjects and political subjects, not so much so, except that it all went into the attempt to psychologically evaluate our allies.

Q: Well, any other things that you recall from that tour of duty?

Admiral Strauss: Well, occasionally, when the director of Strategic Plans couldn't attend meetings of the Joint Chiefs, or the deputy Joint Chiefs, I sat in and occupied the naval part of it. And that was always very interesting. I found that we got along very well with the

Strauss #4 - 318

Army and Air Force. Occasionally there was understandably a difference of objective, but there was never anything that I could call quarrels or hard feelings. They were all peacefully resolved.

Q: So, would you say that the climate improved in that area during your time there?

Admiral Strauss: Very much, yes.

Q: You also got married during that period, didn't you?

Admiral Strauss: Yes, yes, I did.

Q: How had you met your new wife?

Admiral Strauss: During the war there was an elderly lady in London who had been a Miss Peabody of Boston, and she had married Joseph Chamberlain, who was the British Foreign Minister back a ways there.* He was the father of Austen Chamberlain. The story was that Austen admired Miss Peabody, and his father Joseph said, "She's much too good for you," and married her. That may be apocryphal, but

---

*Joseph Chamberlain (1836-1914) was a British statesman noted as a champion of improved municipal housing and sanitation. His two sons were Austen (1863-1937) and Neville (1869-1940), both respected statesmen in their own right.

I've heard it. When Joseph Chamberlain died, she married the dean of St. Margaret's. He was Canon Carnegie, and she was again a widow, Mrs. Carnegie.

My mother and father had met her in England, and knew the family, so they suggested that I call on her. Which I did in the winter of 1941-42, and I was invited from time to time to dine. And also she had Sunday at-homes, and when I wasn't busy I went to some of those. And one time when I went there, among the guests were Ambassador William Phillips, who was political advisor to General Eisenhower, and his daughter Beatrice Phillips, who was in London attached to the Office of Strategic Services, which Mr. Phillips had started before he went to Eisenhower's staff.* Both were Boston friends of the former Miss Peabody.

Well, I was taken with Miss Phillips. In the flat that I shared with these other officers we had a small cocktail party, and I invited her to come to the cocktail party. I never heard from her, and the next time I saw her was when my sister invited her to dinner in Washington here, and that was the start of what I think you can call our romance. That was the start of it. So in 1951, we were married.

---

*William Phillips served as U.S. ambassador to Luxembourg, the Netherlands, Belgium, and Italy. During World War II he was a political advisor to President Roosevelt and General Eisenhower from 1943-44 in the rank of ambassador.

Q: Had your first wife died?

Admiral Strauss: No, we broke up. It was in 1937.

Q: This might be the point to discuss your children and where they are and the sorts of things they're doing.

Admiral Strauss: I have three by the first marriage. One of them, the eldest, takes care of the family finances and lives in Newport and partly in New York. The second one is an M.D., a doctor. He also got a Ph.D in biochemistry and then decided he wanted to be an M.D. and became one. He practices on the West Coast in Santa Monica. My daughter is married to a Frenchman and lives in Neuilly outside of Paris. And my youngest boy is in a company in Alexandria, Virginia. He's representing them on the West Coast just outside of San Francisco. It's a company that tries to solve economic problems by mathematical models, because his expertise is in computers.

Q: Quite a varied spread of activities there.

Admiral Strauss: Yes.

Q: Well, after that tour of duty then you got an

opportunity to go back to sea again in the destroyer flotilla. How did that come about?

Admiral Strauss: Admiral Duncan, who was Vice Chief of Naval Operations, was a friend.* When I had not been selected the first time around, he thought it would be a good idea for me to get a command at sea.** And this, of course, was a flag command. The Navy was just about to form a new flotilla, mostly of DEs, but a couple of experimental DDs and three repair ships.*** This was to be formed, and I was ordered to commission it and take command of it.

Q: Had you known Duncan?

Admiral Strauss: Yes, I had had quite a lot to do with both Admiral Duncan and Admiral Sherman at that time. So, they must have got together on it, because I don't think Admiral Duncan could have done it by himself. But, nevertheless, he pushed it, and I think it was largely due to his pushing it that I got it.

Q: You must have made a favorable impression for him to

---
*Admiral Donald B. Duncan, USN, Vice Chief of Naval Operations, 1951-56.
**This is a reference to not being selected for promotion to rear admiral.
***DEs--destroyer escorts; DDs--destroyers.

try to give you that kind of a boost.

Admiral Strauss: Actually for some reason or other, I became Admiral Sherman's man Friday. I was one of two men Friday, the one of them much closer to him than I was, was Neil Dietrich, a classmate, who was his executive assistant.* But I'd never met Admiral Sherman, and when I came back from command of the Fresno he sent for me and said, "What do you think of the Fresno as a station ship over there in Europe?"

And I said, "Well, I think she's a marvelous ship, but the ship in that job has got a lot of social duties, and I think one with wooden decks would be better and one that had more cabin space." Well, that was the end of that conversation.

A short time after that he was going to take one of his periodic tours of Europe, of his command responsibilities over there, and he asked the director of Strategic Plans if I could go with him on that, which I did. And it was fascinating. We went to England, Spain, and Portugal; we were hunting up the bases in Spain, working for that, and that was one of the things that Admiral Sherman was interested in because he spent several days with Admiral Conolly in England.** So that from then

---
*Captain Neil K. Dietrich, USN, who has been interviewed for a Naval Institute oral history.
**Admiral Richard L. Conolly, USN, Commander in Chief U.S. Naval Forces Eastern Atlantic and Mediterranean, 1946-50.

on I saw something of him and as an extra man I was invited by both Admiral and Mrs. Sherman to take part in different things. I remember one time I dined with him, a dinner with just men. And Ambassador Bullitt was a guest.* I thought he was rather super positive on anything that he said.

Q: I think he'd been ambassador to the Soviet Union.

Admiral Strauss: He was the first ambassador to the Soviet Union, then after that when I went with Admiral Johnson to Le Havre, Bullitt came to Le Havre, and I shook him by the hand.** But that's all, I didn't have a chance to talk to him. I really met him at this dinner at Admiral Sherman's house, which is now the Vice President's house.

Q: Well, from what I've read, the Soviets made it very difficult, so you needed a positive guy to put up with that.

Admiral Strauss: I think that's undoubtedly so.

Q: Well, you developed this great admiration for Admiral

---
*William C. Bullitt, former U.S. ambassador to the Soviet Union (1933-36) and France (1936-41).
**In 1938-39, Strauss was aide and flag lieutenant to Rear Admiral Alfred W. Johnson, USN, Commander Atlantic Squadron, U.S. Fleet.

Sherman.

Admiral Strauss: Oh, yes.

Q: What qualities in him did you admire?

Admiral Strauss: He had a very deep background in everything he did. To show that this isn't only my opinion, General Wedemeyer told me that he'd worked with Admiral Sherman on a planning board.* This was, I think, just on the outbreak of World War II, and he had read up so thoroughly on everything that he undertook that General Wedemeyer was also very much impressed with him I think, like me, he would have been glad to see him President of the United States.

Q: What do you remember about his personality? Was he a friendly, outgoing person?

Admiral Strauss: Ah, yes, yes. I don't mean to say that he was effusive, but I don't think anybody in his presence could fail to realize that he was an outstanding man, an impressive personality. I had great admiration for him.

---

*Brigadier General Albert C. Wedemeyer, USA, served on the War Department General Staff, 1941-43. Forrest Sherman had served in the War Plans Division of the Office of the Chief of Naval Operations (1940-42) and the Joint Strategic Committee at U.S. Fleet headquarters (1942).

Q: He's also been portrayed as a very ambitious officer, but by now he had reached the pinnacle, so you probably didn't see that side of him.

Admiral Strauss: No. I don't suppose anybody, with maybe some exceptions, can get to a high place without being ambitious. I also have an opinion about people who get to the very highest places--George Washington, Hitler, Mussolini--that they can't have any sense of humor, because if you saw yourself as a human being standing up in a suit of fuzzy underwear, you couldn't take yourself that seriously. I think the exception to that is probably Lincoln, who I think had a true sense of humor. People say, "How about Churchill, Roosevelt? I think they both had wit, but not any true humor.

For instance, Consuelo Vanderbilt in her book tells about a party that she attended, as a comparatively young woman, and Churchill was also young.* There was a magician who could do things such as take someone's suspenders off without his knowing it, and he did this with Churchill, and Churchill had to hold his trousers up. He left the room in a huff and wouldn't come back. He was witty, but anything that was against him, I don't think he

___
*Consuelo Vanderbilt Balsan, the former Duchess of Marlborough, recounted the story of her life in The Glitter and the Gold (New York: Harper, 1952).

could take, and I think this is a characteristic of most people who reach the pinnacle in their particular line of work.

Q: Did you see a sense of humor in Admiral Sherman?

Admiral Strauss: Yes, yes. Oh, yes.

Q: Any examples that come to mind?

Admiral Strauss: I can't cite any examples.

Q: Well, you mentioned in the destroyer flotilla that you had some experimental ships. Which ones were those?

Admiral Strauss: I had two destroyers, and I don't remember the names, that were doing radio experiments and so forth. Actually, they were just being completed at that time, but that was their purpose. The flotilla was mostly DEs. Flotilla commanders took turns in commanding the destroyers in the Sixth Fleet. And it was a curious thing that this was a tactical rather than an administrative command. When I first took over, one of my responsibilities was the DEs assigned to the different naval districts. I spent the first part of my tour going

Strauss #4 - 327

to different naval districts and inspecting these DEs. And some of them I gave very mediocre reports to, and I don't think it pleased the district commanders under whom they were, but the idea was to try to bring them up to proper standards. I had one exercise with the Second Fleet, in which some of these DEs took part.

Q: Were these Naval Reserve training ships?

Admiral Strauss: Yes. Some of them were diesel, some of them were steam turbine ships. But then in January of '52 I took the new set of destroyers to the Mediterranean to relieve the ones that were already there.

Q: What was your flagship?

Admiral Strauss: It was the William M. Wood, and actually I didn't want to take her. It was one of these things where you sort of take a card, take any card, and one is forced on you. The ships that I wanted to take, there was some reason that I couldn't do it. We ended up putting this small staff aboard the William M. Wood, and it wasn't a very happy ship. The commanding officer was very difficult, and if I'd done everything I should do, I would have asked for him to be detached, but I put up with him. Later in the tour he was detached, and a very good, very responsible captain was ordered aboard.

Anyway, we went to the Mediterranean and relieved the destroyers there, and took part in a number of exercises. For a while, the ship was detached and was sent to Trieste, and from Trieste we went to Venice, where the Italian admiral in command of the naval district took very good care of us. Then I went with some of the ships to Algiers, where I encountered the French commander of the Mediterranean, Admiral Sala, who had been a captain on Admiral Ramsay's staff during the war as the French liaison officer.* And Admiral Sala was responsible for Red Thackrey getting a Legion of Honor and a Croix de Guerre, and I turned up with a Croix de Guerre, which I'm sure was his responsibility. So I was delighted to see him again as the commander in the Mediterranean.

Q: Did you routinely operate with aircraft carriers?

Admiral Strauss: Yes. I had the NATO destroyers in an exercise called Grand Slam, in which we had British, Italian, and French destroyers. And it was the first time that we'd used the international signal book. And there was a phrase in there, "Say again words twice." And the Italians used this a great deal. You'd send out a voice signal and you'd hear a "Say again-a words-a twice-a". We

_____
*Vice Admiral Léon Marie Pierre Antoine Sala, French Navy.

had a French carrier with us with a French admiral on board, and that was a fascinating experience. I had 31 destroyers and in some parts of the exercise we'd have a screen with the entire 31 destroyers in a circular screen.

Q: How did your role differ from that of a destroyer squadron commander?

Admiral Strauss: You're a big destroyer squadron commander. Except, of course, your squadrons under you have their own commanders, so that you're that much removed from direct contact with the individual ships.

Q: Well, it's unusual, though, for a flotilla commander to have a tactical role, isn't it?

Admiral Strauss: No, no.

Q: I see.

Admiral Strauss: No. That's really what he was, a tactical commander, because at that part of the game, he hadn't any really administrative duties. One of the jobs, of course, is trying to make sure that when the ships go ashore that the crew members behave themselves, because in these foreign ports just one bluejacket hitting a taxi driver can put a black eye on the whole thing.

When we were in Algiers, the consul general came aboard, and he said the son of Sosthenes Behn, who was, I think, chairman of International Telegraph and Telephone Company, a lieutenant in the Naval Reserve, was coming to Algiers to marry the daughter of the Spanish consul general, who had the rank of minister.* And he said that the bride had a lot of friends there and that young Behn didn't have any, and would I come to the wedding and bring some of the officers so as to have an American representation for him.

I was glad to do so, but I was very struck at this wedding ceremony. It was a Catholic ceremony, and my chief of staff Frank Foley was a Catholic.** And I said, "Now you tell me what I should do here." Well, it was a very elaborate wedding. They had priests in gold robes and so forth. But one thing that rather shocked me, they had a photographer in a sweater and trousers who went around during the whole ceremony making snapshots of the proceedings. But, after one or two motions of kneeling and standing up and doing things, I could see that my chief of staff was as bewildered as I, he turned to me and said, "You're flying solo. I can't follow this thing." After that they had a reception, a very pleasant affair.

---
*Sosthenes Behn's son was Lieutenant Edward J. Behn, USNR.
**Captain Francis J. Foley, USN.

Strauss #4 - 331

Q: Well, that was a pleasant interlude in your operations.

Admiral Strauss: Yes.

Q: Did you work with the Royal Navy at all?

Admiral Strauss: Yes, of course, there were British destroyers in this operation Grand Slam. And I got a message from the chief of staff of the British CinC Mediterranean, who had been British director of strategic plans in London when I was there during the war. He was afloat again, and so he sent a signal over to me. He'd seen my name on the list.

Q: It sounds like there was a great deal of international cooperation during that period.

Admiral Strauss: There was. We had a session before the operation started with the French admiral and some of his staff, and it went off very well. Everybody seemed to be happy. I think it was a successful operation.

Q: When you went into Trieste, was there an attempt to get intelligence on Yugoslavia?

Admiral Strauss: Not by us, no. It was at this time that

King George VI died, and the British military commander, a major general, had invited my wife and me to luncheon, and this was canceled because the King had died.* A week later he did invite us there very informally; we had a pleasant luncheon with him. But I think the King's death had probably more influence at the time than almost anything else, you know, because this place, Trieste, was under British military command at that time.

Q: How well were American sailors received ashore in these Mediterranean ports?

Admiral Strauss: I think very well at that time. The Marshall Plan was started and it was successful and NATO was just getting under way.** I saw no evidence of any animosity. There may have been individual cases, but I think our men were pretty well taken care of and received.

Q: Were you still responsible for the Naval Reserve destroyer escorts while you were deployed?

Admiral Strauss: I was still the squadron commander of

---

*King George VI died on 6 February 1952. He succeeded to the throne in 1936 after the abdication of his brother, Edward VIII.
**As Secretary of State, 1947-49, George C. Marshall initiated a program of U.S. aid in order to foster the economic recovery of Europe in the aftermath of World War II.

them, yes. Of course, there was nobody directly riding herd on them during that time.

Q: They pretty much operated individually, though, didn't they, rather than needing a squadron commander?

Admiral Strauss: Yes, that's right. Actually, they didn't operate very much. They spent an awful lot of time in port. The reserve captains on them were the lieutenant commanders, and a great many of them were taking courses at college and doing other things that took up their time. I don't think it was a satisfactory setup, but I don't know what else you could have done. And I got the impression that the district commanders didn't pay too much attention to them.

Q: And you sort of put them on report, when you covered the condition of these ships.

Admiral Strauss: Yes, and I had one unfortunate experience. The Commander Destroyers Atlantic Fleet was Admiral Fahrion, and he would telephone or write to the sea frontier commander that I was coming there to look at such-and-such a district.* And I went to New York to inspect the ones under the Third Naval District. And when I got

---
*Rear Admiral Frank G. Fahrion, USN, Commander Destroyers Atlantic Fleet, 1950-52.

Strauss #4 - 334

there I was ready to inspect them, and I got word that Admiral DeLany, who was the district commander, wanted to see me before I set foot on any destroyer.*

I went up to Church Street to call on him in uniform just as soon as I got there, and he was very unhappy indeed. He said that I had no right to come in and inspect his destroyers, and I told him Admiral Fahrion had gone to the sea frontier commander. He said, "Well, he didn't come to me and they're my destroyers." Well, finally I did inspect them, but I've always felt that Admiral DeLany held it against me. I became very good friends with him afterwards, because he was president of the Naval Historical Foundation.

Q: Well, they were your destroyers too, weren't they?

Admiral Strauss: Well, they were, but, you can see the relationship was a little bit complicated. For instance, I went to Boston and Admiral Thebaud just turned them right over to me.**

Q: Well, he'd known you before.

---
*Rear Admiral Walter S. DeLany, USN, Commandant Third Naval District, 1948-52.
**Rear Admiral Leo H. Thebaud, USN, Commandant First Naval District, 1950-52.

Strauss #4 - 335

Admiral Strauss: Yes, yes, he had. But he was a different sort of man, too.

Q: Do you think DeLany's reaction was based on suspicion, or just what?

Admiral Strauss: No, I think that he considered it a case of somebody horning in on his territory without his permission, or without proper notification. I know Admiral Fahrion afterwards said he was sorry that he hadn't had direct contact with Admiral DeLany.

Q: Oh, I see. Did you effect any improvements during the course of your tenure in those ships?

Admiral Strauss: Yes, I'd like to think so, but I couldn't give you hard statistics. It's like Admiral Whiting.* After he retired, he became head of whatever liquor company makes Early Times bourbon. He had a very good salary by then. The chairman said, "Can you prove to me that we've sold any more bourbon than if you hadn't been there?" Well, it's quite a thing to prove.

Q: Red Whiting you're speaking of, I take it.

---
*Rear Admiral Francis E. M. Whiting, USN, retired on 1 August 1947, at which time he received a tombstone promotion to vice admiral.

Admiral Strauss: Yes.

Q: What impressions do you have of Admiral Fahrion?

Admiral Strauss: He was a fine man. If you played tennis, you were all right, and I used to play tennis with him. He played tennis up until, I think, he was 80, and he was a good Commander Destroyers Atlantic fleet.

Q: Were you disappointed to see that tour come to an end?

Admiral Strauss: Very, yes. Oh, yes. I'd have stayed on there. Admiral Ralph Earle was ordered to relieve me, and he did relieve me in Nice.*

Q: Then it was back to the Navy Department again.

Admiral Strauss: Back to the offices of naval operations and then Admiral Burke was director of Strategic Plans, and Admiral Don Felt, also a classmate, was assistant director of strategic plans.**

---
*Rear Admiral Ralph Earle, Jr., USN.
**Rear Admiral Harry D. Felt, USN, assistant director of the Strategic Plans Division from 1951-53. Admiral Felt's two-volume oral memoir is in the Naval Institute collection.

Q: What did the job involve there? This was more the long-range planning?

Admiral Strauss: Yes. Admiral Burke thought it would be a good idea to have someone sort of detached to figure out where we go from here. Well, it was sort of an amorphous job. The purpose was to examine long-range possibilities.

Q: Well, that was a thing he institutionalized even more when he was CNO, so he obviously believed in the value of it.

Admiral Strauss: Yes. So, Captain George Miller, who was a very thoughtful man, has written a great deal on naval subjects, and was afterwards the deputy head of the Maritime Administration.* And he and I worked on this and put out one or two papers. When I was in London, Field Marshal Montgomery spoke to us and said that if the Allies lost all of Europe, if they didn't lose North Africa, the democracies, England and the United States, could still survive. And I made a talk based on this with appropriate maps and made it to several naval groups, in the Pentagon. I don't know how impressed they were with it, but it was a point of view.

---

*Captain George H. Miller, USN. The oral history of Miller, who was later promoted to rear admiral, is in the Naval Institute collection.

Strauss #4 - 338

Q: What sorts of issues did you look at in this long-range crystal-balling effort?

Admiral Strauss: The part that NATO could play, the possible actions of the Soviet Bloc; that was it.

Q: Did you examine mostly strategic-type issues?

Admiral Strauss: Yes, yes. Not movement plans or anything like that, but just eventualities.

Q: Would you get into new-type weapons systems or ships or technology?

Admiral Strauss: To a certain extent, yes. Not really advanced like aerial warfare from satellites.

Q: Well, for instance, the nuclear submarine was coming along then. Did you try to assess its impact?

Admiral Strauss: Yes.

Q: Any specific cases or issues that you recall?

Admiral Strauss: No, no. During the time I was there, it

wasn't very long, we got out perhaps two or three papers that went to Admiral Burke. And then Miller stayed on afterwards and kept it up for some time, I believe. He became a rear admiral and stayed on that job.

Q: Then you went back over to Europe again.

Admiral Strauss: Then I went back to the U.S. delegation to NATO, and I was supposed to be the director of the political-military division. But, the people at NATO didn't want me to be political-military, so they changed the name of the division to "defense programs." That's really what it was--keeping track of and allocating material to the different NATO countries and keeping track of the size of their forces. My boss was Luke Finlay, who was a lawyer with Exxon, which was then Esso.* He had been lent to the government on several occasions. He graduated number one in the class of 1928 at West Point as an Army engineer but left the Army to become a lawyer and go with Standard Oil of New Jersey, which was when he first went there. He had the rank of minister and was known as Defense Representative on the U.S. NATO delegation.

We had five people with the rank of ambassador in

---

*Brigadier General Luke W. Finlay, AUS, Defense Deputy to U.S. Representative, Europe, 1952-53. He worked for the Standard Oil Company of New Jersey, 1963-69.

Paris at that time.* It used to be rather a joke. I'm not sure I can remember them all, but there was the head of the delegation to NATO. There was the ambassador to France. There was the political head of the NATO delegation, Livvy Merchant, who also had the rank of ambassador.** Another one who was a retired Air Force general, Anderson.*** Then there was the OECD man, and—anyway, there were five of them.

Q: Sort of top-heavy.

Admiral Strauss: Yes.

Q: Why had you had these several moves pretty close together? You hadn't stayed in that job at the Pentagon very long.

Admiral Strauss: Well, I was due to retire, and I really wanted to get away from Washington. Besides, the NATO job sounded interesting.

Q: I see.

---
*David K. E. Bruce was the U.S. ambassador to France from 1951-52; James Clement Dunn was ambassador from 1952-54; and C. Douglas Dillon from 1954-56.
**Livingston T. Merchant, Assistant Secretary of State for European Affairs, 1953-56.
***Major General Frederick L. Anderson, USAF (Retired), Deputy U.S. Special Representative in Europe.

Admiral Strauss: This was a Department of Defense job, not a Navy job. A general came along and was looking for someone and asked me if I'd like it, and I said, "Yes, I would." One of the things that concerned me was that NATO seemed to feel that the European forces were all of NATO, and I tried to let them know and keep to the fore that the NATO Atlantic Command probably really had more forces under it than the European Command. It was an interesting and frustrating job. In the Navy I hadn't been used to all this jockeying for position that you see outside, and you think in a thing that was essentially patriotic that there wouldn't be too much of that, but most of the people came from civil life, and there was a great deal of jockeying for position.

Q: It sounds as if several were successful in jockeying for position if there were five with ambassador rank.

Admiral Strauss. Yes. Oh, yes. They certainly were.

Q: Did you settle into a home in Paris there?

Admiral Strauss: We lived in two apartments. Yes, first in Avenue Amiral Bruix and later in the Rue Bossière. Yes.

Q: Was there a fair amount of social life with that job, entertaining of other nations' individuals?

Admiral Strauss: Not too much. Oh, there was a certain amount. But it wasn't, for instance, as social as London had been back in the Thirties.

Q: Do you remember any of the specific matters that you got involved in while you were there?

Admiral Strauss: Well, there was a thing called the annual review, where you tell what each member nation had provided and then tried to urge them to do some more. And it showed you how difficult it was, because most of these governments were pretty evenly balanced. If you're taking Holland, you say, "You ought to be able to ante up one more antiaircraft battery."

And they'd say, "Well, that's so many men. If we do that, we will either have to increase the time of enlistment from a year to 18 months. That will take people away from the harvest. The farmers will be unhappy, and the government may fall." You see, it's this type of thing that you're up against. Now, whether it was real or not, I think most of the time it was real, but, perhaps if a country didn't wish to comply, it would present such an argument.

Then I was assigned to CoCom. CoCom is the Consultative Commission, it's the body of the NATO countries plus Japan, minus Iceland, that decide what strategic materials can go to the Communist bloc nations. Most countries did this either with their OECD representative, or had one man on it. We had a whole delegation, which is typical of the United States. I was the Department of Defense representative on it and they had a State Department man with the rank of minister who was the head of the U. S. delegation.

We made a determination that no country could sell ships to the Russians that were faster than 14 1/2 knots. Well, the Dutch came in and said that they'd had a big order for some 15 1/2-knot tankers, and that if they lost this contract that perhaps the government would fall. So, the next thing you knew we'd upped our limit on speed to 15 1/2 knots. I used to have to write a monthly report back to the Department of Defense. And, when I finally left, in my last report I said that in my year and a half on the CoCom, I found that if you can sell it, it isn't strategic. Which is a rather a cynical overstatement, but not much of one.

Q: Well, that's a problem we still face today--the transfer of technology and so forth.

Admiral Strauss: There was an article in The Washington Post this morning on this subject, which said that we ought to relax our export control. And then they gave a number of things they felt on which our regulations were unreasonably strict. For instance, some of these electronic heart monitors. The article said, "We won't export them because we claim the technology could be used for military purposes." Whether it's true or not, the article said, they can get them from other countries. A counter argument is that a country with weak technology cannot produce all the things denied her at once. Therefore, for the principal producer to deny a product, makes life a little harder for the U.S.S.R.

Q: Well, while you were there your active duty service came to an end.

Admiral Strauss: That's right.

Q: Were you sorry to retire after 36 years in uniform?

Admiral Strauss: I was very sorry. Actually, yes, yes. But the job went on just the same. There wasn't any change in the job.

Q: And how was that arranged? The position was

civilianized?

Admiral Strauss: No, I was still held on active duty. I mean, though on the retired list, it was still an active duty job under the Department of Defense. But there was one change--Major General Robert Wood came to Paris and USRO wanted him to take over the defense programs division.* Karl Hensel had been under the program of seeing whether strategic items were sneaking through to other countries. He left, and they shifted me into that job. And that was quite interesting because a great many countries had groups that did evade these restrictions. I went, for instance, to Tangier, and the consul general's group found that some of the people in Tangier were transshipping contraband. Goods would come in from one source and these would be "laundered" by being sent on in boats of a different organization.

I had one interesting assignment. I was sent to Berlin, because the company in Berlin that made technical instruments was transferring tracking theodolites to the Communist bloc countries. Ridgway Knight was the acting commissioner in Berlin at that time, and he got the mayor and the president of the company and a couple of other officials and myself together, and he read the riot act to

---

*Major General Robert J. Wood, USA, Deputy to Defense Advisor, France, 1953-55. USRO was the designation of the ambassador and his staff of the U.S. delegation to NATO.

them.* He said that the president of the company must resign, and the mayor was going to be very carefully watched for allowing this thing, "And you're going to have to pay an indemnity for it. I'm going to have an inspector to see that this thing doesn't happen again."

The Department of Defense told me to let them know exactly how this had come out, and I drafted a telegram to send back to the Defense Department. I didn't do it in the embassy, but from the commissioner's office. I said that Ridgeway Knight had handled this thing very effectively and forcibly, and that I felt that the export would stop immediately. And I showed him the telegram. He said, "I can't say that."

I said, "No, but I can. This is going to go out over my signature."

Q: The Eisenhower administration took over while you were there. Did that make any difference in policy--that there was a new Secretary of Defense and so forth?

Admiral Strauss: I don't think so. General Ridgway became the Supreme Allied Commander of NATO, and I had known him.** He was the Army representative on the U.N.'s

---
*Ridgway B. Knight, Deputy Assistant High Commissioner for Germany from 1954-55. In the 1960s-1970s, Knight was ambassador to Syria, Belgium, and Portugal.
**General Matthew B. Ridgway, USA, served as Supreme Allied Commander Europe from 1952-53, when he was selected as Army Chief of Staff.

military staff committee, and I admired him very much. I used to take walks with him. He was very much a soldier, and, of course, he'd been a great parachute commander in the war. The struggle at that time as to who would get Eisenhower's job was between him and Gruenther.*

I was all for Ridgway, because I felt he was a combat soldier and that Gruenther had been most of his life a staff man. Well, again, I was wrong. Ridgway had a rather cold Prussian manner, and he didn't get along all that well with the other nationalities. When Gruenther came along, he was a terrific success. He remembered everybody's children's names, and was nice to their wives, and so forth. So he did a much better job--in that particular post. I don't say in war that the difference would have been what I have cited, but that was so.

Q: I think Eisenhower had a great deal of admiration for Gruenther.

Admiral Strauss: Oh, he was a great brain, and I think a superb staff man, and I don't know that he wouldn't have been a very fine combat soldier, but it's just that things worked out so he never really had the chance, you know. He was a professional bridge player. He umpired some of these

---

*General Alfred M. Gruenther, USA, Supreme Allied Commander Europe, 1953-56.

international matches.

Q: While you were there, did you begin making plans for a second career, a post-retirement career?

Admiral Strauss: No.

Q: How did you then get to Bucknell University?

Admiral Strauss: Well, after I retired I was, of course, looking around for a job, and Judge Eller, who had the job as director, afterwards dean of engineering at Bucknell, called me up and said, "Would you like this job?"* Shortly after I retired, the Director of the U. S. Agency for International Cooperation (now "AID"), John Hollister, asked the chiefs of staff of the three services to nominate an officer so as to have Hollister's deputy chosen from the three.** Admiral Burke with Admiral Howard Orem nominated me as the Navy's man.*** I, of course, couldn't be assured that the choice would be me. Actually, the choice was never made. I couldn't wait forever, and then Judge Eller called me and asked, "How would you like this job?"

I said, "I'm neither an engineer, except inasmuch as

---
*Rear Admiral Ernest M. "Judge" Eller, USN (Ret.), whose oral history is in the Naval Institute collection.
**John B. Hollister, director of the International Cooperation Administration from 1955-57.
***Rear Admiral Howard E. Orem, USN.

all naval officers are engineers, and I'm certainly not a professor."

He said, "Well, come up here anyway." So I came up, and they interviewed me, and I suppose they were very hard up because I got the job in Lewisburg, Pennsylvania. And it's a very fine college, really.

The president was Dr. Odgers, who was a Methodist.* Bucknell was originally a Methodist University, and Judge Eller told me, "Be very careful about drinking." He said, "Don't put bottles in the trash or anything like that. If you want to get rid of them, take them out and drop them in the Susquehanna." Well, it was true that when the president would have you to dinner, you had water, or if you wanted it, Coca-Cola. But, one time he asked me to come to Philadelphia with him on a money-raising effort. He was a member of the Philadelphia Club. And he said, "They make a very fine martini there."

Well, of course, the great responsibility there was getting your four branches through accreditation. You see, we had civil engineering, electrical engineering, chemical engineering, and mechanical engineering. And chemical was the hardest. You not only had to meet the national board's requirements, but there was a special chemical board. Well, we got through, and I was always amused because the Harvard engineering school got blacklisted at one time.

---
*Dr. Merle M. Odgers, president of Bucknell University, 1954-64.

Strauss #4 - 350

Before I took the job, I went up to Harvard and MIT and a couple of other places, and asked what a dean did. Well, I was there something over a year. I got $7,500 a year.

I got a call from the State Department, or AID, saying they were opening up a mission in Tunisia, and would I like the job. Well, this was much more my line of work than the other one, so I jumped at it. I'd agreed to stay a year to see whether I liked them and they liked me. Then I said to Dr. Odgers, "Of course, if you insist, I would stay, but the job in Tunisia hasn't got anybody in it who can remain on if I don't take it." Well, he was very, very good. Perhaps he was delighted. So then I went to Tunisia, and we were there three and a half years.

Q: What sort of work did you do there?

Admiral Strauss: The setting up of a mission and a program to give them economic aid.

Q: What specific projects, for example, were involved?

Admiral Strauss: Well, one of the first things they did, the government started out with $5 million, but you don't just put $5 million into the treasury. You put it in the economy by asking them what they want, and buying it, and then they sell it and generate the money that way. Well, the Tunisians wanted sugar. They wanted fuel oil. Arranging for bids was a complicated procedure. The man who finally put in the low bid, which we had to accept, was not a regular purveyor in the oil business. The companies who owned the Tunisian storage tanks refused to store the winner's oil. We were forced to devise a method whereby oil deliveries had to be made at the rate at which the oil could go direct to consumers.

At that time, the only way a small entrepreneur could raise money was by pawning his wife's jewels. So we started a development bank. For instance, all the cube sugar in Tunisia came from France. The bank now financed a small plant to make cube sugar. It lent money for a factory to make blue jeans and a number of other articles. It was successful. The president of the "Societe Tunisien de Banc," Azzous Materi, became a big shot. He set up a bank in Italy and another country. I left Tunisia before it was time for the loans to be repaid, and that, of course, is the real test of success. I've heard that the bank did very well and that the loans were repaid.

Q: Did you find that a satisfying kind of work?

Admiral Strauss: Oh, yes. We built roads. We started a rice crop. Some of the parts of the country are very poor indeed, and we had a system where the government gave workers who would do ditching, walls, fencing, excavating a certain sum of money and we would give them wheat. And they didn't use our wheat, so that we exchanged our wheat for their hard wheat, the same sort of wheat that you make macaroni and so forth out of. It was an interesting time. At the end I had some trouble, which wasn't the mission's fault.

One of the main things that Mr. Bourguiba wanted to do was to dam a river called the Wed Nabana, "wed" being river.* He wanted to do this to give water to a part of the country called the Sahel, where there wasn't adequate water. This project was very near to his heart. And I worked on this, and AID sent over two or three survey teams to look things over, and then finally the branch of the Agency for International Development that would be responsible ran out of money, so for about a year there was no money.

Finally in Washington they told Tunisia to drill some wells, and see whether that wouldn't supply them the water. You can't drill wells very well in Tunisia because you run into salt water. Well, this incensed the government, that they'd been waiting for the money, hoping to get money, and, of course, I was the AID mission director, so I wasn't very popular. The first ambassador was Lewis Jones; he'd left, and the second ambassador was Newby Walmsley.** We

---
*Habib Bourguiba, was elected President of Tunisia on 25 July 1957.

both had to go up and tell them what the department had decided, and Newby Walmsley said, "If it wasn't so difficult, they would have declared me persona non grata." Well, I was there three and a half years.

Then I had an interlude as an inspector and went to Pakistan to inspect with two others to see how the AID mission in Pakistan was getting on. And then I was ordered to start up the mission in Madagascar. It was a much smaller mission there. We were there two years, and at the end of that time they'd turned the mission back to the embassy. They called it a "delegated post". I went back to Washington and worked in the headquarters of the Agency for International Development for a while. And then finished with them.

Q: You had a trip to Israel also, didn't you?

Admiral Strauss: That was later on when I became an inspector for the State Department, not for AID, and went there, again, with a three-man team to inspect the embassy Tel Aviv and the consulate general Jerusalem. And, of course, at that time the consulate general was divided, part in Jerusalem, part in Jordan. And our team, with diplomatic passports, could get back and forth through

---

**George Lewis Jones, Jr., served as ambassador to Tunisia, 1956-59; Walter Newbold Walmsley, Jr., served as ambassador, 1959-61.

Mandelbaum Gate, but most people couldn't. The consul general, Evan Wilson, finally got permission to rig a walkie-talkie between his two posts, so that when he was on the Jordan side he could tell his wife he'd be home to luncheon, or messages like that.

Well, let's see. What came next? I went up to New York and took exams to be a registered representative with Laidlaw and Company. I've done so many things, people used to say, "Can't you keep a job?" Oh, then I went with the General Electric Company, TEMPO, which was GE's long-range planning group. The head of it was Tom Paine, who left to become head of NASA; he was the first head of NASA.* And my immediate boss was a first-generation Pole, a very fine man called Roman Krzyczkowski. I went to Geneva to be TEMPO's European man. Krzyczkowski was my boss. After Tom Paine lost his job, mine went with it.

Then Krzyczkowski started Interplan, which was a planning group. He was president of Interplan, and I became chairman and stayed in Europe for a little while, and we got a contract in Ireland, which I negotiated for them. And then I came back to the United States and was the Washington rep, and used to go out to Santa Barbara two or three times a year on the job out there. Well,

---

*Thomas O. Paine was a manager with the General Electric Company from 1951-68, when he left to become deputy administrator of the National Aeronautics and Space Administration.

Krzyczkowski died and the vice president Evelyn Putnam, who was a very clever woman, took over. But when the U.S. administration changed, it cut back on the use of outside consultants.

Our first contract we got with NASA through Paine, and we had had an ongoing contract with Naval Research, but then the whole setup changed. They had a civilian who'd been there for years and he used us quite a lot. So we lost that contract, and that was really the end of Interplan. Interplan went out of business. And after that I had no 9:00-to-5:00 job. I became a director of a mutual fund in New York, First Multifund. And from then on I had what the retired people usually do, several unpaid jobs, most of which I still have.

I do want to discuss something of interest that took place since my retirement. Admiral Mountbatten, during his lifetime, designated four military officers to attend his funeral.* And, as I think I mentioned, way back in the Seventies, he said to me, "Elliott, you're coming to my funeral."

Well, of the other three officers--when Mountbatten died, one was incapacitated, two had died. So that I was

---

*Admiral Lord Louis Mountbatten was assassinated by terrorists of the Irish Republican Army on 27 August 1979. He and three others were killed when a bomb exploded on board his small boat, the Shadow V, while he was at his country estate, Classiebawn, in County Sligo, Ireland. His funeral was held at Westminster Abbey on 5 September, with burial in Romsey, Hampshire.

the only one standing up, and for that reason, General Wedemeyer was asked to officiate, because he'd been quite close to Mountbatten, and I think if Mountbatten had thought of it, he would have designated him. And in addition to that, there was a doctor who had been with the Chindits in Burma, and the three of us actually marched in the funeral procession, which started at St. James's Palace and went on to Westminster Abbey. It was a beautiful day, and it was lined with terrific crowds on all sides.

Q: I guess he had pretty much dictated the way it would be, hadn't he?

Admiral Strauss: Yes, before his death, apparently some things had gone wrong with Field Marshal Slim's funeral.* Usually the British manage pageants perfectly. I saw an example last year in the installation of the new dean at Canterbury Cathedral. But Field Marshal Slim's funeral had had some lacunae in it, and apparently Admiral Mountbatten had decided that this wouldn't happen to him. And so he laid the thing out in great detail, and it went off, I should say, completely as he had designated.

Q: What sort of emotional reaction did you have to that

---

*Field Marshal William J. Slim, Commander Fourteenth Army from 1943-45 and Governor-General of Australia, 1953-60. He died on 14 December 1970.

experience?

Admiral Strauss: Well, I was, of course, shocked when I heard of his death. I was up in Maine when I turned on the radio and heard that he'd been assassinated in his boat. I had the same sensation when we were in Madagascar. I was listening to the radio one morning and heard that Lady Mountbatten had died very suddenly.* Because I knew her, not as well as the admiral but very well. I knew her over the years, and so just to pick up or listen to the radio and find someone had died that suddenly was a great shock in both cases.

Q: She was an extremely capable person also.

Admiral Strauss: Yes, she was a personality in her own right and worked very hard. When he was Viceroy of India, and when he was Supreme Allied Commander Southeast Asia and had to cope with this disintegrating war front, she, I would say, had almost an equal part with him in trying to settle things down and taking care of the wounded and the sick and so forth. And as head of St. John's of Jerusalem, she did an outstanding job, and probably the hard work she did, often in unhealthy places, may have contributed to her early death.

---
*Lady Edwina Ashley Mountbatten died on 21 February 1960.

Q: Well, she had had a reputation as a free spirit and a hedonist, really, before World War II, and then she seemed to be transformed by the experience.

Admiral Strauss: Yes, because, as I think I mentioned before, early on they were sort of cafe society.

Q: He was a close friend of Edward VIII, and Edward VIII never did seem to take on his responsibilities as Mountbatten did.*

Admiral Strauss: Yes, yes. My impression of Edward VIII, whom I saw a couple of times, was he wasn't a nonentity at all, that this infatuation you might say ruined him. Because he wanted a job during the war and was made a major general but never was given any opportunity to be anything. He was kept sort of as a liaison officer, and that disgusted him, and he really dropped the bricks on that. I have a feeling that he had the potential to be a good king if he hadn't been sidetracked, but you may say, "Well, that was a weakness. If he had that weakness, that it might have destroyed him anyway." I don't know.

---

*Edward VIII (1894-1972) was Earl Mountbatten's cousin, close friend, and best man at his 1922 wedding. When Edward chose to abdicate his throne in December 1936 in the wake of strong protest at his engagement to a twice-divorced American, Wallis Warfield Simpson, he became the Duke of Windsor and lived in Austria and France. He served as governor of the Bahama Islands, 1940-45.

Strauss #4 - 359

Q: I'm sure it must have been a source of great pride to be picked to represent the United States in Admiral Mountbatten's funeral.

Admiral Strauss: Well, it was. It was evidence of his friendship, because I was very low on the totem pole as far as he was concerned. I would say that Mountbatten had few, if any, intimates. But he had a lot of admirers and a lot of people you could call friends, but they weren't very close to him. I don't know who was close to him. There was a former Chief of Naval Staff, Admiral Charles Lambe, when he was a captain, I always felt was a good friend of Mountbatten, someone that might be close to him.* But I hadn't known any other people; perhaps it's just because I didn't know them that I don't know the extent of their friendship. After Edwina Mountbatten died, we got a notice from him that I'm sure went to all his acquaintances. He said that during her lifetime they'd always welcomed getting Christmas cards that their numerous friends sent them. But that now she was gone, he didn't feel that he cope with them, and he hoped that his friends would remember him but wouldn't send him Christmas cards anymore.

Q: That's interesting. Did you correspond with him

---
*Admiral Sir Charles Lambe, RN, was First Sea Lord, 1959-60, succeeding Mountbatten in that post.

nevertheless?

Admiral Strauss: Yes. I have saved his letters and Christmas cards. And sometime I thought they might be of interest to some collection.

Q: Well, any summing up that you'd like to do on your naval career, Admiral?

Admiral Strauss: Well, if I had it to do over again, under the circumstances at that time, I'd do it. If it was a question of going in today, I'm not so sure, except for command, which is always attractive.

To oversimplify it, the Navy in those days was a good club. Everybody knew one another. Ninety percent of the officers were Naval Academy graduates. And I suppose that if I were the proper age to start today, it wouldn't seem anything out of the ordinary, and I'd be happy in it. I remember after my father had been retired some time, he and Admiral Johnson were talking together one time, and one of them said, "Well, we've seen the best of this. The Navy will never be the same again." And I thought this was just two old men talking together, and really didn't amount to anything, but I realize how right they were. I think if I said the same thing today probably the youngsters would say, "Well this is an old man talking." But I still think that my 30-odd years can't be duplicated again.

Q: Each generation has both its advantages and disadvantages.

Admiral Strauss: Chiefs of Naval Operations whom I respect, like Jim Holloway and Admiral Watkins, all say that the Navy is in better shape today, that's it's never been more heads-up than it is now.* I have a hard time believing it because they've destroyed the rank structure of the Navy and all services, and that happened during the war, when you saw a commander previously, you knew what his background had been and what his qualifications were, although commanders might have had quite different careers.

The fact that you're now an ensign for only one and a half years and there aren't any promotion exams, and that you can get to be a lieutenant commander in six or seven years; I just can't see how the quality of the officer corps is what it once was. Now that may be prejudice, and I may not know what I'm talking about, but it occurs to me that it's very hard to have a completely efficient service unless you have some structure and stick to it.

Q: Well, really, we don't have a means of measuring

---
*Admiral James L. Holloway III, USN, was Chief of Naval Operations, 1974-78; Admiral James D. Watkins, USN, was Chief of Naval Operations, 1982-86.

today's Navy in combat---fortunately. The Navy that you served in in World War II was tested and acquitted itself very well.

Admiral Strauss: Yes. After the first flurry, the naval commanders stayed pretty much through the rest of the war. That wasn't as true of the Army, and, of course, the Air Force was completely a new creation. And the story about Air Force generals having to have a card to show they're old enough to have a drink in a bar is an exaggeration, but not too much of one. So, of course, things are so highly technical now, that the firemen and the seamen of my early days probably couldn't cope with the radars and sonars and so forth. My next question is, can the people of today, under pressure, cope with the sonars and radars, and keep them going and the super-speed gun predictors, and so forth? I just don't know.

Q: Well, I'm sure there are some who are, but I think also that some of the men back in the Twenties or Thirties or Forties--had they faced the same type of equipment--would have mastered it also.

Admiral Strauss: I think that's true. Yes, of course, one of the things now that they have for officers and enlisted men, is much more specialized schooling than we had in my day. That may make a difference. It may overcome this, what seems to me a gap. It's quite possible, the fact that they are better trained. I was shocked to see a ribbon on a bluejacket and also on a chaplain. And I asked the latter what that ribbon meant. It meant that one had had at least six months sea duty during of the past year. Well, I won't comment on that because I couldn't use the right words.

Q: The very fact that you bring it up is a comment.

What would you say were your greatest pleasures and satisfactions, Admiral? Would it be the command tours?

Admiral Strauss: Yes. I think my four commands and my year at the Imperial Defence College were--and I must say that I enjoyed my tour as an assistant naval attaché very much. All in all, I don't think I had any tours in which I was unhappy. I sometimes think, perhaps, getting pushed around as a junior officer--and looking back on it I can well understand why I was pushed around, because I don't think I was a very good junior officer.

Q: Do you have any final thoughts before we conclude this?

Admiral Strauss: I'm happy to have been able to put this on the record, and hope that some of the comments will be of some use to someone someday.

Q: I'm sure they will and I'm grateful to you for having made that contribution.

Admiral Strauss: I'm grateful to you for having been patient enough to listen through it all.

Q: Thank you very much.

Appendices

1. List of Elliott B. Strauss's contributions to the U.S. Naval Institute Proceedings.

2. Manuscript written by Elliott B. Strauss concerning events on board the USS Hannibal in the early 1920s.

Material by Elliott B. Strauss

Published in the U. S. Naval Institute Proceedings

(Ranks shown as of the time of publication)

Lieutenant, Comment on article titled "Petty Officers," August 1933, pages 1191-1192

Lieutenant, "Explosives," December 1931, pages 1612-1615

Lieutenant Commander, "A Home on the Ocean Wave," August 1939, pages 1165-1170

Rear Admiral (Retired), "Stars, Stripes, and Gresham's Law," March 1968, pages 51-57

Rear Admiral (Retired), Comment concerning the Navy's Judge Advocate General's Corps, June 1975, page 83

Rear Admiral (Retired), "A 'Tin Soldier' is a Good Soldier," February 1972, pages 94-97

Rear Admiral (Retired), Comment on article titled "Too Many Senior Officers, Not Enough for Them To Do," December 1974, page 89

Fourteen Decks and No Bottom

Legend has it that the above title describes the ship's characteristics of the USS Abarenda; however, if you trouble to read this article, you may agree that, for a time, they were more nearly those of the USS Hannibal.

Only the old timers will remember that there was a Hannibal on the Navy list, though she met her end as a bomb target as recently as 1944.

The Hannibal was built in 1898 by the British firm of J. Blumer & Company of Sunderland. She was bought by the U.S. Navy that same year to serve as a collier for the coal starved fleet in the Spanish American War. In 1911 she was assigned to the U.S. Survey Squadron but had time out during World War I as a subchaser tender in Plymouth, England, after which she resumed her surveying role.

In 1923, when this part of her story begins, she was a participant in an international marine survey effort to rechart areas where obsolete charts were a danger to commerce. Hannibal was assigned the waters between the Isle of Pines and Cuba. The town of Batabano, in this gulf, is a sugar port and a major center for sponges. Charts of adjoining waters were from original Spanish surveys and certain islands were shown as much as ten miles out of place.

The Hannibal displaced 4,000 tons, was 274 feet

overall and had an all-out speed of seven knots. She had a single screw, two scotch boilers and an iron hull (which would "dish" under too vigorous a blow from a chipping hammer). Her hull was painted white; her upper works, spar colored.

The other ships of the Navy Survey Squadron were two former yachts, the Niagara and the Nokomis. These were sleek and chic and faster than the Hannibal, and rather looked down their classical bows at her. However, they had virtually no stowage space, a commodity the latter had in abundance.

These three ships reported directly and separately to the Hydrographer of the Navy in Washington. They surveyed separate areas. There was no intermediate administrative or tactical superior, and thereby hangs this tale.

At this period, Hannibal's home port was Philadelphia, where she spent the summer turning her collected data into charts. She was based on Key West during the survey season which ran from December to May.

At the time of the 1923-24 season the commanding officer of the Hannibal was Commander E. C. S. Parker, of the Naval Academy class of 1902; her executive officer was Lieutenant Commander S. L. H. Hazard of the class of 1904. Other officers who figure prominently in this history were Lieutenant Emil Swanson, a mustang; the ship's doctor; the boatswain; plus a miscellaneous list of junior officers, petty officers, and nonrated men.

When outfitted for her survey duties, the Hannibal was accompanied by a former coal barge, which was decked over for officers' quarters with a superimposed tent to house the enlisted men, and four 34-foot, coal-burning steam launches. This impedimenta was picked up from the Key West base and convoyed to the survey grounds. On reaching the proper area, the barge was towed by the launches to a chosen anchorage, where it became a houseboat for the launch crews. The steam launches served as sounding boats. They, with the aid of hand leads, and quintants to locate their positions, ran the survey lines in water to the depth of ten fathoms. The parent ship ran soundings with its fathometer in deeper water, usually a number of miles from the barge and its boats.

Before leaving Key West in December of 1923, it became evident to observers in the ship that the captain's sobriety was in question. After reaching the Cuban survey grounds, this was no longer a question--he was quite evidently and permanently drunk. He seldom left his cabin and it was discovered that his tipple was absinthe. The effect of this can be imagined--discipline irtually disappeared. Its disappearance extended to the houseboat and its launches. The four very junior sounding-boat officers, with their mustang lieutenant "housemother," were incapable of keeping rum out of their steam launches. Wonderful to relate the sounding work went on, but for the rest, both in the Hannibal and in its auxiliaries, any resemblance to a Navy ship was purely accidental.

At this juncture, it is probable that the situation could have been saved by the executive officer taking the always drastic step of relieving the commanding officer. He did not, and in a partial extenuation, it must be stated that for him to have succeeded he needed the backing of the medical officer. This officer, recently married, had installed his young wife in quarters in Havana, at the other end of Cuba. He spent little time in the ship, but was habitually on undocumented leave in the metropolis. The medical officer was happy with things as they were and could not be counted on to take any steps to upset the status quo.

The executive officer, feeling himself unable to cope with conditions in the ship, removed himself to the houseboat and "took charge" there.

One officer, a big man physically with backbone of the same order, was Lieutenant Swanson. He was not intimidated by events and, for his part, attempted to impose the needed discipline. As might be expected, his popularity with the more obstreperous members of the crew was not high. Some of those, returning from shore leave late one night, threw a brick through the transom of his cabin. Fortunately his location was such it missed him. Later, seven of the unruly group massed to raid his room with the intent to assault him. Ensign Walfrid Nyquist (class of '21) stationed himself at the break in the deck with his .45

pistol and announced that if the attempt was made, six of the seven would be permanently unsuccessful. The expedition was abandoned.

While the ship was in Key West for R & R, a party was held in the naval base, which some of the Hannibal officers attended. An altercation arose between a ship's officer and one attached to the base. The Hannibal officer returned aboard, roused a few of his friends, returned to the base, called out his opponent now dressed in his pajamas, and severely punched him. This time Commander Parker exercised command judgment. Knowing that there would be repercussions ashore, he got the ship underway and stood out.

The denouement and the captain's downfall came about in this fashion: One day while the ship was in Key West, the captain chased a young seaman from his cabin up on deck. The terrified young man jumped over the side and swam ashore. The captain ordered that the incident not be logged, so the seaman was never declared a deserter. He made his way home and reported the goings-on to his parents who notified their congressman. He, in turn, reported the incident to the Navy Department.

In March of 1924, the Atlantic Fleet was wintering in Guantanamo. Hannibal was ordered thither. On anchoring, a boat from the flagship came alongside.

Marine guards went aboard and took Commander Parker away.

A court of inquiry was held at which a number of iniquities besides those recounted above came to light. A star witness was Boatswain Ullman. When subjected to the "Did you or did you not see . . .?" type of question, he "stonewalled" by droning on about the extreme temperatures in the tropics, the hardships to the men, etc. However, in response to the question as to whether he remembered a particular day, he electrified the gathering by saying, "Yes, that was the day the captain tried to crucify the boatswain's mate." Further questioning brought out that the captain, displeased because the boatswain's mate refused to drink with him, ordered the carpenter's mate to erect a cross on the quarter deck. Fortunately, the captain went on drinking, and the project fell through.

The upshot of the court of inquiry was that Commander Parker was assigned to St. Elizabeths Hospital where he retired that same year and where he remained for some years. His brother was a serving congressman, which may have influenced the leniency in the disposition of the case.

Commander William T. Conn (class of 1902) was ordered detached as executive officer of the _Idaho_ and to command _Hannibal_. He came aboard with a cleanup squad of officers and leading petty officers. Most of the officers in the ship were detached, as were all members of the crew considered in any way involved in the events recounted above. Under Commander Conn's stern, but just command,

<u>Hannibal</u> sailed calmer seas.

The concatenation of circumstances which resulted in this scandal could probably never be duplicated. A new set of regulations is not required to guard against commanding officers on detached duty who are hooked on absinthe. However, the events do make one appreciate the usefulness of an unbroken chain of command.

Index

to

Reminiscences of Rear Admiral Elliott B. Strauss

U.S. Navy (Retired)

Acuff, Captain Jasper T., USN (USNA, 1921B)
   At the end of the war, complained to Strauss about an officer he'd transferred off the Charles Carroll (APA-28) in 1944, 254

Africa
   See Algeria; Morocco; North Africa; Somalia; South Africa; Tunisia

Agency for International Development (AID)
   Strauss was nominated as director of this agency in the mid-1950s, 348; sent aid to Tunisia in the late 1950s, 352; Strauss sent to Pakistan and Madagascar to evaluate the AID missions there in the early 1960s, 353

Algeria
   British banker entertained Concord (CL-10) officers during shakedown cruise to Algiers in 1923-24, 37; Concord's propellers accidently sank a French tug in the Algiers harbor, 37; the Charles Carroll (APA-28) transported Moroccan troops to Algiers in 1944, 252; Destroyer Flotilla Six visited Algiers in the early 1950s, 328; Strauss and other officers were asked to attend the wedding in Algiers of an American reserve officer to the daughter of the Spanish minister, 330

Amphibious Exercises
   Discussion of some participants in amphibious exercises off Culebra in 1937-38, 154, 157, 167

Amphibious Force Europe
   Instituted in the early 1940s to help the British increase the serviceability of their landing craft prior to the Normandy invasion, 230-231

Anderson, Captain Walter S., USN (USNA, 1903)
   As naval attaché in London in 1936, represented the U.S. Navy at the funeral of King George V, 126-127; pursued by those seeking good seating for the coronation of King George VI, 129; lived in a Washington, D.C. nursing home prior to his death in 1981, 129; nationally ranked tennis player, 130; as Commander Battleships in 1941, indirectly held responsible for loss of battleships at Pearl Harbor, 130-132; letter of thanks from King Edward VIII, 130-131; Strauss's relationship with Anderson, 133-135; at the coronation of King George VI in 1937, 135; Strauss's assessment of Anderson, 141, 144-145, 218-219; contacted by the director of naval intelligence in the mid-1930s to get after Strauss to gather information about Alfred Mahan for a biography, 209; visited with Strauss when the USS Fresno (CL-121) visited England in 1947, 295

Andrews, Captain Charles L., Jr., USN (USNA, 1919)
   During World War II, Andrews worked with reserve
   Lieutenant Douglas Fairbanks on a project using records
   to make deceptive sounds, 244

Arkansas, USS (BB-33)
   Strauss assigned to this battleship as a gunnery officer
   in 1926, 68; modernized in the mid-1920s, 69; plane
   catapult was on top of a gun turret, 69; Strauss's duties
   as turret officer, 70--71, 73-74; claustrophobic gunner's
   mate on board, 74-75; watch sections, 76

Arkansas, USS (BM-7)
   Because Strauss's father was serving in this monitor when
   his son was born in 1903, the child was appointed to the
   ship's mess, 2-3

Army-Navy Football Game
   Strauss's recollections of attending this football
   classic in New York in the early 1920s, 20-21

Artificial Harbors
   See Harbors

Asiatic Fleet
   Commander in Chief Asiatic Fleet, Admiral Joseph Strauss,
   was allowed a naval yacht for his family in the early
   1920s, 5

Astor, William Vincent
   Friendship with President Franklin Roosevelt in the
   1930s, 98-99

Backhouse, Admiral Sir Roger, RN
   As Commander in Chief of the Mediterranean Fleet in the
   1930s, fired his chief of staff, Admiral Sir Bertram
   Ramsay, 246

Atlantic Squadron, U.S. Fleet
   Title changed from Training Detachment, U.S. Fleet, in
   the late 1930s, 164-165; see also Training Detachment,
   U.S. Fleet

Aurora, HMS
   Strauss toured this British cruiser as a naval attaché in
   the mid-1930s, 150-151

Aviation
    Arkansas (BB-33) plane catapult was on top of a gun turret in the mid-1920s, 69; The Manley (DD-74) had carrier plane guard duty in the early 1930s, 110-111; Strauss was turned down for aviation duty because of a slight eye problem, 115; see also Battleship Aviation

Baker, Midshipman Kenneth, USN
    Anecdote concerning his resignation from the Naval Academy in the early 1920s, 25-26; anecdote about temporary religious conversion in an effort to escape mandatory chapel attendance, 26

Ballentine, Rear Admiral John J., USN (USNA, 1918)
    When Ballentine joined Admiral Richmond K. Turner's staff in early 1946, Strauss's duties diminished, 275-276

Bartlett, Lieutenant Commander Harold T., USN (USNA, 1911)
    Arkansas (BB-33) first lieutenant's reaction to the decorated wardroom of the Florida (BB-30) in 1927, 75

Baruch, Herman
    U.S. ambassador to Holland in 1947 entertained the crew of the Fresno (CL-121) during that cruiser's visit to Rotterdam, 287-288

Bastedo, Captain Paul H., USN (USNA, 1908)
    Strauss's recollections of Bastedo as chief of staff to Commander U.S. Naval Forces Europe during World War II, 231-232

Battleship Division Two
    Competition among unit ships, 78-81; staff officers in the mid-1920s, 79-80

Battleships
    Strauss toured Vickers Works in England in the 1930s where a King George V-class battleship was under construction, 126, 151; see also Arkansas (BB-33); Connecticut (BB-18); Florida (BB-30); Mississippi (BB-41); Nevada (BB-36); New York (BB-34); West Virginia (BB-48); Wyoming (BB-32); North Dakota (BB-29)

Beatty, Admiral of the Fleet David
    Strauss marched in Beatty's funeral in 1936, 123; attempted to equalize the status of various naval officer specialties in the 1920s, 229

Behn, Lieutenant Edward J., USNR
    Married the daughter of the Spanish minister to Algeria in an elaborate wedding attended by Strauss in the early 1950s, 330

Berkeley, HMS
    Lost during the August 1942 Dieppe raid, 200

Biesemeir, Captain Harold, USN (USNA, 1918)
    Former commanding officer of the Charles Carroll (APA-28) was mistakenly told by Admiral Ernest King that he'd never make captain, 251

Bitterman, Lieutenant Commander Frank J., USN (USNA, 1941)
    As first lieutenant of the Fresno (CL-121) in 1947, was unhappy about the cruiser's deployment schedule, 287

Blake, Vice Admiral Sir Geoffrey, RN
    As liaison officer to Admiral Harold Stark in the mid-1940s, acted as best man at the wedding of an American petty officer and a British service woman, though he didn't approve, 292

Bleasdale, HMS
    Strauss rode in this Canadian ship during the August 1942 Dieppe raid, 199-201

Blue, Lieutenant (junior grade) John Stuart, USN (USNA, 1925)
    Anecdote from his service as aide to President Franklin Roosevelt in the early 1930s, 99

Bolte, Lieutenant Colonel Charles L., USA
    Anecdote about Bolte as a military observer in London at the start of U.S. involvement in World War II, 188-189

Bonsal, Philip W.
    As deputy chief of the U.S. mission to The Hague in 1947, attended a reception when the Fresno (CL-121) visited Rotterdam, 293

Boone, Rear Admiral Walter F., USN (USNA, 1921A)
    Assessed by Strauss as director of the Strategic Planning Division of OpNav in the late 1940s, 307-308

Bourguiba, Habib
    President of Tunisia in the late 1950s wanted to dam the Nabana river, 352-353

Bradley, General of the Army Omar N., USA (USMA, 1915)
   Commented in the late 1940s that naval officers were
   mostly "fancy Dans," 308

Brady, Captain Parke H., USN (USNA, 1930)
   As naval attaché in Rotterdam in 1947, entertained the
   crew of the Fresno (CL-121) at his own expense, 288

Brazil
   The cruiser Concord (CL-10) visited Pernambuco during
   Mardi Gras in 1924, 41; Rear Admiral Ernest Von Heimburg
   was so taken with Rio de Janeiro during a visit in 1947
   that he asked to be the next head of the U.S. naval
   mission there, 282; high-quality 5-inch guns made in
   Brazilian factory, 282

Brind, Vice Admiral Sir Eric J. P., RN
   Strauss visited with Brind, who was president of the
   Royal Naval College at Greenwich, during a 1947 Northern
   European deployment in the Fresno (CL-121), 294-295

Bronson, Captain Amon, Jr., USN (USNA, 1896)
   Assessed as skipper of the Arkansas (BB-33) in the mid-
   1920s, 77-78

Brooks, USS (DD-232)
   Recommisioned from the reserve fleet for World War II,
   52; neutrality patrols off Nova Scotia and Panama, 167-
   170, 173; 5-inch guns removed, 171, 173; discussion of
   officers, 171-172

Brown, Lieutenant Commander John J., USN (USNA, 1912)
   Naval Academy officer in the early 1920s reprimanded a
   midshipman who attempted to shirk mandatory chapel
   attendance, 26

Brown, Rear Admiral Wilson, USN (USNA, 1902)
   As Superintendent of the Naval Academy in the late 1930s,
   brought along a staff officer from a previous assignment,
   even though he knew of this officers wild ways, 155-156

Browne, Commodore Davenport, USN (USNA, 1917)
   As Commandant of the 12th Naval District in early 1945,
   helpful to Charles Carroll (APA-28) skipper Strauss in
   quickly removing the executive officer who was found to
   be homosexual, 255

Bryan, Lieutenant Commander Hamilton V., USN (USNA, 1913)
   As first lieutenant of the Florida (BB-30) in 1927,
   decorated the battleship's wardroom, 75

Bucknell University
   Strauss was chosen as director of the engineering department here in 1956, 348-349; discussion of the engineering program, 349-350

Bullitt, William C.
   Strauss met this former ambassador to the Soviet Union and France at a dinner party given by CNO Admiral Forrest Sherman in the early 1950s, and found him to have an overly positive outlook, 323

Burke, Admiral Arleigh A., USN (USNA, 1923)
   Didn't stand out as exceptional as a midshipman at the Naval Academy, 22; Strauss felt Burke's promotion to commodore is an example of the best use of the rank, 256; promotion to rear admiral held up as a result of his work during the unification crisis of the late 1940s, 303, 309-310; as director of Strategic Plans in the early 1950s, 312-313, 336-337, 339; nominated Strauss as director of the U.S. Agency for International Cooperation in the mid-1950s, 348

Byrnes, James F.
   As Secretary of State in January 1946, admonished military participants in United Nations committee to be more circumspect since press leaks were inevitable, 273

Campbell, Commander Gordon, RN
   Strauss met this World War I hero during a cruise to South Africa in the Concord (CL-10) in 1923-24, 38-39

Canada
   Canadians played a prominent role in the August 1942 Dieppe raid, 197-201, 211-212; in 1977, a Canadian television documentary show concluded that the Dieppe raid was necessary, but that the Canadian troops were too inexperienced to have been relied on so heavily, 201-203

Carusi, Commander Eugene C., USNR (USNA, 1928)
   Beachmaster injured during June 1944 Normandy invasion, 236

Cease, Ensign John M., Jr., USN
   Despite Strauss's initial misgivings when Crease was assigned as the gunnery officer of the Brooks (DD-232) in the late 1930s, he turned out to be a fine addition to the destroyer, 172

Charles Carroll (APA-28), USS
　　Commanding officer Strauss had the executive officer relieved in early 1945 because he was homosexual, 251, 254-255; role in the invasion of South France in 1944, 252; transported Moroccan troops from Naples to Algiers in 1944, 252; had been a passenger liner before the war, 252; officers in 1944, 253; engineer transferred off at San Francisco, 253-254; service in the South Pacific in early 1945, 256-257; preparations for amphibious assaults, 260; officer contingent, 260-262; junior officer killed during Okinawa landing, 261; at Okinawa, 262-263; R&R in Hawaii, 263-264; ship's namesake, 265; trip to Manus Island without zigzagging in mid-1945, 266-267; intended for use in the invasion of Japan, 267

Chilean Navy
　　Purchased decommissioned light cruisers from the United States in 1951, 314-315; characterized as the best Navy of the South American countries, 315-316

Christiania (Oslo), Norway
　　Strauss's recollections from liberty here during a summer cruise in the early 1920s, 28, 31

Christie, Lieutenant Commander Ralph W., USN　(USNA, 1915)
　　Strauss's recollections of Christie as torpedo officer at the Naval Torpedo Station in the early 1930s, 92

Churchill, Sir Winston
　　Selected Lord Louis Mountbatten to be Chief of Combined Operations in late 1941, 190; his advisors had to rein him in on some of his wilder ideas, 197; gave approval to Dieppe raid in 1942, 197; ironic that he was not elected on the heels of victory in World War II, 304; Churchill's doctor invaded his privacy with a book in the mid-1960s, 304-305; anecdote showing he lacked a sense of humor about himself, 325-326

Clark, Rear Admiral Frank H., USN　(USNA, 1893)
　　As Commander Destroyers Scouting Fleet in the late 1920s, was lenient with the Toucey (DD-282) when she lost part of her top mast in a brush with a tender, 82-83

Clark, Major General Mark W., USA　(USMA, 1917)
　　Expedition to North Africa in the early 1940s, 229-230

Coaling Ship
　　Strauss's experiences during summer midshipman cruises in the early 1920s, 28

Coast Guard, U.S.
　Inspections of merchant shipping off Panama in the late
　1930s, 168-169

Cold Weather Operations
　Difficulties encountered by the Brooks (DD-232) during
　neutrality patrols off Nova Scotia in 1939-40, 167-168

Combined Operations
　Lord Louis Mountbatten selected for this vice admiral's
　billet as a captain in 1941, 190; American officers were
　integrated right into the staff, not used as liaisons,
　191, 247; tentative planning for the Normandy invasion,
　194-196; planned and participated in 1942 Dieppe raid,
　197-201, 211-212; in on planning for the landings on
　North Africa, 219-221

Commodores
　Strauss feels there are three reasons that captains
　attain the wartime rank of commodore, 256

Communist Bloc Countries
　NATO groups monitored contraband being filtered into
　Communist countries in the early 1950s, 343-346; see also
　Soviet Union

Concord, USS (CL-10)
　Shakedown cruise to Africa in 1923-24, 37-43; sank French
　tug in Algiers harbor, 37-38; took on hardworking
　American merchant seaman at St. Helena, 40-41; crew was
　well received in African ports during cruise, 42;
　discussion of officers in the early 1920s, 44, 47-48;
　seaworthiness and handling characteristics, 47, 49-50,
　178; embarked admiral insisted that a large hull number
　be painted on the bow, 50-51

Connecticut, USS (BB-18)
　Lost use of her propellers during a midshipman summer
　cruise in the early 1920s, 29

Conolly, Admiral Richard L., USN (USNA, 1914)
　Conolly's quote on types of Chiefs of Naval Operations,
　213; as Commander U.S. Naval Forces Eastern Atlantic and
　Mediterranean in 1947, used the Fresno (CL-121) as his
　flagship, 288-289; assessed by Strauss, 289-290; Strauss
　tried to convince him that CinCNELM was the best job in
　the Navy, 289; visited by CNO Admiral Forrest Sherman in
　the early 1950s, 322

Consultative Commission (CoCom)
   This association of NATO countries plus Japan decided
   what strategic materials can go to Communist bloc nations
   in the early 1950s, 343

Cook, Allen Blow
   English professor at the Naval Academy in the late 1930s
   gave midshipmen protocol and cultural training, 164

Costobadie, Lieutenant Commander Ackroyd N. P., RN
   Anecdote concerning Costabadie as an officer on Combined
   Operations staff in 1942 and his boss, Captain John
   Hughes-Hallett, 204

Couble, Lieutenant (junior grade) Alexander J., USN (USNA, 1920)
   Couble, a division officer in the Concord (CL-10) in
   1924, was upset about having a merchant seaman picked up
   in St. Helena assigned to his division--until the man
   proved to be extremely hardworking, 41

Cramp's Ship and Engine Building Company
   Quality of work on the USS Concord (CL-10) in the early
   1920s, 36-37, 43

Craven, Captain Francis S., USN (USNA, 1911)
   Assessed as captain of the Nashville (CL-43) in the early
   1940s, 175-176; required that a department head be on
   deck at all times, 180

Cripps, Sir Richard Stafford
   Strauss was disappointed with Cripps's address to
   students at the Imperial Defence College when the
   Chancellor of the Exchequer spoke in 1948, 303-304

Crosley, Lieutenant (junior grade) Floyd S., USN (USNA, 1919)
   One-eyed junior officer assigned to the Naval Academy in
   the early 1920s, 21

Cruisers
   CNO Admiral Forrest Sherman wanted to keep one
   antiaircraft class cruiser in commission in the late
   1940s-early 1950s, 312; see also Fresno, (CL-121);
   Concord, (CL-10); Indianapolis, (CA-35); Little Rock,
   (CL-92); Nashville, (CL-43); Phoenix (CL-46); Toledo (CA-
   133); Trenton (CL-11); HMS Aurora

Cuba
  U.S. Navy ships surveyed off Cuba in the mid-1920s, 52-56; U.S. destroyers exercised off Guantánamo in the late 1920s, 85; some larger ships smuggled liquor on board when they went into Guantánamo in the 1920s, 109; the Fresno (CL-121) made her shakedown cruise to Guantánamo in 1947, 281, 283-284

Culebra
  Amphibious exercises off Culebra during the winter of 1937-38, 154, 157

Cutts, Midshipman Richard M., Jr., USN (USNA, 1923)
  Strauss's Naval Academy roommate was an expert shot, 23

Damage Control
  Not taken too seriously in the Concord (CL-10) in the mid-1920s, 46

Davis, Rear Admiral Arthur C., USN (USNA, 1915)
  Advised Strauss not to take a staff job with Admiral Richmond K. Turner in the fall of 1945, 269

de Booy, Rear Admiral Alfred
  Strauss had a reunion with de Booy--whom he had known in London in the 1930s when both were naval attachés--when the Fresno (CL-121) visited Rotterdam in 1947, 286

de Gaulle, General Charles
  Was not immediately recognized when he visited the U.S. Navy headquarters in London in 1942, 213

DeLany, Rear Admiral Walter S., USN (USNA, 1912)
  As Commandant of the Third Naval District in the 1950s, furious that Strauss had been sent to inspect reserve destroyers in his district, 333-335

Denfeld, Admiral Louis E., USN (USNA, 1912)
  Strauss's recollections of saying goodbye to CNO Denfeld when he left office in 1949, 302-303, 309

Denmark
  Rear Admiral Alfred Johnson gave dinner for Prince Knud in Copenhagen in the late 1930s, 162-163

Dennison, Captain Robert L., USN (USNA, 1923)
  Strauss wrote reports on the weekly meetings of the Military Staff Committee of the Security Council of the United Nations for Dennison, who was on the Military Diplomatic Committee of OpNav in 1946, 276

Destroyer Flotilla Six
  Background to Strauss's taking command in 1951, 321; makeup of flotilla, 321, 326; Strauss's duties as commander, 326-327, 329-330, 332-333; exercised in the Mediterranean, 328; took part in NATO exercise Grand Slam, 328-329, 331; unsatisfactory arrangement of reserve destroyers in this flotilla, 332-335

Destroyers
  "Hunt"-class destroyers played predominant role in August 1942 Dieppe raid, 198-201; Strauss was unsatisfied with operations of reserve destroyers operating with Destroyer Flotilla Six in the early 1950s, 332-335; see also Brooks (DD-232); Joseph Stauss (DDG-16); Manley (DD-74); Reuben James (DD-245); Toucey (DD-282); William M. Wood (DD-715)

Deyo, Rear Admiral Morton L., USN (USNA, 1911)
  Strauss's assessment of Deyo, 239-240; Admiral Richmond Kelly Turner's assessment of Deyo, 240

Diane
  French naval yacht used to chase Arab dhows across the Red Sea in the mid-1920s, 39

Dieppe Raid
  Prime Minister Winston Churchill wanted an operation that would get the Canadians more involved in the war, 197-198; Combined Operations staff planned 1942 raid, 198; narrative of action, 198-201; in 1977, a Canadian documentary concluded that the raid was necessary, but that the Canadians were too inexperienced to have been relied on so heavily, 201-203; Strauss feels that the wrong lessons were learned from the raid, 211-212

Dietrich, Captain Neil K., USN (USNA, 1923)
  Close to his boss, CNO Admiral Forrest Sherman, in the early 1950s, 322

Discipline
  Trouble with the crew of the Hannibal (AG-1) in the mid-1920s, 64-65; quality of the crews of the Toucey (DD-282) and the Blakeley in the late 1920s, 86; in the Manley (DD-74) in the early 1930s, 104-105

Djibouti
  Strauss's recollections of Djibouti from his cruise there in 1923-24 in the Concord (CL-10), 38-39

Doyle, Captain James H., USN (USNA, 1920)
  When Doyle joined Admiral Richmond K. Turner's staff in early 1946, Strauss's duties on the staff diminished, 275-276

Draemel, Commander Milo F., USN (USNA, 1906)
  Strauss's friendship with Draemel, who was on the staff of Commander Battleship Division Two in the mid-1920s, 80

Drexler, Ensign Henry C., USN (USNA, 1924)
  Killed in a turret explosion in the Trenton (CL-11) in 1924, 72

Dulles, John Foster
  Represented the State Department on the trusteeship committee at the first General Assembly of the United Nations in January 1946, 272-273

Duncan, Admiral Donald B., USN (USNA, 1917)
  As Vice Chief of Naval Operations in 1951, role in getting Strauss assigned as destroyer flotilla commander, 321

Edward VIII, King
  Letter of thanks to American naval attaché Captain Walter Anderson prior to his abdication in 1936, 130-131; reception of German delegation during diplomatic corps levee in 1936, 146-147; abdication in December 1936, 147-148; assessed by Strauss, 358

Eisenhower, General Dwight D., USA (USMA, 1915)
  Strauss felt General Eisenhower should have made a British officer his Supreme Allied Commander chief of staff rather than relying on Lieutenant General W. B. Smith, 226; daring decision to go ahead with Normandy invasion in June 1944, 235

Elbrick, Burke
  First secretary of the U.S. embassy in Lisbon in 1941 hosted Strauss on his way to London, 183-183

Elizabeth, Queen
  Graciousness at London party in 1948, 306

Eller, Rear Admiral Ernest M., USN (Ret.) (USNA, 1925)
  As director of the engineering department at Bucknell University, asked Strauss to be his successor in the mid-1950s, 348-349

Elliott, Lieutenant Commander Richard M., Jr., USN
   Manley (DD-74) executive officer killed by a depth charge
   explosion on board in 1918, 97

Engineering Plant
   Discussion of the plant in the Toucey (DD-282) in the
   late 1920s, 84-85; in the Manley (DD-74) in the early
   1930s, 102

English Channel
   Difficulties for the Fresno (CL-121) holding gunnery
   practice in the channel in 1947, 286

Enlisted Personnel
   Quality of enlisted men in the 1920s and 1930s, 33-34,
   102-103; training in the early 1930s, 103-104, 362-363;
   relationship between officers and enlisteds in the Manley
   (DD-74) in the early 1930s, 112

Erwin, Ensign Marcus, Jr., USN (USNA, 1923)
   Killed in a gun turret explosion in the Mississippi, (BB-41) in 1924, 72

Everett, Washington
   Guns removed from the Brooks (DD-232) here in the late
   1930s, 170-171, 173

Fahrion, Rear Admiral Frank G., USN (USNA, 1917)
   As Commander Destroyers Atlantic Fleet in the early
   1950s, got Strauss to inspect the reserve destroyers in
   various districts, 333-335; assessed by Strauss, 336

Fairbanks, Lieutenant Douglas E., Jr., USNR
   Strauss's recollections of Fairbanks, who reported to him
   in London during World War II, 243-245

Fechteler, Admiral William M., USN (USNA, 1916)
   Lieutenant Fechteler offered Ensign Strauss a drink at an
   Annapolis restaurant during Prohibition, 18; assessed as
   popular junior officer, 21-22; example of sense of humor
   as Chief of Naval Operations in the early 1950s, 308

Finlay, Brigadier General Luke W., AUS (USMA, 1928)
   As Defense Deputy to U.S. Representative, Europe, in the
   early 1950s, 339

Flanigan, Commander Howard A., USN (Ret.) (USNA, 1910)
   Strauss's recollections of Flanigan as Admiral Harold
   Stark's deputy chief of staff in the early 1940s, 214-217

Florida, USS (BB-30)
   Anecdote concerning this battleship's wardroom after it was decorated by the first lieutenant in 1927, 75; expression "Florida fashion" was supposed to be complimentary, but came to mean something else, 78

Fog
   Measures taken to prevent groundings and collisions after 1923 incident at Point Arguello when seven destroyers collided, 113-114

Forrestel, Lieutenant Commander Emmet P., USN (USNA, 1920)
   Assumed an attaché position in Italy in the mid-1930s that was originally to be offered to Strauss, 117

France
   The Fresno (CL-121) visited Le Havre during Northern European deployment in 1947, 293-294

French Navy
   At Djibouti in the mid-1920s, 39-40; participated in NATO exercise Grand Slam in the early 1950s, 329, 331

Fresno, USS (CL-121)
   Discussion of her 5-inch guns, 179-180; fitting out at Kearny, New Jersey in 1946, 279; quality of ship's officers, 279-280; shakedown cruise to Guantánamo, 280-281, 283-284; sent to Uruguay for inauguration of new President in 1947, 281-282; armament, 283; some necessary parts for this cruiser were still in short supply due to the recent war, 284-285; Strauss upgraded the cabin silver, 284-285; deployment to Northern Europe in 1947, 285-290, 293-295; some members of the crew were reluctant to go on Northern European cruise, 285-287; Strauss's satisfaction with this command, 296-298; considered as a station ship in Europe in the late 1940s, 322

Frost, Commander Holloway H., USN (USNA, 1910)
   Strauss's recollections of Frost as commanding officer of the Toucey (DD-282) in the late 1920s, 81-84, 296-297

Fullinwider, Commander Simon P., Jr., USN (USNA, 1917)
   Strauss was pleased that Fullwinder, executive officer of the Nashville (CL-43) in the early 1940s, didn't smoke, 175

Furer, Captain Julius A., CC, USN (USNA, 1901)
   Represented the naval attachés stationed in London at the funeral of King George V in 1936, 127; toured HMS Aurora in the mid-1930s, 150

General Alava, USS (AG-5)
    Naval yacht allocated to Commander in Chief Asiatic Fleet
    in the early 1920s, 5

General Electric Company
    Strauss's employment as a civilian in G.E.'s long-range
    planning group, TEMPO, in the late 1960s, 354

Geodesy and Geophysics
    Strauss presented a paper by the Navy Hydrographic Office
    at a conference of scientists in Edinburgh in 1936, 148-
    149

George V, King
    Strauss marched in King George's funeral in 1936, 123;
    126-128

George VI, King
    Strauss's recollections of his coronation in May 1937,
    135-139; Strauss spoke with him during his visit to the
    Imperial Defence College in 1948, 302; death in 1952, 332

Germany, Federal Republic of
    Acting American commissioner in Berlin punished a German
    company that was accused of supplying technology to
    Communist bloc countries in the early 1950s, 345-346

Ghormley, Vice Admiral Robert L., USN (USNA, 1906)
    Strauss's impression of Ghormley as Commander U.S. Naval
    Forces in Europe in 1941, 187; Strauss feels Ghormley was
    prematurely relieved as Commander South Pacific Force in
    1942, 187-188; Joseph Strauss's opinion of Ghormley from
    duty with him in 1914, 187-188

Gibb, Lieutenant Commander Edwin D., USN (USNA, 1918)
    Assessed as commanding officer of the Manley (DD-74) in
    the early 1930s, 97

Gillette, Lieutenant Commander Norman C., USN (USNA, 1913)
    Strauss's assessment of the skipper of the Manley (DD-74)
    in the early 1930s, 97; injured while ice skating, 106-
    107

Great Britain
    Conservatism of military in late 1940s, 304; see also
    London; Royal Navy; Imperial Defence College; Royal Naval
    College; Edward VIII; King George V; King George VI;
    Queen Elizabeth; Princess Margaret

Griffin, Captain Robert M., USN (USNA, 1911)
    Guarded his prerogatives as commanding officer of the New York (BB-34) in the late 1930s, even though his was a flagship, 158

Gruenther, General Alfred M., USA (USMA, 1919)
    NATO Supreme Allied Commander Europe in the mid-1950s compared to his predecessor, 347-348

Gunnery Duty
    Strauss felt duty as a turret officer was one of the most professional jobs in the Navy, 70-71, 74

Guns
    Discussion of the 12-inch/50-caliber guns in the Arkansas (BB-33) in the mid-1920s, 70-71; safety precautions in the Arkansas, 73; turrets in King George V-class battleships, 126; 5-inch guns removed from the Brooks (DD-232) in the early 1940s, 171; discussion of rapid-fire 5-inch guns, 179-180; one lesson learned during the August 1943 Dieppe raid was that 4-inch guns were not heavy enough to permanently distract the enemy, 211; Brazilian factory that made high-quality 5-inch guns in the mid-1940s insisted on training machinists who had not worked on previous guns, 282

Habitability
    Conditions in the older battleships in the early 1920s, 29-30

Hamilton, Lieutenant Colonel Pierpont M., USA
    Awarded the Medal of Honor for his bravery at Arzeu in November 1942, 220-221

Hammond, Lieutenant Commander Paul L., USNR
    "Banished" from Washington by CNO Admiral Ernest King because of his familiarity with President Franklin D. Roosevelt in 1942, 189; introduced Strauss to Admiral Lord Louis Mountbatten, 190; his prediction about Commander Howard Flanigan came true, 215

Handy, Major Thomas T., USA
    Favorable assessment of Handy when he took part in amphibious exercises off Culebra in 1937-38, 157

Hannibal, USS (AG-1)
　　Surveyed off the coast of Cuba in the mid-1920s, 52-53, 66; discussion of officers, 53-54, 59-61; description of ship, 55-56; crewman left ship after being diagnosed as having a brain tumor, 57-58; junior officer deserted the ship at Key West after writing a bad check to cover a gambling debt, 60-61; reported directly to the hydrographer of the Navy, 63; outrageous behavior of the skipper, officers, and men before Strauss joined the crew led to the removal of the commanding officer in 1924, 63-65

Hansen, Helland
　　This Norwegian explorer was the main attraction at a geodesy conference in Edinburgh in 1936, 148-149

Harbors
　　Officer on Mountbatten's Combined Operations staff in the early 1940s was credited with originating the concept, of artificial harbors 195, 217; importance to Normandy invasion planning, 234-235, 238

Hart, Colonel Franklin A., USMC
　　Anecdote about Hart meeting a Royal Navy officer from the wealthy family of a large liquor manufacturer during World War II, 195-196

Hartman, Lieutenant Commander Kenneth P., USN (USNA, 1923)
　　Former naval observer with the British in the early days of World War II was frustrated that no one seemed interested in learning from British combat experiences, 182-183

Hatch, Lieutenant Commander William G. B., USN (USNA, 1913)
　　Easygoing as commanding officer of the Blakeley (DD-150) in the late 1920s, 85

Hawaii
　　Liberty in Honolulu during midshipmen summer cruise in the early 1920s, 32; the beach at Waikiki in 1945 compared unfavorably with what Strauss remembered from the early 1920s, 264

Hazard, Lieutenant Commander Stanton L. H., USN (USNA, 1904)
　　Hannibal (AG-1) executive officer in 1924 failed to put his skipper on report after some outlandish episodes, 64

Hearst, Mrs. William Randolph
   Strauss was detailed to accompany Mrs. Hearst throughout
   all the social duties entailed by the New York World's
   Fair in 1939, 159-161

Heffernan, Lieutenant John B., USN   (USNA, 1917)
   Assessed as junior officer in the Arkansas (BB-33) in the
   mid-1920s, 77-78

Hensel, Captain Karl G., USN   (USNA, 1923)
   While on Defense Department duty with NATO in the early
   1950s, was in charge of section monitoring strategic
   items being dispensed to foreign countries, 345

Hillsinger, Colonel Loren B., USA   (USNA, 1932)
   Injured during the August 1942 Dieppe raid, 200

Hiss, Alger
   Strauss's recollections of this State Department official
   from their joint attendance of the first session of the
   United Nations General Assembly in January 1946, 270,
   275-276

Holland
   When the Fresno (CL-121) visited Rotterdam in 1947, she
   was the first American naval vessel to go to Holland
   since World War II, 286; Strauss saw caged prisoners of
   war awaiting repatriation during 1947 visit, 286-287;
   hospitality toward Fresno crew, 287-288; concerns in NATO
   in the early 1950s, 342-343

Hollister, John B.
   As director of the International Cooperation
   Administration in the mid-1950s, asked for nominations
   for his replacement, 348

Hughes-Hallett, Captain John, RN
   As officer on Vice Admiral Mountbatten's Combined
   Operations staff in the early 1940s credited with
   originating the idea of building artificial harbors, 195,
   217; as naval commander of August 1942 Dieppe raid, 199-
   200, 203; assessed by Strauss, 203-204; donned a
   private's uniform to get a firsthand taste of how they
   were handled in transports, 204; as skipper of the
   Illustrious in 1948, lent Strauss his cabin in the
   carrier when he came to witness an exercise, 204-205

Humphreys, Lieutenant (junior grade) Charles W., USN (USNA, 1923)
   Arkansas (BB-33) gun turret officer in the mid-1920s got an excellent evaluation during a battle practice even though he hit one less target than Strauss, 71

Huse, Captain John O., USN (USNA, 1919)
   Huse was supposed to go with Strauss to North Africa in 1942, but weather prevented the trip, 228; discussion with Vice Admiral Louis Mountbatten about the quality of American versus British engineer officers, 228-229; designated Commander Amphibious Force Europe briefly in the early 1940s, 230-231

Hutchins, Captain Gordon, USN (USNA, 1913)
   As deputy naval commander of the U.S. forces involved in the June 1944 Normandy invasion, 216-217

Illustrious, HMS
   Commanding officer, Captain John Hughes-Hallett, loaned Strauss his cabin when the latter visited to witness an exercise in 1948, 204-205

Imperial Defence College, London
   The model for the U.S. National War College, 122; when Strauss was selected to attend in 1947, he was concerned that he had had too much English duty, 296; Strauss's recollections from attending IDC in 1948, 299-301; King George VI visited in 1948, 302; speakers, 300, 303-304

Indian Head, Maryland
   Naval Proving Ground at Indian Head had to be moved to Dahlgren, Virginia, early in the 20th Century to protect ships in the Chesapeake, 5

Indianapolis, USS (CA-35)
   Sunk in July 1945, the skipper was held accountable because he had not zigzagged, 266

Ingersoll, Rear Admiral Stuart H., USN (USNA, 1921A)
   Assessed as director of the Strategic Planning Division in the early 1950s, 308

Intelligence
   Intelligence gathering aspects of attaché duty in London in the mid-1930s, 126, 150-152; one reason for the assistant attaché billet in London was to help keep track of Japanese merchant activity, 206-209

Interplan
    Strauss worked as a civilian with this planning
    consultant firm in the 1960s, 354-355

Israel
    Strauss was sent to Israel as an inspector for the State
    Department in the mid-1960s, 353-354

Italian Navy
    Italian admiral in charge of the Venice naval district
    was hospitable to Destroyer Flotilla Six in the early
    1950s, 328; took part in NATO exercise Grand Slam in the
    early 1950s, 328

Jackson, Lieutenant (junior grade) Frederick H. W., USN
(USNA, 1921B)
    Hannibal (AG-1) officer drowned at Philadelphia in
    October 1925, 54

Jacobs, Helen Hull
    Tennis champion lived with the U.S. ambassador to England
    and his family in the mid-1930s, 145

Japan
    The United States kept track of Japanese merchant
    shipping in the 1930s through information provided from
    Lloyd's of London, 206-209

Jellicoe, Admiral of the Fleet John R.
    Strauss marched in Jellicoe's funeral in 1935, 123

Johnson, Captain Alfred W., USN (USNA, 1899)
    Anecdote about Johnson as director of naval intelligence
    in the late 1920s, 87; discussion of his family, 152-153;
    anecdote about how his parents met, 152-153; assessed as
    Commander Training Detachment, U.S. Fleet, in late 1930s,
    154-155; requested and received a change in title to
    Commander Atlantic Squadron, U.S. Fleet in the late
    1930s, 165-166; felt his generation had the best of naval
    duty, 360

Johnston, Captain Rufus Z., USN (USNA, 1895)
    Strauss's association with Johnston, who was chief of
    staff to Commander Battleship Division Two in the mid-
    1920s, 80

Joint Chiefs of Staff (JCS)
    When Strauss attended JCS meetings for his boss while
    serving in the Strategic Planning Division in the early
    1950s, he found that the services seemed to get along
    together well, 317-318

Joseph Strauss, USS (DDG-16)
    Named in honor of Strauss's father, 4; quality of
    materials used in outfitting this ship benefited from
    being several years after the end of World War II, 284

Kamikazes
    Strauss feels the Japanese were foolish to go after
    destroyer screens when they could have wreaked more havoc
    by attacking transports, 262-263

Kane, Lieutenant Commander John D. H., USN (USNA, 1918)
    During duty in the Bureau of Navigation in 1937, set
    Strauss up as aide to Commander Training Detachment, U.S.
    Fleet, Rear Admiral Alfred Johnson, 152

Kaplan, Captain Leonard, USN (USNA, 1922)
    Controversy over his class standing at the Naval Academy
    fueled by prejudice, 24-25; did a good job as naval
    constructor at Kearny, New Jersey, shipyard during
    fitting out of the Fresno (CL-121), 279

Kenney, General George C., USAAF
    Army Air Forces Chief of Staff in early 1946 unhappy
    about length of transatlantic voyage to England when it
    would have been much quicker to fly, 272; remark on the
    Nuremburg trials, 272; disagreed with suggestion in
    January 1946 to give away Okinawa for trusteeship, 272-
    273

Key West, Florida
    Characterized as a wild city in the mid-1920s during
    Prohibition, 60; Hannibal (AG-1) junior officer deserted
    after writing a bad check to cover a gambling debt at a
    Key West bar, 60-61

King, Admiral Ernest J., USN (USNA, 1901)
    Had a reserve naval officer who was on a first-name basis
    with President Roosevelt transferred to London in 1942 to
    get him out of Washington, 189; opposed to the selection
    of Rear Admiral Alan Kirk of U.S. naval commander for the
    June 1944 Normandy invasion, 232-233; mistakenly told an
    officer, who later retired as a rear admiral, that he'd
    never made captain, 251

Kirk, Rear Admiral Alan G., USN (USNA, 1909)
    Strauss's long-standing relationship with Kirk, with whom
    he served in the mid-1920s, 80, 232; appointed as the
    U.S. naval commander for the Normandy invasion against
    the wishes of CNO Admiral Ernest King, 232-233;
    involvement in Normandy invasion, 233-234, 239; King
    George VI asked Strauss about Kirk during a visit to the
    Imperial Defence College in 1948, 302

Knight, Ridgway
    As an acting commissioner in Berlin in the early 1950s,
    lent strong support when a NATO discovered that a German
    firm was supplying technology to Communist bloc
    countries, 345-346

Knoll, Captain Denys W., USN (USNA, 1930)
    As staff officer for Admiral Richmond K. Turner in early
    1946, 272

Knud, Prince
    Rear Admiral Alfred Johnson gave a dinner party for
    Danish Prince Knud in Copenhagen in the late 1930s, 163

Korean War
    Drain on resources in Washington, 314

Leadership
    Training at the Naval Academy in the early 1920s, 23-24;
    some skippers were better than others at bringing along
    their executive officers to prepare them for command,
    111-112; Strauss feels that in order to attain the
    highest levels, leaders cannot have a sense of humor,
    325-326

Le Breton, Captain David M., USN (USNA, 1904)
    Anecdote about Le Breton as assistant director of naval
    intelligence in the late 1920s, 87

Lefavour, Lieutenant William R., USN (USNA, 1931)
    Assessed as executive officer of the Brooks (DD-232) in
    late 1930s, 171-172

Leigh, Captain Richard H., USN (USNA, 1891)
    As assistant chief of the Bureau of Navigation in the
    late 1910s, nominated Strauss's sister as sponsor of the
    Reuben James (DD-245)

Levasseur, Ensign Julian J., USN (USNA, 1923)
    Gun turret officer in the Mississippi (BB-41) narrowly
    escaped death after an explosion in the 1920s, 72

Liquor
　　Toucey (DD-282) skipper, lenient with some other transgressions, was intolerant of anyone caught bringing alcohol on board, 83; liquor not frequently smuggled on board ships in the 1920s, 109; pink gin was a popular liquor served by the Royal Navy in the 1930s, 125; anecdote from Strauss's time as director of the engineering department at Bucknell University in the mid-1950s, 349; see also Prohibition

Lisbon, Portugal
　　As neutral city in 1941, both German and British planes used airfields here, 183-184

Little Rock, USS (CL-92)
　　The Fresno (CL-121) was sent to Northern Europe in 1947 to replace the Little Rock when she experienced some mechanical difficulties, 285

Lloyd's of London
　　The United States established attaché billets in the mid-1930s in order to keep tabs on Japanese merchant activities with information available through Lloyd's, 206-209

London
　　As junior naval attaché in London in 1935-36, Strauss marched in the funerals of King George V and admirals of the fleet David Beatty and John Jellicoe, 123; social aspects of embassy duty in the mid-1930s, 123-125, 138-139, 146-147; size of the embassy contingent in the 1930s, 125; Strauss's accommodations in London in the mid-1930s, 139-140; Strauss was in London during the several days preceding the Pearl Harbor attack, 184-186; Strauss's recollections of the blitz, 185-186; Strauss's accommodations in the early 19402, 228-230; Strauss was concerned that the debris in the Thames would present problems for the Fresno (CL-121) during a visit to London in 1947, 295; conditions still austere in 1948, 302

Long Island, USCGC
　　Ferried troops during the June 1944 Normandy invasion, 236

Lovat, Lieutenant Colonel Lord
　　Heroic action during August 1942 Dieppe raid, 199

MacArthur, Brigadier General Douglas, USA　(USMA, 190) (USMA, 1903)
　　Made an honorary Knight Commander of St. Michael and St. George by the British after World War I, 9

McGregor, Midshipman Charles, USN (USNA, 1864)
Strauss's great-uncle attended the Naval Academy up in Newport, Rhode Island, during the Civil War, 2

McReynolds, James C.
Former U.S. Attorney General asked Strauss to carry some seasickness medicine to Eleanor Roosevelt before a transatlantic voyage in January 1946, 270-271

McVay, Captain Charles B. III, USN (USNA, 1920)
As commanding officer of the Indianapolis (CA-35) when the cruiser was sunk in July 1945, criticized for not zigzagging, 266-267

Madagascar
Strauss's recollections of visiting Madagascar in the Concord (CL-10) in 1923-24, 38-39; Strauss was sent here to evaluate the aid mission in the early 1960s, 353

Mahan, Rear Admiral Alfred Thayer, USN (Ret.) (USNA, 1859)
As a naval attaché in London in the mid-1930s, Strauss was tasked by Captain William Puleston, Director of Naval Intelligence and naval author, to gather information for a biography on Mahan, 209-210

Manley, USS (DD-74)
Depth charge explosion during World War I killed the executive officer, 97; discussion of officers in the early 1930s, 97, 101; assigned as guard while President Franklin Roosevelt fished, 98; engineering plant, 102; enlisted personnel, 102-104, 112; discipline, 104-105; living conditions, 105; food, 105-106; test fired torpedoes at the Newport Torpedo Station, 106, 108-109; Strauss was acting skipper when the commanding officer was laid up in sick bay, 107; plane guard duty, 110-111; spent winter at Navy yard at Boston, 112-113

Margaret, Princess
Behavior verged on rudeness at a London party Strauss attended in 1948, 305

Marine Corps, U.S.
Strauss was more impressed by the behavior of Marines embarked in the Charles Carroll (APA-28) in 1945 than Army troops, 260

Maxse, Major General Sir Ivor
Strauss contacted Maxse in the mid-1930s on the behalf of Captain William Puleston, who was writing a biography of Alfred T. Mahan, 209

Mayo, Commander Claude B., USN (USNA, 1906)
    As executive officer of the Florida (BB-30) in the mid-1920s, his effort to fire up and instill pride among the crew backfired, 78

Medals and Decorations,
    Strauss's father was made an honorary Commander of the Order of St. Michael and St. George by the British after World War I, 3, 9; Brigadier General Douglas MacArthur received the same decoration as Strauss's father, 9; Strauss received the Croix de Guerre for his World War II service, 328

Miller, Captain George H., USN (USNA, 1933)
    Worked with Strauss in the long-range planning section of the Strategic Planning Division of OpNav in the early 1950s, 337-339

Minckler, Lieutenant Commander Campbell H., USN (USNA, 1921A)
    Assessed as a bright man with many vices as flag secretary to Commander Training Detachment, U.S. Fleet, in the late 1930s, 155-156

Mines
    Strauss's father oversaw the laying of a mine barrage in the North Sea during World War I, 3

Mississippi, USS (BB-41)
    Gun turret explosion on board in 1924, 72

Montgomery, Field Marshal Bernard L.
    While working in the long-range planning section of the Strategic Planning Division in the early 1950s, Strauss expanded on an idea he'd heard Montgomery address some years earlier concerning the importance of North Africa, 337

Moon, Rear Admiral Don P., USN (USNA, 1916)
    Strauss's recollections of Moon as Commander Task Force 125 during the June 1944 Normandy invasion, 238-239

Morgan, General Sir Frederick
    Strauss's recollections of Morgan as chief of staff to the Supreme Allied Commander in the early 1940s, 195, 225-227

Morocco
    Weather conditions taken into account by those planning
    the North African invasion during World War II, 219-220;
    a NATO section discovered that contraband was being
    laundered in Tangier in the early 1950s for transport to
    Communist bloc countries, 345

Mountbatten, Lady Edwina
    Anecdote about a potentially embarrassing situation in
    1942 when both she and her husband drove cars to the same
    event, even though gasoline was in short supply, 223;
    death in 1960, 357, 359; assessed by Strauss, 357-358

Mountbatten, Admiral of the Fleet Lord Louis
    Funeral in 1979 compared with King George V's in 1936,
    127; Strauss's presence at his funeral was specifically
    requested, 194, 355-357, 359; had a wild reputation in
    London in the mid-1930s, 140; early promotions were
    earned, 141; introduced to Strauss by Paul Hammond, 190;
    Strauss's relationship with Mountbatten, 193-194; assessed
    by Strauss, 194, 196, 222-223, 224; in 1977 suggested
    Strauss for a Canadian documentary on the Dieppe raid,
    201-203; resentment towards, 221-222; exasperation about
    quality of British engineering officers, 228-229; showed
    Indian bias when discussing the India-Pakistan situation
    at the Imperial War College in 1948, 300; corresponded
    with Strauss, 360 see also Combined Operations

Murfin, Captain Orin G., USN (USNA, 1897)
    Strauss's impressions of Murfin as captain of the Concord
    (CL-10) in the mid-1920s, 44; when the admiral embarked
    in the Concord insisted that a big 10 be painted on the
    bow, Murfin had it removed as soon as the admiral was
    relieved, 50

Murphy, Robert D.
    Expedition to North Africa in the early 1940s with
    General Mark Clark, 229-230

Nashville, USS (CL-43)
    Skipper's skill at shiphandling in the early 1940s, 49-
    50; hosted British cruiser at New York in the early 1940s
    that had been in action in the Mediterranean, 170;
    Strauss was pleased that smokers refrained from smoking
    in the charthouse, 175; expended a lot of ammunition
    during the war shooting at fishing boats, 175-176;
    relieved the British garrison at Iceland in July 1941,
    176-177; handling characteristics, 177-178; Strauss's
    navigation duties, 178-179; gunnery practice, 179;
    additional watches for department heads, 180; see also
    Wentworth, Captain Ralph S.; Craven, Captain Francis S.

National War College
   Patterned on the Imperial Defence College in London, 122;
   Strauss attended briefly in late 1947, 299

NATO
   See North Atlantic Treaty Organization

Naval Academy, U.S.
   Moved to Newport, Rhode Island during the Civil War, 2;
   Strauss attended a cram school before entering the
   academy in 1919, 7, 9-11; entrance examinations, 10-11;
   Strauss's plebe year, 12; life in Bancroft Hall, 13-14;
   Strauss saw professors more as umpires than as teachers,
   14-15; academics, 14-15, 23; discipline, 16; upperclass
   privileges in the early 1920s, 17-18; social life, 18-19;
   Log magazine, 19; discussion of Strauss's classmates, 22-
   23; leadership training, 23-24; drill practice, 27;
   summer cruises, 28-33; see also Cook Allen Blow

Naval Institute, U.S.
   Interest in Proceedings among officers in the mid-1920s,
   67-68; both Strauss and his father were Proceedings
   authors, 68

Naval Intelligence, Office of (ONI)
   Attachés in London in the mid-1930s relayed information
   back to ONI, 126, 150-52, 206-209

Naval Torpedo Station, Newport, Rhode Island
   As explosives officer here in the early 1930s, Strauss's
   division oversaw the making of primers for fixed and bag
   ammunition, 88-90, 94-95; some workers resisted the face
   masks worn as a safety precaution when working around
   tetryl, 89; use of female employees in the early 1930s,
   90, 93; civil service employees, 92-95

Naval Training Station, Newport, Rhode Island
   Strauss's duties as training and commissary officer in
   the mid-1930s, 116-119; association with the Naval War
   College, 121

Naval War College
   Association with the Naval Training Center, Newport, in
   the mid-1930s, 121; Strauss was never particularly
   interested in attending the program, 121-122; junior
   course sometimes seen as a place to park junior officers
   in the 1930s, 122

Navigation
   Strauss's duties as navigator of the Nashville (CL-43) in
   the early 1940s, 178-179

Navy Hydrographic Office
    Strauss presented a paper by this organization at a
    geodesy conference in Edinburgh in 1936, 148-149

Netherlands
    See Holland

Neutrality Patrols
    Made by the Brooks (DD-232) off Nova Scotia and Panama in
    1939-40, 167-170, 173

Nevada, USS (BB-36)
    Strauss's father was the second commanding officer of
    this battleship from 1916 to 1918, 3, 8

Newport, Rhode Island
    Social activities in the 1930s, 96, 119-121; weather
    conditions at Newport, 112-113; interest in the Navy,
    120-121; see also Naval Torpedo Station, Newport; Naval
    Training Station, Newport; Naval War College

New York, USS (BB-34)
    Sent to England for the coronation of King George VI in
    May 1937, 135-137; quality of officers embarked in this
    battleship in 1918, 158;

Nicaragua
    Measures taken to ensure honesty of Nicaraguan elections
    in the late 1930s, 154

Niagara, USS (SP-136)
    Used for surveying off Cuba in the mid-1920s, 53

Normandy Invasion
    Chief of Combined Operations Vice Admiral Louis
    Mountbatten held a planning conference in Scotland in the
    early 1940s with those he felt would be the commanders
    involved in this June 1944 operation, 195-197; rift among
    the staff officers of the U.S. naval forces involved in
    the invasion, 216-217; unusual first impression by a
    British officer when he returned from Normandy, 223-224;
    planning by the staff of Commander U.S. Naval Forces
    Europe, 224-226, 233-235; discussion of leaders involved,
    225-226; Utah Beach, 235, 237; Omaha Beach, 235;
    aftermath, 235-238; supplies and logistics, 242-243

North Africa
    General George Patton conferred with the Combined
    Operations staff in 1942 while planning for the landings
    on North Africa, 219-221; Strauss was scheduled to go to
    North Africa in 1942, but bad weather canceled the trip,
    228; Field Marshall Bernard Montgomery and Strauss spoke
    on the great importance of North Africa to Britain and
    the United States, 337

North Atlantic Squadron (Royal Navy)
    Attended Tennis Week at Bar Harbor, Maine, in the late
    1920s, 88; social engagements at Newport in the early
    1930s, 96

North Atlantic Treaty Organization (NATO)
    The Strategic Planning Division of OpNav was concerned
    with setting up a command structure for NATO at its
    inception in 1949, 311-312, 317; Destroyer Flotilla Six
    participated in exercise Grand Slam in the early 1950s,
    328-329, 331; role of NATO studied by the long-range
    planning group of the Strategic Planning Division in the
    early 1950s, 338; Strauss concerned that the Atlantic
    portion of NATO have as much prominence as the European
    aspect, 341; concerns of the defense programs section in
    the early 1950s, 342; Consultative Commission, 343;
    Strauss was in charge of a program monitoring the
    transfer of contraband to foreign countries, 345

North Dakota, USS (BB-29)
    Midshipmen transferred to this battleship during their
    summer cruise in the early 1920s when the Connecticut
    (BB-18) lost her propellers, 29

North Sea
    Strauss's father oversaw the laying of a mine barrage in
    the North Sea during World War I, 3

Nuremburg Trials
    Comment on trials by General George Kenney, the Army Air
    Forces Chief of Staff in 1946, 272

Nutter, Lieutenant David L., USN (USNA, 1923)
    Anecdote from his service as flag lieutenant to Commander
    Training Detachment, U.S. Fleet, in the late 1930s, 162

Nyquist, Ensign John W., USN (USNA, 1921)
    Hannibal (AG-1) officer was forced to protect another
    officer at gunpoint from the wrath of some members of the
    crew in the early 1920s, 65

Ochiltree, Lieutenant (junior grade) Thomas H., USN (USNA, 1922)
Collided his small boat with another during survey work off Cuba in the mid-1920s, 56-57

Odgers, Dr. Merle M.
Anecdote concerning alcohol and Odgers, who was president of Bucknell University in the mid-1950s, 349-350

Okinawa
Charles Carroll (APA-28) participated in landings in the spring of 1945, 261, 262-264; when a United Nations committee considered giving away trusteeship of Okinawa in January 1946, someone leaked the story to the press, 272-273

O'Leary, Captain Forrest M., USN (USNA, 1920)
As a division commander in mid-1945, rode the Charles Carroll (APA-28) to Hawaii for R&R, 264

Olmstead, Midshipman Jerauld L., USN (USNA, 1922)
Controversy over his top standing in his Naval Academy graduating class, 24-25

Ordnance
Discussion of making ammunition primers at the Naval Torpedo Station in the early 1930s, 88-91

Orem, Rear Admiral Howard E., USN (USNA, 1922)
Nominated Strauss as director of the U.S. Agency for International Cooperation in the mid-1950s, 348

Pakistan
Strauss was sent to Pakistan to evaluate the aid mission there in the early 1960s, 353

Paley, William
Strauss sat next to the chairman of the Columbia Broadcasting System at a luncheon hosted by Lady Louis Mountbatten in mid-1944, 223

Panama
Strauss's recollections from liberty here in the early 1920s, 31-32; neutrality patrols off Panama in 1939-40, 168-170, 173

Paris
Top-heavy with U.S. ambassadors in the early 1950s, 339-340; Strauss's accommodations in the early 1950s, 341

Parker, Commander Edward C. S., USN (USNA, 1902)
   Unstable, heavy-drinking captain of the Hannibal (AG-1)
   was removed from his ship in 1924, 63-65

Patton, Major General George S., Jr., USA (USMA, 1909)
   Consulted with Vice Admiral Louis Mountbatten's Combined
   Operations staff while planning for the North African
   invasion, 219-221

Pell, Herbert Claiborne, Jr.
   Strauss family friend visited the Charles Carroll (APA-
   28) at San Francisco in mid-1945, 265

Pernambuco (Recife), Brazil
   The Concord (CL-10) visited Pernambuco during Mardi Gras
   in 1924, 41

Phoenix, USS (CL-46)
   After being decommissioned, this light cruiser was sold
   to Argentina in 1951, and was sunk in 1982 during the
   Falklands War, 315

Planning
   Various possibilities studied by the long-range planning
   section of the Strategic Plans Division of OpNav in the
   early 1950s, 336-339

Pound, Lieutenant (junior grade) Harold C., USN (USNA, 1925)
   Anecdote from his tour as White House aide in the early
   1930s, 99

Pridham-Wippell, Admiral Sir Henry D., RN
   As Commander in Chief Plymouth in 1947, entertained
   Strauss when the Fresno (CL-121) was temporarily based in
   Plymouth, 298-299

Prisoners of War
   Strauss saw caged German prisoners of war awaiting
   repatriation during a 1947 visit to Holland, 286-287

Prohibition
   Ensign Strauss offered a drink at an Annapolis restaurant
   shortly after graduation in 1923, 18; not enforced at Key
   West during the mid-1920s, 60, 62; West Coast-based crews
   often went into Mexico to drink, 109-10

Promotions
   Strauss laments the passing of promotions for junior
   officers based on examinations, as was the case in the
   1920s and '30s, 114-15

Puleston, Captain William D., USN (USNA, 1902)
    As Director of Naval Intelligence in the 1930s, set up a
    network of attachés to keep track of Japanese merchant
    shipping, 206; tasked Strauss with gathering information
    in England from associates of Alfred Mahan for a
    biography he was writing, 209-210; other books by
    Puleston, 210

Pyle, Ernest T.
    Strauss's recollections of this popular war correspondent
    from April 1945 when he rode in the Charles Carroll (APA-
    28), 257-259

Q-boats
    Strauss met the Royal Navy officer who was decorated for
    his skillful use during World War I of these disguised
    merchant ships, 38-39

Queen Elizabeth, RMS
    Soon after she'd been decommissioned as a troop
    transport, this liner carried a distinguished group of
    delegates to attend the first United Nations General
    Assembly in London in January 1946, 270

Quinn, Ensign Bertrand D., USN (USNA, 1924)
    Collided his small boat with another during survey work
    off Cuba in the mid-1920s, 56-57

Ramsay, Admiral Sir Bertram H., RN
    Allied Naval Commander in Chief assessed by staff officer
    Strauss, 196, 245-247; held in great esteem by the
    British, 224; responsibilities during June 1944 Normandy
    invasion, 241-242; death in January 1945, 242, 247;
    brought out of retirement for World War II, 246; as
    commander of Dover, 246-247; completely integrated
    American officers into his staff, 247

Reeves, Lieutenant Commander John W., Jr., USN (USNA, 1911)
    Strauss's recollections of Reeves as engineer officer in
    the Concord (CL-10) in the mid-1920s, 44-46

Reeves, Admiral Joseph Mason, USN (USNA, 1894)
    As Commander in Chief U.S. Fleet in the mid-1930s, took
    measures to silence a commander who gained prominence
    through various books he'd written, 81-82

Reuben James, USS (DD-245)
    Strauss's sister christened this destroyer in 1919 that
    became the first American ship lost in World War II, 181

Ribbentrop, Joachim von
   As German ambassador to Great Britain in 1936, gave King
   Edward VIII a "Heil Hitler" salute during diplomatic
   corps levee, 146-147

Ridgway, General Matthew B., USA (USMA, 1917)
   Strauss's assessment of Ridgway as Supreme Allied
   Commander Europe in the early 1950s, 346-347

Rodgers, Commander Christopher Raymond Perry, USN (USNA, 1904)
   Aristocratic as commanding officer of the Hannibal (AG-1)
   in the mid-1920s, 53-54; reaction to collision of two
   small boats doing survey work, 57; social call to the
   mayor of Batabanó, 59; reaction when a Hannibal (AG-1)
   junior officer deserted ship and went into hiding after
   writing a bad check, 61; when he heard that Strauss was
   being considered as an attaché in the mid-1930s,
   mistakenly assumed he wouldn't want to leave Newport,
   116-117

Rodman, Admiral Hugh, USN (Ret.) (USNA, 1880)
   Represented the United States at the coronation of King
   George VI in 1937, flying his flag in the USS New York
   (BB-34), 136-137

Roenigk, Commander John G., USN (USNA, 1934)
   Strauss's favorable assessment of his Fresno (CL-121)
   executive officer in the mid-1940s, 279-280

Roosevelt, Eleanor
   Though suspicious of the former First Lady initially,
   Strauss was won over by her charm during their
   transatlantic voyage in January 1946, 270-271

Roosevelt, Franklin D.
   President Roosevelt presented the Manley (DD-74) with the
   flippers of a sea turtle he had caught while the
   destroyer guarded his fishing expedition in the early
   1930s, 98

Rowell, Commander G. W., RN
   As planning officer to Commander Allied Naval Forces
   during World War II, sensible attitude toward rank
   discrepancies, 242

Royal Navy
   Cooperation with the U.S. Navy in the 1930s, 125, 150-151; British officer mugged outside the Brooklyn Navy Yard in the early 1940s, 170; discrepancies in quality and rank of some British billets as compared to American, 228-229, 242-243, 248; difference in staff style between U.S. and Royal navies, 248-249; participated in NATO exercise Grand Slam in the early 1950s, 331; see also North Atlantic Squadron

Royal Naval College, Greenwich
   Strauss asked permission for the Fresno (CL-121) to fire a naval salute when approaching Greenwich in 1947, but learned that Queen Elizabeth I had banned salutes in the 16th century because they broke windows, 294

Russell, Captain Guy, RN
   Russell's trip to North Africa in 1942 was delayed due to bad weather, 228

Russell Islands
   Water was slightly too deep for the anchor of the Charles Carroll (APA-28) during a visit in early 1945, 256; party for the skippers of ships at anchorage there, 257-258

Ryder, Commander Robert Edward Dudley, RN
   Strauss shared a desk in a London office with Dudley, a war hero, in 1942, 192-193

St. Helena
   Strauss's recollections of this island from his visit in the Concord (CL-10) in 1924, 40-41

Sala, Vice Admiral Léon M. P. A., FN
   Sala, French Commander of the Mediterranean in the early 1950s, ran into Strauss, with whom he'd served on a staff during World War II, in Algiers, 328

San Francisco
   The Charles Carroll (APA-28) visited in mid-1945 while the city was crowded with delegates attending a United Nations meeting, 264-265

Seasickness
   Strauss experienced this malady while serving in the Concord (CL-10) in the mid-1920s, 86; Manley (DD-74) crewman who suffered from chronic seasickness found that when the destroyer went through a severe storm in the early 1930s, he was too scared to be sick, 86-87

Schiff, Lieutenant John M., USNR
   Reserve officer became Strauss's housemate in London in the early 1940s, 229; rented apartment to Strauss in New York in the mid-1940s, 229, 278

Seattle, Washington
   Hospitable to midshipmen during summer cruise in the early 1920s, 32

Shadman's School, Washington, D.C.
   Strauss attended this school in preparation for entering the Naval Academy in 1919, 7, 9-11

Sharks
   Filipino messboys who would dive for lobsters at Cuba in the mid-1920s had to be protected from sharks, 58

Sharp, Air Commodore A. C. H., RAF
   Took Strauss along to a 1948 London party attended by Queen Elizabeth and Princess Margaret, 304-305

Sherman, Admiral Forrest P., USN (USNA, 1918)
   There was some initial resentment of Sherman when he became Chief of Naval Operations in 1949, but he proved to be one of the best CNOs ever, 309; asked President Truman to lift promotion ban on Captain Arleigh Burke, 310; wanted flag officer insignia that distinguished the officer's specialty, 310; issues studies as CNO, 311-312; wanted to establish U.S. naval bases in Spain, 314, 322; relationship with Strauss, 321-323; assessed by Strauss, 323-326

Shiphandling
   Handling characteristics of the Concord (CL-10), 47, 49-50, 178; skilled handling of the Nashville (CL-43) by her commanding officer in early 1940s, 50; the Toucey (DD-282) lost part of her topmast when she brushed the boat boom of a tender in the late 1920s, 82-83; daring, but skillful handling of the Manley (DD-74) by her skipper in the early 1940s, 97-98; Strauss's first experiences at actual shiphandling were in the Manley, 107; handling characteristics of the Brooks (DD-232), 171; characteristics of the Nashville, 178

Short, Brigadier General Walter C., USA
   Strauss's recollections of Short when he was the Army commander during amphibious exercises off Culebra in 1937-38, 157

Slayton, Commander Charles C., USN (USNA, 1907)
    Popular Naval Academy officer to whom the class of 1923 dedicated its yearbook, 16

Slessor, Air Marshal Sir John, RAF
    Assessed as Commandant of the Imperial Defence College in 1948, 301; Strauss was asked to write a paper refuting a paper by Slessor in the late 1950s urging less concentration on conventional warfare, since the next war would undoubtedly be nuclear, 312-313

Slim, Field Marshal William J.
    His funeral in 1970 affected Lord Louis Mountbatten's plans for his own funeral, 356

Smith, C. Alphonso
    Distinguished Naval Academy English professor in the early 1920s, 14

Smith, Lieutenant (junior grade) Harry T., USN (USNA, 1922)
    Hannibal (AG-1) officer deserted the ship in the mid-1920s and went into hiding for many years after writing a bad check to cover a gambling debt at a Key West bar, 60-62

Smith-Hutton, Captain Henri H., USN (USNA, 1922)
    Strauss was annoyed that Smith-Hutton, naval attaché to France in 1947, didn't attend a reception given by the Fresno (CL-121) when she visited Le Havre, 293

Smoot, Captain Roland N., USN (USNA, 1923)
    Favorable assessment of Strauss's Naval Academy classmate, 22-23; as captain detailer in 1947, convinced him that attending the Imperial Defence College would be an asset to his career, 296

Somalia
    The Concord (CL-10) visited Berbera over Christmas 1923, 38, 40

Somerville, Vice Admiral Sir James, RN
    Brought out of retirement to serve in World War II, 246

South Africa
    Strauss's favorable recollections of visiting South Africa in the Concord (CL-10) in 1923-24, 38-39

South America
    The United States sold various decommissioned ships to
    South American navies in the early 1950s, 314-315;
    Strauss was not impressed by the navies of South America,
    with the exception of the Chilean Navy, 315-316

Soviet Union
    British Admiral Sir Frederick Morgan was one of the first
    men that Strauss ever heard speak of the postwar threat
    posed by the Russians, 227; see also Consultative
    Commission

Spain
    CNO Admiral Forrest Sherman was interesting in
    establishing U.S. naval bases in Spain in the early
    1950s, 314, 322

Spitfire
    Shot down by Canadian antiair fire during August 1942
    Dieppe raid, 200, 212

Stark, Admiral Harold R., USN (USNA, 1903)
    Chose Strauss for assignment to Vice Admiral Louis
    Mountbatten's Combined Operations staff in 1942, 190;
    assessed by Strauss, 212-214, 218-219

Stevens, Lieutenant Commander Leslie C., CC, USN (USNA, 1919)
    Stevens's comment about bosses before he left London for
    duty as naval attaché in Moscow in the mid-1930s, 133;
    requested a Stetson hat from Moscow, 140

Strategic Plans Division, OpNav
    Officers assigned to this division in the late 1940s,
    307; staff kept too busy with minutiae, 311; worked on
    command structure of NATO, 311-312, 317; concerned with
    the allocation of material, 312-313; studied feasibility
    of foreign bases, 314; decommissioned naval vessels sold
    to foreign navies, 314-316; long-range planning in the
    early 1950s, 337-339

Strauss, Beatrice Phillips
    Met her husband in London in the early 1940s, and married
    him in 1951, 319

Strauss, Rear Admiral Elliott B., USN (USNA,1923)
   Family and background, 1-7, 181; wives and children, 68,
   87-88, 319-320; schooling, 6-11; midshipmen at Naval
   Academy, 1919-23, 12-36; duty in the Concord (CL-10),
   1923-25, 36-52, 86, 88; duty in the Hannibal (AG-1),
   1925-26, 52-67; turret officer in the Arkansas (BB-33),
   1926-27, 68-81; engineer officer in the Toucey (DD-282),
   1927-30, 81-87; duty in the Blakeley (DD-150), 1930, 85-
   87; explosives officer at the Naval Torpedo Station,
   1930-32, 88-96; executive officer in the Manley (DD-74)
   1932-34, 92, 97-114; training and commissary officer at
   the Naval Training Station, Newport, 1934-35, 116-;
   assistant naval attaché in London, 1935-37, 123-152; flag
   secretary to Commander Training Detachment/Atlantic
   Squadron, U.S. Fleet, 1937-39, 146, 152-167; commanding
   officer, USS Brooks (DD-232), 1939-40, 167-173; navigator
   in the Nashville (CL-43), 1940-41, 49-50, 170, 173-181;
   naval observer in London and duty on the Combined
   Operations Staff, 1942-43, 182-224; staff, Commander U.S.
   Naval Forces Europe, 1943-44, 224-251; commanding
   officer, USS Charles Carroll (APA-28), 1944-45, 251-267;
   Military Staff Committee, Security Council, U.N., 1946,
   268-278; commanding officer, USS Fresno (CL-121), 1946-
   47, 24, 165, 278-295; student, Imperial Defence College,
   1948, 122, 140, 204-205; 295-306; head of the Strategic
   Applications and Policy Branch of the Strategic Planes
   Division, 1949-51, 302-303, 307-318, 322-325; Commander
   Destroyer Flotilla Six, 1951-52, 297, 321-322; 326-336;
   head of Long Range Plans Branch, OpNav, 1952, 336-339;
   director of defense programs, NATO, 1952-56, 339-348;
   director of engineering at Bucknell University, 1956-57,
   348-350; chief of the American Aide Mission to Tunisia,
   1957-60, 350-353; various assignments with AID in the
   early 1960s, 353; State Department inspector in Israel in
   the mid-1960s, 353-354; various civilian jobs in the late
   1960s, 354

Strauss, Admiral Joseph, USN (USNA, 1885)
   Brief discussion of Strauss's father's distinguished
   career, 2-5,8; decorated by the British after World War
   I, 3, 9; USS Joseph Strauss (DDG-16) named in his honor,
   4, 284; career advice to his son, 54-55; had article
   published in Naval Institute Proceedings in 1901, 67-68;
   thoughts on Alfred Thayer Mahan, 210; felt his generation
   had the best of naval duty

Surveying
   Survey duty viewed as the epitome of seamanship, 54-55;
   description of work, 56-57, 66; effect of new survey
   charts on merchant shipping insurance rates, 67

Swanson, Lieutenant Emil, USN
　Hannibal (AG-1) officer, a stern disciplinarian, had to be protected at gunpoint from the wrath of some crew members in the early 1920s, 65

Sweitzer, Brigadier General Nelson B., USA (USMA, 1853)
　Strauss's grandfather served on General George McClellan's staff during the Civil War, 1-2

Task Force 21
　As commander of Task Force 21 in 1947, Strauss had the authority to decide whether officers and men in his group would be allowed to marry English girls, 290-292

Thach, Ensign James H., Jr., USN (USNA, 1923)
　Strauss's assessment of his classmate and Concord (CL-10) shipmate in 1924, 47-48

Thackrey, Captain Lyman A., USN (USNA, 1921A)
　As deputy commander of U.S. naval forces during the June 1944 Normandy invasion, 216, 225; staff in 1943, 233, 249; held Strauss in London until after the June 1944 Normandy invasion, 251; received the Legion of Honor and a Croix de Guerre, 328

Thebaud, Rear Admiral Leo H., USN (USNA, 1913)
　As Commandant of the First Naval District in the early 1950s, cooperated completely with Strauss when he came to inspect reserve destroyers in his district, 334

Thomas Jefferson, USS (APA-30)
　Moved briskly on transit from South Pacific to Hawaii in mid-1945, 264

Thwing, Commander James G., USNR
　As executive officer of the Charles Carroll (APA-28) in 1945, was a last-minute addition to the crew before a Pacific deployment, 255; assessed by Strauss, 261

Todd, Captain Forde A., USN (USNA, 1904)
　Anecdotes from his service as aide to President Woodrow Wilson in the mid-1910s, 100; longtime association with Strauss, 101

Toledo, USS (CA-133)
　Underwent shakedown training along with the Fresno (CL-121) in early 1947, 281

Tonga
　Anecdote about Queen Salote of Tonga at the coronation of King George VI in 1937, 136

Torpedoes
Strauss made suggestions for more realistic testing of torpedoes while serving at the Naval Torpedo Station in the early 1930s, 91; the Manley (DD-74) test-fired torpedoes at Newport in the early 1930s, 106, 108-109; see also Naval Torpedo Station, Newport

Toucey, USS (DD-282)
Lost part of her topmast after brushing the boat boom of a tender in the late 1920s, 82-83; discussion of the engineering plant, 84-85

Training
Leadership training at the Naval Academy in the early 1920s, 23-24; quality of training of enlisted personnel in 1920s, 103-104, 362-363; boot training at Newport in the mid-1930s, 116-119

Training Detachment, U.S. Fleet
Staff officers in the late 1930s, 155-156; duties in the late 1930s, 157, 166; Strauss's duties as flag secretary to the commander, 159-163; title of unit changed to Atlantic Squadron, U.S. Fleet, in the late 1930s, 164-165

Trenton, USS (CL-11)
Gun turret explosion in October 1924, 72

Trieste
King George VI died in February 1952 while Destroyer Flotilla Six visited Trieste, 328, 331-332

Truman, Harry
President Truman was unhappy about all the squabbling going on among the armed forces during the unification crisis in the late 1940s, 303, 309-310

Truscott, Brigadier General Lucian K., Jr., USA
Considered to be one of the best amphibious landing officers of World War II, 219, 289

Turkey
In the early 1950s, hoped to get motor torpedo boats from the U.S. Navy, 314

Tunisia
Strauss's duties as Chief of the American Foreign Aide Mission to Tunisia in the late 1950s included overseeing financial and agricultural matters, 350-353

Turner, Rear Admiral Richmond Kelly, USN (USNA, 1908)
    As director of the War Plans Division in December 1941,
    was lucky not to have the Pearl Harbor fiasco held
    against him, career-wise, 132; Strauss's anecdotes about
    his boss, Turner, when they were in London after World
    War II, 132-133; opinion of Rear Admiral Morton Deyo,
    240; Strauss was recommended to him as a staff officer in
    the fall of 1945, 268-269; heavy drinker, 271-272;
    Strauss filled in for Turner at U.N. committee meetings
    in January 1946, 273; staff officers in 1946, 275-277;
    assessed by Strauss, 276

Turtles
    The Manley (DD-74) passed through a massive spread of sea
    turtles off the southern coast of California in the early
    1930s, 98

Ullman, Boatswain David L., USN
    Hannibal (AG-1) boatswain's run-in with the skipper in
    the mid-1920s when he refused to drink, 64

Unification
    Strauss's recollections of this squabble among the armed
    forces in the late 1940s, 302-303, 308

U.S. Naval Forces in Europe
    Officers on this staff in 1941, 186, 188-189, 214-217;
    see also Ghormley, Vice Admiral Robert L.; Stark, Admiral
    Harold R.

United Nations
    The Charles Carroll (APA-28) visited San Francisco in
    mid-1945 while the city was crowded with U.N. delegates,
    264-265; distinguished delegates to first U.N. General
    Assembly in London in January 1946, 269-270; committee
    considered giving away trusteeship of Okinawa, 272-273;
    explanation of political organization, 274; headquarters
    originally established at Hunter College, 274-275;
    military staff committee opposed introduction of press to
    meetings, 276-277

Uruguay
    The Fresno (CL-121) was sent to represent the United
    States at the inauguration of Uruguay's new President in
    1947, 281-282

Vernou, Captain Walter N., USN (USNA, 1901)
    Assessed as aide to President Roosevelt in the early
    1930s, 99

Vian, Vice Admiral Sir Philip, RN
   Involvement in planning for the June 1944 Normandy invasion, 226, 233-234, 239

Vickers Works
   Strauss and other U.S. naval attaché visited this British shipyard in the mid-1930s, 126, 150-151

Von Heimburg, Rear Admiral Ernest H., USN
   Embarked in the Fresno (CL-121) in 1947 for the trip to Montevideo for the inauguration of Uruguay's new President, 281-282; requests duty as head of the naval mission to Brazil, 282

Wadbrook, Lieutenant (junior grade) William P. E., USN (USNA, 1923)
   Hannibal (AG-1) officer was supposed to accompany the skipper on a social call at Cuba in the mid-1920s, until it was discovered that he had just shaved his head, 59

Walmsley, Walter Newbold, Jr.
   U.S. ambassador to Tunisia in the late 1950s had the unpleasant task of letting that country know that aid had run out to help with an irrigation project, 352-353

Walvis Bay, South-West Africa
   The Concord (CL-10) was credited with standardizing the spelling of this body of water after a visit in 1924, 40

Ware, Commander James G., USN (USNA, 1910)
   Strauss gave his seat at the coronation of King George VI to Ware, who was executive officer of the New York (BB-34) in 1937, 135

Wassner, Captain Erwin
   Assessed as less than tactful as German naval attaché in London in the mid-1930s, 150

WAVES
   Strauss saw his first American female naval personnel in a Navy plane in which he was riding on the day the Japanese surrender was announced, 268

Wedemeyer, General Albert C., USA (USMA, 1919)
   While serving on the War Department General Staff in the early 1940s, very impressed with future Chief of Naval Operations Forrest Sherman, 324; at Lord Mountbatten's funeral in 1979, 356

Weeden, Lieutenant (junior grade) William W., Jr., USN (USNA, 1924)
    Arkansas (BB-33) boat officer informed that the captain's gig had caught fire from the skipper in the mid-1920s, 69-70

Wentworth, Captain Ralph S., USN (USNA, 1912)
    As commanding officer of the Nashville (CL-43) in the early 1940s, skill as a shiphandler, 49-50: Strauss's assessment of Wentworth, 174

Wernher, Major General Sir Harold
    As one of the richest and most influential men in England in 1942, value to Mountbatten's Combined Operations staff, 192

West Germany
    See Germany, Federal Republic of

West Virginia, USS (BB-48)
    Postponement of this battleship's commissioning in the fall of 1923 caused Strauss to request assignment to another ship, 36, 49

Whiting, Vice Admiral Francis E. M., USN (Ret.) (USNA, 1912)
    Asked by the liquor company he worked for in his career after retiring from the Navy to prove his worth to the firm, 335

Wilkinson, Vice Admiral Theodore S., USN (USNA, 1909)
    Favorably assessed by Strauss, 240; death in 1946, 240-241

William M. Wood, USS (DD-715)
    Strauss's Destroyer Flotilla Six flagship in the early 1950s was not a happy ship, 327

Williams, Rear Admiral George W., USN (USNA, 1890)
    As Commander Destroyer Squadrons Scouting Fleet in the mid-1920s, insisted that his flagship, the Concord (CL-10), have a large hull number painted on the bow, which was immediately removed when he left the ship, 50

Willson, Captain Russell, USN (USNA, 1906)
   Poor health held him back from greater prominence in the Navy, 141-142; commended for his valuable contributions during World War II, 142; went after the billet of Superintendent of the Naval Academy in early 1940s, 142-143; death in 1948, 143; assessed by Strauss, 143-144; recommended Strauss to Admiral Richmond K. Turner for his staff in the fall of 1945, 268

Wilson, Rear Admiral George B., USN (USNA, 1914)
   As chief of staff to Admiral Harold Stark in the early 1940s, most people found his assistant more effective for getting things done, 215

Wilson, Rear Admiral Henry B., USN (USNA, 1881)
   Popular as Naval Academy Superintendent in the early 1920s, 16-17; allowed Midshipman Strauss to ride in a car with his father and the Superintendent despite a rule forbidding it, 17-18

Wilson, Woodrow
   Anecdote about elderly man who came to see President Wilson during a New Year's Day open house at the White House, 100

Wood, Major General Robert J., USA (USMA, 1930)
   As Deputy to Defense Advisor, France, in the mid-1950s, 345

World War I
   Strauss's father oversaw the laying of the North Sea mine barrage, 3; see also Q-boats

Wright, Captain Jerauld, USN (USNA, 1918)
   Strauss's housemate in London in the early 1940s, 228-229; expedition to North Africa in the early 1940s, 229-230

Wyoming, USS (BB-32)
   Strauss umpired target practice in this battleship in the mid-1920s, 74-75

www.ingramcontent.com/pod-product-compliance
Lightning Source LLC
Chambersburg PA
CBHW082148070526
44585CB00020B/2138